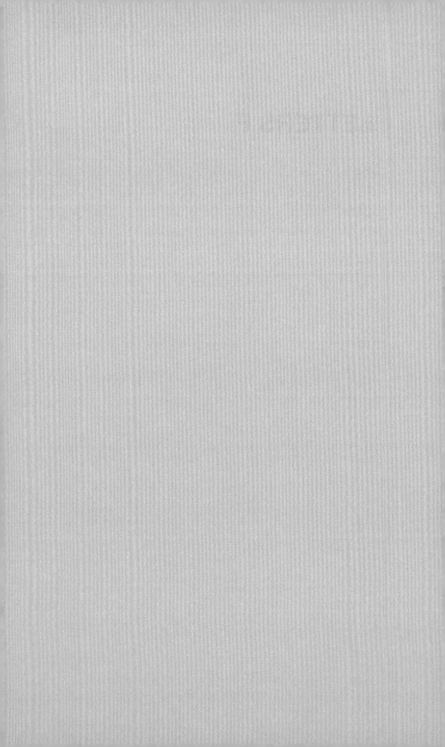

LETTERS FROM A STOIC

Also available in the same series:

Beyond Good and Evil: The Philosophy Classic
by Friedrich Nietzsche (ISBN: 978-0-857-08848-2)

Meditations: The Philosophy Classic
by Marcus Aurelius (ISBN 978-0-857-08846-8)

On the Origin of Species: The Science Classic
by Charles Darwin (ISBN: 978-0-857-08847-5)

Tao Te Ching: The Ancient Classic
by Lao Tzu (ISBN: 978-0-857-08311-1)

The Art of War: The Ancient Classic
by Sun Tzu (ISBN: 978-0-857-08009-7)

The Game of Life and How to Play It: The Self-Help Classic
by Florence Scovel Shinn (ISBN: 978-0-857-08840-6)

The Interpretation of Dreams: The Psychology Classic
by Sigmund Freud (ISBN: 978-0-857-08844-4)

The Prince: The Original Classic
by Niccolo Machiavelli (ISBN: 978-0-857-08078-3)

The Republic: The Influential Classic
by Plato (ISBN: 978-0-857-08313-5)

The Science of Getting Rich: The Original Classic
by Wallace Wattles (ISBN: 978-0-857-08008-0)

The Wealth of Nations: The Economics Classic
by Adam Smith (ISBN: 978-0-857-08077-6)

Think and Grow Rich: The Original Classic
by Napoleon Hill (ISBN: 978-1-906-46559-9)

The Prophet: The Spiritual Classic
by Kahlil Gibran (ISBN: 978–0–857–08855-0)

Utopia: The Influential Classic
by Thomas More (ISBN: 978-1-119-75438-1)

The Communist Manifesto: The Political Classic
by Karl Marx and Friedich Engels (978-0-857-08876-5)

A Room of One's Own: The Feminist Classic
by Virginia Woolf (978-0-857-08882-6)

LETTERS FROM A STOIC
The Ancient Classic

SENECA

With an Introduction by
DONALD ROBERTSON

CAPSTONE
A Wiley Brand

This Capstone edition first published 2021
Introduction copyright © Donald Robertson

Moral letters to Lucilius (Epistulae morales ad Lucilium) by Seneca

Translated by Richard Mott Gummere

A Loeb Classical Library edition; volume 1 published 1917; volume 2 published 1920; volume 3 published 1925

Registered office
John Wiley & Sons Ltd, The Atrium, Southern Gate, Chichester, West Sussex, PO19 8SQ, United Kingdom

For details of our global editorial offices, for customer services and for information about how to apply for permission to reuse the copyright material in this book please see our website at www.wiley.com.

A catalogue record for this book is available from the Library of Congress.

ISBN 9781119751359 (hardback)
ISBN 9780857088796 (epdf)
ISBN 9781119751434 (epub)

Cover Design: Wiley

Set in 12/16pt, NewBaskervilleStd by SPi Global, Chennai, India.

10 9 8 7 6 5 4 3 2 1

C9781119751359_250923

CONTENTS

An Introduction   ix

About Donald Robertson   xxxiii

About Tom Butler-Bowdon   xxxiv

Chapter One   On the Use of Time   1

Chapter Two   On Discursiveness in Reading   5

Chapter Three   On True and False Friendship   9

Chapter Four   On the Terrors of Death   13

Chapter Five   On the Philosopher's Mean   19

Chapter Six   On Sharing Knowledge   23

Chapter Seven   On Crowds   27

Chapter Eight   On the Philosopher's Seclusion   33

Chapter Nine   On Philosophy and Friendship   39

Chapter Ten   On Living to Oneself   49

Chapter Eleven   On the Blush of Modesty   53

Chapter Twelve   On Old Age   57

Chapter Thirteen   On Groundless Fears   63

Chapter Fourteen   On the Reasons for Withdrawing
                    from the World   71

Chapter Fifteen   On Brawn and Brains   79

Chapter Sixteen   On Philosophy, the Guide of Life   85

CONTENTS

Chapter Seventeen   On Philosophy and Riches   91

Chapter Eighteen   On Festivals and Fasting   97

Chapter Nineteen   On Worldliness and Retirement   105

Chapter Twenty   On Practising What You Preach   113

Chapter Twenty One   On the Renown Which My Writings
              May Bring You   119

Chapter Twenty Two   On the Futility of Half-Way Measures   125

Chapter Twenty Three   On the True Joy Which Comes from
              Philosophy   133

Chapter Twenty Four   On Despising Death   139

Chapter Twenty Five   On Reformation   151

Chapter Twenty Six   On Old Age and Death   155

Chapter Twenty Seven   On the Good Which Abides   161

Chapter Twenty Eight   On Travel as a Cure for Discontent   167

Chapter Twenty Nine   On the Critical Condition of Marcellinus   171

Chapter Thirty   On Conquering the Conqueror   177

Chapter Thirty One   On Siren Songs   185

Chapter Thirty Two   On Progress   191

Chapter Thirty Three   On the Futility of Learning Maxims   195

Chapter Thirty Four   On a Promising Pupil   201

Chapter Thirty Five   On the Friendship of Kindred Minds   203

Chapter Thirty Six   On the Value of Retirement   207

Chapter Thirty Seven   On Allegiance to Virtue   213

Chapter Thirty Eight   On Quiet Conversation   217

Chapter Thirty Nine   On Noble Aspirations   219

Chapter Forty   On the Proper Style for a Philosopher's
              Discourse   223

Chapter Forty One   On the God Within Us   231

CONTENTS

Chapter Forty Two   On Values   237

Chapter Forty Three   On the Relativity of Fame   241

Chapter Forty Four   On Philosophy and Pedigrees   243

Chapter Forty Five   On Sophistical Argumentation   247

Chapter Forty Six   On a New Book by Lucilius   253

Chapter Forty Seven   On Master and Slave   255

Chapter Forty Eight   On Quibbling as Unworthy
                of the Philosopher   265

Chapter Forty Nine   On the Shortness of Life   273

Chapter Fifty   On Our Blindness and Its Cure   279

Chapter Fifty One   On Baiae and Morals   283

Chapter Fifty Two   On Choosing Our Teachers   289

Chapter Fifty Three   On the Faults of the Spirit   297

Chapter Fifty Four   On Asthma and Death   303

Chapter Fifty Five   On Vatia's Villa   307

Chapter Fifty Six   On Quiet and Study   313

Chapter Fifty Seven   On the Trials of Travel   321

Chapter Fifty Eight   On Being   325

Chapter Fifty Nine   On Pleasure and Joy   341

Chapter Sixty   On Harmful Prayers   351

Chapter Sixty One   On Meeting Death Cheerfully   353

Chapter Sixty Two   On Good Company   355

Chapter Sixty Three   On Grief for Lost Friends   357

Chapter Sixty Four   On the Philosopher's Task   365

Chapter Sixty Five   On the First Cause   371

AN INTRODUCTION

BY DONALD ROBERTSON

Lucius Annaeus Seneca, also known as Seneca the Younger, is one of the most compelling and yet paradoxical figures in Roman history.

Ancient historians, particularly Tacitus, Suetonius, and Cassius Dio, provide us with important details about his life. These mainly regard Seneca's relationship with Nero, with whose rule as emperor his own story is intertwined. Our information from these sources is very sparse and its reliability has often been questioned.

Seneca himself was a very prolific writer. Yet if we turn to his works for clues about his life and character, we encounter another notorious problem – he was carefully *constructing* his own public image.

THE SENECA ENIGMA

Seneca's writings employ rhetorical methods to paint a picture of his life that is, in many ways, quite at odds with the historical evidence. For instance, those who read only the *Moral Letters*, written to his friend Lucilius, are bound to form a very different impression of Seneca than those who consult other Roman sources about his life. Indeed, what Seneca tells us about himself often says more about *how he wished to appear* than about how he actually was in reality. For example, he was by profession a rhetoric tutor. However, he says very little in his writings about his passion for rhetoric, his position as an imperial speechwriter, or his relationship with Nero's court. He wants to present himself, first and foremost, as a Stoic philosopher.

A second example is the way Seneca describes his banishment to the island of Corsica. Corsica was a thriving colony for wealthy Romans, long known for exporting wine. Seneca almost certainly lived in relative luxury there, probably accompanied by his wife, and attended by a large retinue of slaves. Perhaps slaves even carried him around Corsica in a sedan chair, his typical mode of transportation in the later writings (e.g. *Moral Letters*, 55). Seneca chose, however, to portray himself as stranded on a 'barren rock' where he eked out a very austere and lonely existence, surrounded by uncivilized foreigners. In doing so, Emily Wilson notes, he appears to be drawing inspiration from the earlier writings of the poet Ovid, who was exiled to a remote town called Tomis, beside the Black Sea, at the edge of the Roman Empire on the so-called Scythian Frontier. Corsica, by contrast, is off the coast of Italy, just two days' sailing from the port of Ostia, near Rome. Today, it's a popular holiday destination.

The enduring success with which Seneca reconstructed his own persona is perhaps best illustrated by the curious way in which another man's face was, for many decades, mistaken for his. Seneca tells us that he suffered throughout life from some kind of chronic lung condition, possibly pulmonary tuberculosis. He says that he 'became totally emaciated' through illness and often felt like taking his own life. He was only stopped by the thought that his loving father, who was now advanced in years, would be distraught at losing his son. However, Seneca's writings often contain conflicting accounts. He also says that it was philosophy that saved him from committing suicide:

> My studies were my salvation. I ascribe it to philosophy that I recovered and got stronger. It is to her that I owe my life, and that is the least of what I owe her. (*Moral Letters*, 78.3)

This and similar remarks about his inner struggle, and his embrace of simplicity and austerity, shape the perception many readers form of Seneca the man.

A bronze bust discovered at Herculaneum in 1794 was believed at first to depict Seneca, whose appearance was otherwise unknown at the time. The face was suitably haggard, slightly emaciated, with straggly hair and beard, and an intense, perhaps even angst-ridden, expression. This image was widely replicated and found its way into works of art and book illustrations. Today it frequently accompanies quotations from Seneca on the Internet. However, it is not Seneca.

This bust is now known as the Pseudo-Seneca and is believed to be modelled on an earlier Greek sculpture, perhaps of the poet Hesiod. In 1813, a double-herm – a single sculpture composed of two busts – was discovered, dating from the third century CE, which depicts Socrates and Seneca back to back. Seneca's name is conveniently engraved upon his chest. Real Seneca looks *completely* different from Pseudo-Seneca. He is an overweight, bald-headed man, with a double chin, heavy jowls, pursed lips, and an emotionless, perhaps slightly aloof expression.

Of course, we can't tell much about Seneca's character from his facial appearance. What we do know is that Seneca's modern readers have tended to come away from his writings with an image of him more like Pseudo-Seneca than real Seneca. In real life, perhaps unsurprisingly, Seneca looked less like our stereotypes of an anguished poet-philosopher and more like a typical billionaire Roman senator. 'It seems the face of a businessman or bourgeois', as James Romm put it, 'a man of means who ate at a well-laden table'. Seneca's writings had once again created an image that proved to be dramatically at odds with the truth.

With these notes of caution in mind, we may proceed to examine the main events of Seneca's highly eventful life.

SENECA'S FAMILY

Seneca was born around 4 BCE, in Corduba, in the Roman province of Hispania – modern-day Córdoba in Spain. However, he tells us that we should view the details of his birth as trivial.

> As for the fact of my birth: consider what it really is, in itself. Being born is a trivial thing, uncertain, with equal chance of turning into something good or bad. It's certainly the first step to everything else, but it's not better than everything else just because it came first. (*On Benefits*, 3.30)

Seneca came from a moderately wealthy family of Roman-Spanish knights of the eques, i.e. equestrian class. His writings create the impression of a lifelong desire to rise above, what seemed to him, relatively humble and provincial origins. It was not by accident that Seneca sought to attract the attention of the emperors Caligula and Claudius, and was finally appointed tutor to Nero, ultimately establishing himself at the centre of the imperial court as the emperor's right-hand man. He was a determined social climber who fought hard to be accepted into the highest echelons of Roman society.

Although Corduba had been his family's ancestral home, and his birthplace, Seneca's father brought him to Rome as a small child, where he was raised and educated. His father bore the same name and is therefore known as Seneca the *Elder*, or sometimes Seneca the Rhetorician. He was a historian who became famous for his work on the art of declamation. Seneca's mother, Helvia, was an educated woman, to whom he addressed an open letter of consolation, which, as we'll see, survives today.

Seneca was the middle of three brothers. His elder brother, Novatus, was adopted by the rhetorician Junius Gallio, from whom he took the name Gallio himself. Gallio was appointed consul and later made governor of the Roman province of Achaea, in modern-day Greece, in 52 CE, under Emperor Claudius. He is mentioned in the New Testament, where the apostle Paul is arraigned before him (*Acts* 18.12–17).

Seneca's younger brother, Mela, was the father of the poet Lucan, who authored the epic *Pharsalia*, which lauds the great Roman Republican hero of the civil war, Cato of Utica. Lucan was a Stoic, like his uncle Seneca, and they seem to have been quite close.

Seneca had a wife at the time of his death, Pompeia Paulina, but we know very little about her or their marriage. Some historians believe that this was his second marriage and he'd earlier been wedded to a woman whose name is unknown. He mentions having one son who died in infancy, about whom virtually nothing is known. Later in life, Lucan, his highly talented but ill-fated nephew, was perhaps the closest Seneca had to a son.

EDUCATION AND INFLUENCES

Seneca's life at Rome was defined by several dramatic reversals of fortune, owing to his falling in or out of favour with successive Roman emperors. Indeed, it's no exaggeration to say that the drama of his real life often rivals that found in the celebrated tragedies written by him. He was born during the reign of Augustus, the founder of the Roman Empire, who died when Seneca was around eighteen years old. Indeed, over the course of his life, Seneca would witness the successive rule of all five emperors from the Julio-Claudian dynastic line: Augustus, Tiberius, Caligula, Claudius, and Nero.

Seneca the Elder had his son educated in philosophy and rhetoric. The father greatly admired a Greek Stoic called Attalus, who became his son's first and main teacher in philosophy. Seneca the Younger speaks fondly of him several times:

> This was the advice, I remember, which Attalus gave me in the days when I practically laid siege to his class-room, the first to arrive and the last to leave. Even as he paced up and down, I would challenge him to various discussions; for he not only kept himself accessible to his pupils, but met them half-way. His words were: 'The same purpose should possess both master and scholar – an ambition in the one case to promote, and in the other to progress.' (*Moral Letters*, 108)

Little is known about Attalus, and although he authored several works, none of them survive. Curiously, Seneca has nothing to say about the most famous Roman Stoics of his lifetime. Thrasea and his circle are ignored. The most influential Stoic of this era, Musonius Rufus, has been called the 'Roman Socrates' by modern scholars. He was mentor to the leaders of the Stoic Opposition against Nero's rule, and later became the teacher of Epictetus. Musonius was about forty years old when Seneca died, but he's not mentioned even once in Seneca's writings.

In 20 CE, when he was aged around twenty-five, Seneca became quite ill from a lung condition. He travelled to Alexandria in the Roman province of Egypt, where his uncle Gaius Galerius served as prefect. While there he learned that his tutor, Attalus, had been exiled by Emperor Tiberius. Either in Rome, or perhaps later in Alexandria, Seneca became a student of the School of the Sextii. Dating from around 50 BCE, it was one of the first major schools of philosophy to have originated in Rome, although they apparently wrote in Greek. Little is known of their teachings except that they were a unique hybrid of philosophical ideas, including elements of Stoicism and Pythagoreanism. Seneca held the school's founder, Quintus Sextius, in exceptionally high regard:

> We then had read to us a book by Quintus Sextius the Elder. He is a great man, if you have any confidence in my opinion, and a real Stoic, though he himself denies it. (*Moral Letters*, 49)

Although they were an eclectic school of philosophy, Seneca preferred to call the Sextians Stoics, thereby bolstering his own credentials as a Stoic teacher. As far as we know, Seneca had never travelled to Greece – an omission that would potentially have weakened his status as an expert on Stoic philosophy in the eyes of fellow Romans.

In addition to reading the works of Sextius, Seneca became the student of an otherwise unknown Sextian philosopher called Sotion.

It was but a moment ago that I sat, as a lad, in the school of the philosopher Sotion: but a moment ago that I began to plead in the courts, but a moment ago that I lost the desire to plead, but a moment ago that I lost the ability. (*Moral Letters*, 49)

Seneca describes Sotion's views on reincarnation and vegetarianism, which are clearly influenced by those of Pythagoras – although the Sextians claimed to arrive at the same conclusions based on different arguments.

CAREER AT ROME

After spending about a decade convalescing in Egypt, Seneca finally returned to Rome in the year 31, during the rule of Tiberius. He soon rose to the office of quaestor, the first rung on the Roman *cursus honorum*, or course of offices, which earned him the right to sit in the senate. The elderly Emperor Tiberius finally passed away in 37 CE. According to some accounts, he was poisoned or smothered by Caligula, his grand-nephew and adopted grandson, who succeeded him as emperor.

Seneca appears at first to have pursued a promising legal career. However, according to the historian, Cassius Dio, he was almost executed by Caligula, merely because he 'pleaded a case well in the senate while the emperor was present'. Presumably, Caligula didn't like the direction in which Seneca was influencing the senate and therefore saw his eloquence as a threat:

Gaius [Caligula] ordered him to be put to death, but afterwards let him off because he believed the statement of one of his female associates, to the effect that Seneca had a consumption in an advanced stage and would die before a great while. (*Cassius Dio*, 59.19)

It was perhaps following this incident that Seneca 'lost the desire to plead' and, as he puts it, later also the ability. Around this time, shortly after his return to Rome, he became known more as a writer and rhetorician. *The Consolation to Marcia*, believed to be the earliest of his known works, is thought to date from around 40 CE, when he was approaching middle age. It is, like his other consolations, an open letter, although it reads more like a modern essay. Marcia was a wealthy and influential Roman noble, the daughter of Aulus Cremutius Cordus, a famous historian. She had been mourning the loss of her son for three long years. Seneca employs typical Stoic arguments, not so much to console her empathically as to persuade her to accept her loss, finish her period of mourning, and move on. We can probably infer from Seneca's continued output as a writer, and reports of his growing celebrity, that his early letters sparked public interest and were well received.

Meanwhile in the political realm, Caligula's rule was becoming increasingly tyrannical. In 39 CE, the emperor exiled his own sisters, Julia Livilla and Agrippina the Younger, for involvement in a failed plot to overthrow him. As we'll see, both of these powerful women were friends of Seneca and their stories are closely interlinked. In 41 CE, Caligula was assassinated by a faction of his own praetorian guard. Reputedly, a group of praetorians sympathetic to imperial rule found his uncle, Claudius, cowering in fear behind a curtain, where he was hiding from the assassins. They whisked him away to the safety of their camp where he was acclaimed emperor in place of his nephew. Seneca's troubles, however, were about to worsen.

EXILE

After being acclaimed emperor, Claudius permitted Julia and Agrippina to return from exile to Rome. But before a year had passed, Julia was in trouble again. Claudius' wife, the Empress Messalina, accused Julia and Seneca of committing adultery with one another. They were both found guilty. Julia was exiled first, probably to a nearby island off the Italian coast, where Claudius shortly after ordered her death. Seneca, on the other hand, wasn't banished from Rome until the following year, which suggests there may have been more wrangling over his sentence. Messalina wanted the death penalty but Claudius, after some delay, sentenced Seneca to be exiled to Corsica instead. Technically he was 'relegated', the mildest form of exile, which meant he avoided losing any property or being stripped of his citizenship. You could, therefore, call this an act of clemency on the emperor's part as Seneca got off much more lightly than Julia.

Around 42 CE, shortly after he arrived in Corsica, Seneca wrote another open letter of consolation. This one was to his own mother, Helvia, whom he sought to console not over a bereavement, as would be the norm for the genre, but over the grief caused to her by his own exile. In it, as noted earlier, Seneca portrays himself Stoically enduring a harsh and barren environment:

> What can be found barer or more precipitous on every side than this rock? What more barren in respect of food? What more un-couth in its inhabitants? More mountainous in its configuration? Or more rigorous in its climate? (*Helvia*, 6)

In 44 CE, Seneca published another open letter of consolation. His fame as a writer seemed to be growing thanks to the popularity of these letters. This one was addressed to a freedman called Polybius who served as secretary to Claudius, and had considerable influence at court. Seneca urges Polybius, who had recently lost his brother, to console himself by focusing on the happiness that serving Claudius bestowed upon him. He says things like 'raise yourself up, and fix your eyes upon Caesar whenever tears rise to them; they will become dry on beholding that greatest and most brilliant light'. He tells Polybius to write a panegyric praising Claudius' reign, which might be read 'by all future ages', adding 'for he himself will afford you both the noblest subject and the noblest example for putting together and composing a history'.

The letter eventually turns from being a consolation of Polybius into a plea for mercy directed to his master, the emperor. While taking the opportunity to beg, via Polybius, for an imperial pardon, Seneca also heaps praise on Claudius for his clemency and other virtues. As we'll see, this could not be further removed from the way Seneca later chose to portray Claudius in writing. Seneca concludes by bemoaning the fact that his 'mind is dimmed and stupefied' by the tedium of his long exile. He writes of the difficulty in consoling another while he is steeped in his own sorrows. He complains that his Latin has suffered because around him, on Corsica, he 'hears nothing but a rude foreign jargon, which even barbarians of the more civilised sort regard with disgust'. Once again, his real circumstances appear to have been far more comfortable than he implies.

RETURN

In 48 CE, the Emperor Claudius had his wife, Messalina, executed. Ironically, she was accused of a crime of infidelity not unlike the one for which she had demanded Seneca's execution. Shortly thereafter, Claudius married Agrippina the Younger, the sister of Caligula mentioned earlier. Agrippina soon had her new husband, the emperor, recall Seneca from exile. After eight years honing his art and building his reputation as a writer, Seneca finally got his wish to return to the centre of power. But his recall would have costs.

Agrippina hired Seneca, presumably based on his growing reputation as a writer, to become the rhetoric tutor of her twelve-year-old son, Lucius Domitius Ahenobarbus, the future Emperor Nero. Claudius, after marrying Agrippina, had adopted the boy, her son from a previous marriage. As Lucius/Nero was three years older than the emperor's natural son, Britannicus, Nero effectively supplanted him and became second in line to the throne. Rival camps emerged supporting each of the boys, and Seneca's destiny was now bound to the faction supporting Nero.

Agrippina was a formidable woman who wielded considerable political influence behind the scenes. She promoted her son's status at court by, for example, dismissing the tutors of his rival Britannicus and replacing them with relative unknowns. Seneca, by contrast, was chosen to become Nero's tutor in part because his fame improved her son's public image. He was immediately advanced to the office of praetor, one of the most senior administrative positions in the Roman government. Roman adolescents would normally study literature and the basics of oratory under a grammarian. They would proceed to the more advanced study of formal rhetoric at around fifteen, with philosophy coming years later. So it's unlikely that Nero's lessons at this time focused directly upon Stoic philosophy, although Seneca presumably tried to incorporate some moral instruction.

THE REIGN OF NERO

In 54 CE, Emperor Claudius died after eating some mushrooms. Agrippina, who employed an expert poisoner called Locusta, was widely believed to have had her husband's meal laced with deadly belladonna. Her son Nero was therefore proclaimed emperor, aged only sixteen. Seneca went from being Nero's rhetoric tutor to his political advisor and speechwriter. (We might compare his role to that of today's presidential chief of staff and spin doctor.) Tacitus said the speech Seneca wrote for Nero to deliver following Claudius' death was 'just as elegantly-written as one would expect from that celebrity', confirming that Seneca's fame as a rhetorician had grown. Seneca became Nero's right-hand man and closest advisor, sharing influence with a military man, the praetorian prefect, Burrus.

As we've seen, while in exile Seneca had praised Claudius and urged Polybius to write a panegyric to him. Now Claudius had been killed off, though, and the political tides had changed direction. Seneca responded by publishing a biting satire ridiculing and degrading him, called *The Pumpkinification of the (Divine) Claudius*, in which he hailed Nero as the glory of Rome:

[Just as the sun god] brightly gleams on the world and renews his chariot's journey, so cometh Caesar; so in his glory shall Rome behold Nero. Thus do his radiant features gleam with a gentle efful-gence, graced by the flowing locks that fall encircling his shoulders. (*Pumpkinification*, 4)

Now that Nero was emperor, Seneca was increasingly expected to praise him in public and extol his virtues. Nero rewarded his advisor with 'gifts' of money and property that quickly transformed Seneca into one of the richest men in Rome. Seneca's friends and family also benefited. His elder brother, Gallio, was made consul, the highest political office in the empire; Mela, his younger brother, was made a procurator; Lucan, his nephew, was made a quaestor; Pompeius Paulinus, Seneca's brother-in-law, was made an imperial legate; and Annaeus Serenus, one of his closest friends, was appointed commander of the night watch.

At first, Seneca's position perhaps seemed like an acceptable arrangement. Historians often view the first five years of Nero's reign, the *Quinquennium Neronis*, as promising, owing to the benevolent guiding influence of Seneca and Burrus. However, by accepting all these gifts and favours, Seneca was placing himself, and his friends, in a vulnerable position. Nero, in other words, had an increasing amount of leverage over Seneca. What could possibly go wrong?

MURDER OF BRITANNICUS

A year into Nero's reign, the question of his claim to the throne came to a head. His step-brother, Britannicus, was about to turn fifteen, making him an adult under Roman law. Whereas Nero had merely been adopted by Claudius, Britannicus was his flesh and blood, and therefore had a strong claim to the throne. However, Locusta the poisoner was now in Nero's service. 'All of a sudden, unsurprisingly, Britannicus dropped dead', as Emily Wilson puts it. Thus began Nero's spiralling descent into paranoia and tyranny.

The murder of Britannicus caused public outrage, in part because he was still only a child. Seneca responded by composing and publishing another open letter, this time addressed to the emperor, and titled *On Clemency*. In it he encourages Nero to show forgiveness and mercy towards his opponents. Seneca also used it as an opportunity to praise his former student as a paragon of virtue and a philosopher-king in the making. More importantly, perhaps, he also used it to publicly assert Nero's innocence of any killing:

> You, Caesar, have granted us the boon of keeping our state free from bloodshed, and that of which you boast, that you have not caused one single drop of blood to flow in any part of the world, is all the more magnanimous and marvellous because no one ever had the power of the sword placed in his hands at an earlier age. (*On Clemency*, 11)

Although Seneca does not mention the death of Britannicus, the timing makes it obvious that he was seeking to acquit Nero in the court of public opinion. The slyness with which Seneca here claims that Nero, who retained a poisoner, had never spilled a drop of blood, is very typical of his writings – it's technically true but obviously intended to mislead.

Many readers of the letter found it hard to believe that Seneca could have had the gall to shamelessly praise and exonerate Nero in the aftermath of his younger brother's murder. However, as Wilson suggests, 'the evidence that Seneca did indeed compose this work right after the death of Britannicus is incontrovertible. Some hope to excuse Seneca's comments by claiming that they can perhaps be read in a more nuanced way. Perhaps Seneca's letter's should be seen as part of the genre known as mirrors of princes', seeking to convey not Nero's true reflection but the potential within him for virtue. However, Seneca's letter would have been widely circulated, and we must assume that many Romans would have taken them at face value. Seneca does not only say that Nero has the *potential* for wisdom and virtue, 'a great mind and great gentleness', but that he already possesses these gifts. Moreover, Seneca's claim that not even 'one single drop of blood' had ever been spilled at Nero's behest, probably came across to some as a twisted joke. Yet it may be that, in private, Seneca was troubled by the death of Britannicus. After all, the brutal murder of children is a theme that recurs in his plays, most notably *Thyestes*.

SUPER-RICH SENECA

In 56 CE, shortly after these events, Seneca was appointed consul, the most senior political office in the Roman senate. Men who had attained consular rank were esteemed as nobles alongside the hereditary patrician class. Moreover, as soon as Britannicus had been killed off, Nero 'loaded his best friends with gifts', according to Tacitus, presumably dividing up his dead brother's property among his closest advisors. This has been taken by some historians to explain, at least in part, how Seneca rose from moderately well-off provincial origins to become, under Nero, one of the richest men in the empire. Cassius Dio makes the extraordinary claim that Seneca was worth over 300 million sesterces, which would make him the Roman equivalent of a Warren Buffet or Jeff Bezos. Typically, only the Roman emperor himself or his closest associates might command such wealth. Hence another ancient source, the poet Martial, dubbed him 'Super-rich Seneca'.

Unsurprisingly, Seneca also seems to have owned many properties and a great deal of land throughout Italy, and possibly also in Egypt. We don't know how many slaves he owned, but given his considerable wealth and property, at a rough estimate, they may have numbered over a thousand. As an example of his extravagance, we're told that Seneca owned 500 identical citrus-wood tables with legs of ivory, used for hosting massive banquets. That may sound implausible to modern readers, but it was not unusual for Rome's elite to pride themselves on holding vast banquets, akin to festivals, where hundreds of guests would be entertained. One such banquet, hosted by Lucius Verus, the brother of Marcus Aurelius, reputedly cost 6 million sesterces to put on. Expensive furniture and tableware were highly prized status symbols in elite Roman society.

In 58 CE, a Roman senator called Publius Suillius, who was indicted by Seneca and others for judicial corruption, brought the counter-charge of financial corruption against Seneca. He accused Seneca, perhaps owing to lingering resentment over his exile, of having a vendetta against anyone who had aligned themselves with the Emperor Claudius. However, he also accused Seneca of having enriched himself at the public expense in the short space of four years, i.e. since Nero became emperor. 'In Rome, he spread his nets to catch the wills of childless men', alleged Suillius, while 'Italy and the provinces were sucked dry by his insatiable usury'.

This latter allegation is supported by Cassius Dio's claim that Seneca, wishing suddenly to call in a 40 million sesterce loan made to native Britons under Roman rule, 'resorted to severe means' in demanding repayment. Some historians believe this was one of several events that provoked the famous 61 CE uprising against Roman rule in Britain, led by Queen Boudica.

Suillius was found guilty of corruption and sent into exile, forfeiting half his estate. According to Tacitus, Seneca then attempted to go after the man's son in court as well, but 'the emperor interposed his veto, on the ground that vengeance was satisfied'. In this instance, ironically, his wayward student Nero actually showed more clemency than Seneca. However, worryingly for Seneca, it demonstrated that Nero was now willing to publicly question the wisdom of his teacher's actions.

MURDER OF AGRIPPINA

By 59 CE, Seneca's influence over Nero was waning. The emperor sidelined his powerful mother and plotted to have her murdered. He employed the bizarrely elaborate method of having Agrippina set sail in a boat rigged to collapse, with the intention of crushing and/or drowning her. However, she narrowly escaped and swam back to shore. Seneca and Burrus may have known of this entire scheme. In any case, Nero was forced to seek their help when it failed. Tacitus reports that 'Seneca took the initiative. He looked at Burrus and asked if the military should be ordered to carry out the killing' (*Annals*, 14.7). Burrus agreed and sent a group of praetorians to clean up Nero's mess by completing the assassination.

Tacitus adds that when the soldiers cornered Agrippina, in her bedroom, she pointed at her womb and yelled 'Strike here!', knowing that they had been sent to kill her by her own child. Cassius Dio, on the other hand, claims that her last words were the power-crazed 'Let him kill me, as long as he rules!' Nero was now infamous as the murderer not only of his own brother, but also his mother – and Seneca and Burrus were both thoroughly entangled in his crimes. Nero's tyranny only grew worse from this point on.

Seneca composed a letter to be read before the senate, which claimed that Agrippina, having been discovered plotting against her son, had voluntarily taken her own life. Upon hearing it, Thrasea Pateus, the leader of a faction of scholars and senators referred to as the 'Stoic Opposition', stood up and silently walked out in protest, thereby risking his own life. Nero became increasingly suspicious that those Stoics who saw him as a tyrant were planning to overthrow him. The following year, Nero sent Rubellius Plautus, a relative of his and perceived as a rival to the throne, into exile. Plautus was accompanied by his mentor, the famous Stoic teacher, Musonius Rufus. However, Nero was still too afraid to lift a finger against Thrasea, his staunchest opponent in the senate.

Around this time, Nero instigated a festival called *Juvenalia*, or Games of Youth, in commemoration of the day he reached manhood and began shaving his beard. It was an enormous, grossly extravagant festival, sinister insofar as Nero used the opportunity to humiliate his political opponents by forcing them to engage in indecent performances on stage before huge audiences. 'Now, more than ever', says Tacitus, 'not only these performers but the rest as well regarded the dead as fortunate.' At the climax, we're told that Gallio, Seneca's elder brother, would introduce Nero himself, who craved celebrity, as the headline act. He would sing, accompanying himself on the lyre, although apparently his vocals weren't very good and he 'moved his whole audience to laughter and tears at once'.

Nero created a special corps of 5000 soldiers, the size of an entire legion, called 'Augustans', who surrounded the crowd and led the cheering and applause, forcing compliance under threat of execution. Tacitus says that while Nero sang, Seneca and Burrus, the latter presumably in command of the guards, were on the stage beside him, continually prompting the audience to wave their arms and togas in appreciation of their emperor's performance. The crowd were forced to call out: 'Glorious Caesar! Our Apollo, our Augustus, another Pythian! By thyself we swear, O Caesar, none surpasses thee.' One man in the audience refused to participate, though – Thrasea Pateus, the leader of the Stoic Opposition.

LEAVING NERO

In 62 CE, Burrus, who had been a restraining influence on the emperor, died mysteriously. Suetonius mentions the rumour that Nero had him poisoned. Two new praetorian prefects were appointed, Faenius Rufus and Ofonius Tigellinus. Rufus did little to discourage Nero's excesses. Tigellinus actively encouraged them by, among other things, convincing Nero that his exiled relative Plautus and other Stoics were plotting a coup. Nero finally snapped and had Plautus assassinated.

Seneca, now in desperation, responded by trying to distance himself from his former student. He even asked to turn over his wealth to Nero so that he could retire in peace. Seneca was probably afraid that Nero might eventually have him killed in order to recover his wealth. This was a common threat hanging, like the Sword of Damocles, over the heads of conspicuously wealthy men in the ancient world.

In 64 CE, the Great Fire consumed much of Rome. Nero was suspected of starting it, or at least allowing it to burn unstopped, so that he might rebuild the city in accord with his own designs. The Christians were ultimately blamed for starting the fire and many were rounded up and executed, including St Paul.

Following the death of Burrus, Seneca had increasingly withdrawn from public life. He appears to have been continually on the move, perhaps a precaution against assassination. He focused on writing his *Moral Letters*, *On Providence*, and *Natural Questions*, all dedicated to his friend Lucilius. Despite obvious concerns, Seneca still found himself praising the emperor as 'a man passionately devoted to truth, as he is to the other virtues'. By this point, such flattery must have seemed remarkably at odds with the increasingly violent and despotic nature of Nero's rule. In any case, according to Tacitus, Nero 'in his hatred of Seneca, grasped at all methods of suppressing him'. The perfect opportunity was about to arise.

ENDGAME: THE PISONIAN CONSPIRACY

In 65 CE, Epaphroditus, a freedman who served as secretary to the emperor, gave Nero some information: a group led by a popular senator named Gaius Calpurnius Piso was planning to overthrow him and seize power. Nero responded with swift force, carrying out a violent purge of his enemies. Many prominent individuals were implicated in the plot. Some were exiled. Piso was ordered to commit suicide, along with other ringleaders including the praetorian prefect, Faenius Rufus, and the tribune, Subrius Flavus. The same fate would be visited on Seneca and his nephew Lucan. Tacitus reports the following remarkable twist:

> It was rumoured that Subrius Flavus and the centurions had de-
> cided in private conference, though not without Seneca's knowl-
> edge, that, once Nero had been struck down by the agency of Piso,
> Piso should be disposed of in his turn, and the empire made over
> to Seneca; who would thus appear to have been chosen for the
> supreme power by innocent men, as a consequence of his distin-
> guished virtues. (*Annals*, 15.65)

It's worth pausing for a moment to imagine what history may have been like if such a plot had succeeded in replacing Nero with Seneca, a Stoic man of letters, as the emperor of Rome.

In fact, Nero engaged in a total purge of the Stoic Opposition to his rule. The philosopher, Musonius Rufus, who had returned after the death of Plautus, was sent once again into exile, and several of his Stoic followers were either killed or exiled. Thrasea was finally put on trial for treason. His crimes were mainly to have publicly abstained, in numerous ways, from expressing praise or support for Nero as emperor, including not applauding at his festivals when prompted to do so by Burrus and Seneca. Defiant until the last, Thrasea is reputed to have said at his trial: 'Nero can kill me but he cannot harm me.' Nero had him executed. Barea Soranus, another prominent Stoic, and distant relative of the future emperor Marcus Aurelius, was executed for alleged conspiracy against Nero. Thrasea's son-in-law Helvidius Priscus, and his friend, Paconius Agrippinus, were put on trial at the same time and exiled.

As it happens, Epaphroditus was also the owner of a slave named Epictetus, who would become famous. Epictetus was probably just reaching manhood in Roman terms, aged around fifteen, when these events unfolded. Nevertheless, it's likely that he had a ringside seat to observe the drama at Nero's court. This would shape his own attitude towards imperial power and corruption. Epictetus later gained his freedom and studied Stoic philosophy under Musonius Rufus. He went on to become arguably the most famous teacher of philosophy in Roman history. It's clear from his *Discourses* that he greatly admired Musonius Rufus and revered the members of the Stoic Opposition as moral heroes.

In the years following the Pisonian conspiracy, opposition mounted to Nero's rule, until eventually his legions in Gaul rebelled against him. Though they were defeated, the rebellion spread until Nero, abandoned by his praetorian guard, committed suicide. His death was followed by the chaotic Year of the Four Emperors, which led to the reign of Emperor Vespasian, the founder of the Flavian dynasty.

We're told that, years earlier during the purge that followed the Pisonian conspiracy, when Nero's praetorian guards came for Seneca, he exclaimed:

For to whom had Nero's cruelty been unknown? Nor was anything left him, after the killing of his mother and his brother, but to add the murder of his guardian and tutor. (*Annals*, 15.62)

If he truly spoke these words, it was a last-minute confession. He directly contradicts the public assertions of Nero's innocence (of the death of his brother, Britannicus) that we can read for ourselves in his *On Clemency*. Seneca would also be contradicting the false assertion made in his speech to the senate that Nero's mother, Agrippina had chosen to kill herself. At the end of his life, Seneca can admit to his friends the truth: that Nero had murdered his mother and younger brother.

Readers often notice that Seneca's name is never mentioned in the *Lectures* of Musonius Rufus, the *Discourses* of Epictetus, the *Meditations* of Marcus Aurelius, or indeed the writings of any other Roman Stoic. That may be because his name had been deliberately suppressed by other Stoics, a practice scholars term *damnatio memoriae*. According to the historian Cassius Dio, after Nero murdered his mother, Thrasea told his friends:

> If I were the only one that Nero was going to put to death, I could easily pardon the rest who load him with flatteries. But since even among those who praise him to excess there are many whom he has either already disposed of or will yet destroy, why should one degrade oneself to no purpose and then perish like a slave, when one may pay the debt to nature like a freeman? As for me, men will talk of me hereafter, but of them never, except only to record the fact that they were put to death. (*Cassius Dio*, 62.15)

Seneca, without question, was the most obvious target of this statement.

Tacitus reports that the dying Seneca made a point of emphasizing to his friends that by leaving them with 'his sole but fairest possession – the image of his life' he had bequeathed them something much more valuable than any writings or possessions. Yet, as we've seen, the image of Seneca's life is tainted by, among other things, being inseparably intertwined with Nero's corrupt regime. The Stoic emperor, Marcus Aurelius, writing to himself over a century after Seneca's death, refers to Nero as a cruel tyrant much like Phalaris, and compares him to a wild beast, a moral degenerate 'drawn this way and that by the puppet-strings of impulse' (*Meditations*, 3.16). Yet Seneca repeatedly portrayed Nero as a wise and *virtuous* ruler, almost a philosopher-king.

Nevertheless, Seneca's letters and essays, not to mention his tragedies, have inspired countless people throughout the centuries. It is not the image of his *real* life, therefore, that is Seneca's greatest legacy but rather the image of philosophy as a way of life that he depicted in these writings, especially the *Moral Letters* that he wrote in the years immediately prior to his execution.

THE *MORAL LETTERS*

The *Moral Letters, or Letters to Lucilius*, are Seneca's best-known writings today. The letters include some of Seneca's most memorable sayings, and remain one of our best sources for understanding Stoic philosophy.

There are 124 letters in total. In Letter 8, Seneca mentions his retirement from politics, which happened in 62 CE following the death of his friend Burrus, Nero's praetorian prefect. So these letters are believed to have been written during the last three years of Seneca's life.

Like his essays on *Natural Questions* and *On Providence*, which were written around the same time, they are addressed to a friend called Lucilius. Seneca describes him as an equestrian who was serving as the procurator of Sicily, and it's implied that he came originally from the ill-fated Roman city of Pompeii, in Campania. However, Lucilius is unknown except through Seneca's remarks about him, and it is therefore uncertain whether he was a real person or a character invented for use as a literary device. The consensus among modern scholars is that these letters, probably like all of Seneca's extant writings, were intended for publication.

The *Moral Letters* are perhaps Seneca's finest writings, written in pithy epigrammatic style and containing his most cherished philosophical reflections. Many letters begin with some reference to an everyday, mundane event, which gives him the pretext to launch into an aspect of Stoic teachings. The discussion proceeds, in an apparently unsystematic and informal way, to cover typical Stoic themes such as the goal of life, dealing with old age and death, the nature of virtue, the passions, sensory pleasures, and the dangers of attachment to external things. How Seneca handles this last theme is of particular interest, given his vast wealth.

This Capstone edition includes Letters 1–65, which are historically the most published of the three 'books' of letters. They provide a full impression not only of Seneca's influences and teachings, but in their details give the modern reader a sense of what it was like to be alive in mid-first-century Rome and its provinces: its climate, geography, food, festivals, government, household management, and not least the relations between the upper classes and their slaves (see Letter 47).

On this last issue, Seneca's view is comparatively enlightened: while he in no way calls for an end to the practice, he does demand that slaves be treated as human beings, and be fed well, praised, entertained, and promoted where appropriate. He includes fascinating details, such as the fact that his household includes Harpasté (see Letter 50), a blind, female clown belonging to his wife who had come to her as the result of a legacy. 'I particularly disapprove of these freaks', Seneca ruefully says, yet he also seems amused by the woman, and there's no mention of removing her. He sees the welfare of servants and slaves as a responsibility.

EPICUREANISM VS STOICISM

It's striking that Seneca often mentions Epicurus and his philosophy, in seemingly favourable terms, throughout the first thirty or so letters, and occasionally thereafter. Some have taken this to mean that Seneca's thought was eclectic or that he was sympathetic to Epicurean philosophy, as opposed to Stoic teachings only. I think this is mistaken. Seneca elsewhere is just as scathing about the Epicureans as Epictetus and other Stoics were. For instance, in *On Benefits*, he writes:

> In this part of the subject we oppose the Epicureans, an effeminate and dreamy sect who philosophise in their own paradise, amongst whom virtue is the handmaid of pleasures, obeys them, is subject to them, and regards them as superior to itself. (*On Benefits*, 4.2)

When he praises Epicurus, it's typically an example of a clever argumentative strategy: to praise the thinker's character before attacking his opinions. (In a sense, this is the opposite of the *ad hominem* fallacy, which attacks the character in order to try to refute the ideas.) Although Seneca says that Epicurean philosophy contains a few good sayings, he also subtly undermines their value by claiming that they're commonly found also in the writings of other authors. It's as though he's saying, as we would put it today, what's good in Epicurus isn't original and what's original isn't good. In Letter 2, where Seneca says that he's happy to sneak over to the 'enemy camp' in order to steal some of their ideas, Epicureans are nevertheless 'the enemy'. These little nuances are typical of Seneca's style of writing.

It's clear, and in fact one of Seneca's major themes, that he believes Epicurus was wrong to view the goal of life as consisting in pleasure, even when construed as the stable pleasure of total peace of mind (*ataraxia*). The true goal of life, for Seneca, as for all Stoics, is virtue (*arete*), which we could also describe as a form of *moral wisdom*.

The *Moral Letters* provide an education in how to live wisely, by seeing beyond the value mistakenly invested in external goods such as wealth and reputation by the majority of people. Instead, the Stoic Sage lives in accord with virtue, which he views as its own reward. Even though Seneca may have failed to embody this philosophy in practice, it is nevertheless the type of person he clearly wished he could have been, and perhaps wanted to become until the end.

FURTHER READING

Bartsch, S., & Schiesaro, A. (2018). *The Cambridge Companion to Seneca*. New York: Cambridge University Press.

Griffin, M. T. (2003). *Seneca: A Philosopher in Politics*. Oxford: Clarendon.

Griffin, M. T. (2016). *Nero: The End of a Dynasty*. London & New York: Routledge.

Inwood, B. (2009). *Reading Seneca: Stoic Philosophy at Rome*. Oxford: Clarendon.

Romm, J. S. (2014). *Dying Every Day: Seneca at the Court of Nero*. New York: Alfred A. Knopf.

Star, C. (2019). *Understanding Classics: Seneca*. London: Bloomsbury.

Wilson, E. (2018). *The Greatest Empire: A Life of Seneca*. Oxford: Oxford University Press.

NOTE ON THE TEXT

This Capstone edition, *Letters from a Stoic*, is based on Richard Mott Gummere's 1917 translation of the *Moral Letters to Lucilius*. Gummere's footnotes are retained where they help to explain terms, phrases, and people that may be foreign to the contemporary reader. A few additional footnotes have been added for the same reasons. Gummere also includes sources for quotations or texts that Seneca himself includes or mentions.

ABOUT DONALD ROBERTSON

Donald Robertson is a writer, trainer, and cognitive behavioural psychotherapist. He specializes in the relationship between ancient philosophy and modern evidence-based psychological therapy. Donald is the author of six books on philosophy and psychotherapy, including Stoicism and the Art of Happiness (2013) and How to Think Like a Roman Emperor: The Stoic Philosophy of Marcus Aurelius (2019). He provided the Introduction for the Capstone edition of the Meditations by Marcus Aurelius.

ABOUT TOM BUTLER-BOWDON

Tom Butler-Bowdon is the author of the bestselling 50 Classics series, which brings the ideas of important books to a wider audience. Titles include *50 Philosophy Classics*, *50 Psychology Classics*, *50 Politics Classics*, *50 Self-Help Classics*, and *50 Economics Classics*. As series editor for the Capstone Classics series, Tom has written Introductions to Plato's *The Republic*, Machiavelli's *The Prince*, Adam Smith's *The Wealth of Nations*, Sun Tzu's *The Art of War*, Lao Tzu's *Tao Te Ching*, and Napoleon Hill's *Think and Grow Rich*. Tom is a graduate of the London School of Economics and the University of Sydney. www.Butler-Bowdon.com

ON THE USE OF TIME

From Seneca to his friend Lucilius.

Continue to act thus, my dear Lucilius – set yourself free for your own sake; gather and save your time, which till lately has been forced from you, or filched away, or has merely slipped from your hands. Make yourself believe the truth of my words – that certain moments are torn from us, that some are gently removed, and that others glide beyond our reach. The most disgraceful kind of loss, however, is that due to carelessness. Furthermore, if you will pay close heed to the problem, you will find that the largest portion of our life passes while we are doing ill, a goodly share while we are doing nothing, and the whole while we are doing that which is not to the purpose. What man can you show me who places any

1

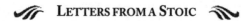

value on his time, who reckons the worth of each day, who understands that he is dying daily? For we are mistaken when we look forward to death; the major portion of death has already passed. Whatever years lie behind us are in death's hands.

Therefore, Lucilius, do as you write me that you are doing: hold every hour in your grasp. Lay hold of today's task, and you will not need to depend so much upon tomorrow's. While we are postponing, life speeds by. Nothing, Lucilius, is ours, except time. We were entrusted by nature with the ownership of this single thing, so fleeting and slippery that anyone who will can oust us from possession. What fools these mortals be! They allow the cheapest and most useless things, which can easily be replaced, to be charged in the reckoning, after they have acquired them; but they never regard themselves as in debt when they have received some of that precious commodity – time! And yet time is the one loan which even a grateful recipient cannot repay.

You may desire to know how I, who preach to you so freely, am practising. I confess frankly: my expense account balances, as you would expect from one who is free-handed but careful. I cannot boast that I waste nothing, but I can at least tell you what I am wasting, and the cause and manner of the loss; I can give you the reasons why I am a poor man. My situation, however, is the same as that of many who are reduced to slender means through no fault of their own: every one forgives them, but no one comes to their rescue.

What is the state of things, then? It is this: I do not regard a man as poor, if the little which remains is enough for him. I advise you, however, to keep what is really yours; and you cannot begin too early. For, as our ancestors believed, it is too late to spare when you reach the dregs of the cask. Of that which remains at the bottom, the amount is slight, and the quality is vile. Farewell.

ON DISCURSIVENESS IN READING

Judging by what you write me, and by what I hear, I am forming a good opinion regarding your future. You do not run hither and thither and distract yourself by changing your abode; for such restlessness is the sign of a disordered spirit. The primary indication, to my thinking, of a well-ordered mind is a man's ability to remain in one place and linger in his own company. Be careful, however, lest this reading of many authors and books of every sort may tend to make you discursive and unsteady. You must linger among a limited number of master-thinkers, and digest their works, if you would derive ideas which shall win firm hold in your mind. Everywhere means nowhere. When a person spends all his time in foreign travel, he ends by having many acquaintances, but no friends.

And the same thing must hold true of men who seek intimate acquaintance with no single author, but visit them all in a hasty and hurried manner. Food does no good and is not assimilated into the body if it leaves the stomach as soon as it is eaten; nothing hinders a cure so much as frequent change of medicine; no wound will heal when one salve is tried after another; a plant which is often moved can never grow strong. There is nothing so efficacious that it can be helpful while it is being shifted about. And in reading of many books is distraction.

Accordingly, since you cannot read all the books which you may possess, it is enough to possess only as many books as you can read. 'But', you reply, 'I wish to dip first into one book and then into another.' I tell you that it is the sign of an overnice appetite to toy with many dishes; for when they are manifold and varied, they cloy but do not nourish. So you should always read standard authors; and when you crave a change, fall back upon those whom you read before. Each day acquire something that will fortify you against poverty, against death, indeed against other misfortunes as well; and after you have run over many thoughts, select one to be thoroughly digested that day. This is my own custom; from the many things which I have read, I claim some one part for myself.

The thought for today is one which I discovered in Epicurus;[1] for I am wont to cross over even into the enemy's camp – not as a deserter, but as a scout. He says: 'Contented poverty is an honourable estate.' Indeed, if it be contented, it is not poverty at all. It is not the man who has too little, but the man who craves more, that is poor. What does it matter how much a man has laid up in his safe, or in his warehouse, how large are his flocks and how fat his dividends, if he covets his neighbour's property, and reckons, not his past gains, but his hopes of gains to come? Do you ask what is the proper limit to wealth? It is, first, to have what is necessary, and, second, to have what is enough. Farewell.

---

[1]Fragment 475 from Hermann Usener's *Epicurea* (1887). Usener's numbering system for Epicurus is used throughout this edition of Seneca's *Letters*.

ON TRUE AND FALSE FRIENDSHIP

You have sent a letter to me through the hand of a 'friend' of yours, as you call him. And in your very next sentence you warn me not to discuss with him all the matters that concern you, saying that even you yourself are not accustomed to do this; in other words, you have in the same letter affirmed and denied that he is your friend. Now if you used this word of ours[1] in the popular sense, and called him 'friend' in the same way in which we speak of all candidates for election as 'honourable gentlemen', and as we greet all men whom we meet casually, if their names slip us for the moment, with the salutation 'my dear sir' – so be it. But if you consider any man a friend whom you do not trust as you

---

[1] i.e. a word which has a special significance to the Stoics.

trust yourself, you are mightily mistaken and you do not sufficiently understand what true friendship means. Indeed, I would have you discuss everything with a friend; but first of all discuss the man himself. When friendship is settled, you must trust; before friendship is formed, you must pass judgement. Those persons indeed put last first and confound their duties, who, violating the rules of Theophrastus,[2] judge a man after they have made him their friend, instead of making him their friend after they have judged him. Ponder for a long time whether you shall admit a given person to your friendship; but when you have decided to admit him, welcome him with all your heart and soul. Speak as boldly with him as with yourself. As to yourself, although you should live in such a way that you trust your own self with nothing which you could not entrust even to your enemy, yet, since certain matters occur which convention keeps secret, you should share with a friend at least all your worries and reflections. Regard him as loyal, and you will make him loyal. Some, for example, fearing to be deceived, have taught men to deceive; by their suspicions they have given their friend the right to do wrong. Why need I keep back

---

[2]Successor to Aristotle in the Peripatetic School.

any words in the presence of my friend? Why should I not regard myself as alone when in his company?

There is a class of men who communicate, to anyone whom they meet, matters which should be revealed to friends alone, and unload upon the chance listener whatever irks them. Others, again, fear to confide in their closest intimates; and if it were possible, they would not trust even themselves, burying their secrets deep in their hearts. But we should do neither. It is equally faulty to trust everyone and to trust no one. Yet the former fault is, I should say, the more ingenuous, the latter the more safe. In like manner you should rebuke these two kinds of men – both those who always lack repose, and those who are always in repose. For love of bustle is not industry – it is only the restlessness of a hunted mind. And true repose does not consist in condemning all motion as merely vexation; that kind of repose is slackness and inertia. Therefore, you should note the following saying, taken from my reading in Pomponius[3]: 'Some men shrink into dark corners, to such a degree that they see darkly by day.' No,

---

[3]Pomponius Secundus, a contemporary of Seneca. Statesman in the time of Tiberius, Caligula, and Claudius. Poet and writer of tragedies and letters.

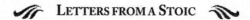

men should combine these tendencies, and he who reposes should act and he who acts should take repose. Discuss the problem with Nature; she will tell you that she has created both day and night. Farewell.

CHAPTER FOUR

ON THE TERRORS OF DEATH

Keep on as you have begun, and make all possible haste, so that you may have longer enjoyment of an improved mind, one that is at peace with itself. Doubtless you will derive enjoyment during the time when you are improving your mind and setting it at peace with itself; but quite different is the pleasure which comes from contemplation when one's mind is so cleansed from every stain that it shines.

You remember, of course, what joy you felt when you laid aside the garments of boyhood and donned the man's toga, and were escorted to the forum; nevertheless, you may look for a still greater joy when you have laid aside the mind of boyhood and when wisdom has enrolled you among men. For it is not boyhood that still stays with us, but something

13

worse – boyishness. And this condition is all the more serious because we possess the authority of old age, together with the follies of boyhood, yea, even the follies of infancy. Boys fear trifles, children fear shadows, we fear both.

All you need to do is to advance; you will thus understand that some things are less to be dreaded, precisely because they inspire us with great fear. No evil is great which is the last evil of all. Death arrives; it would be a thing to dread, if it could remain with you. But death must either not come at all, or else must come and pass away.

'It is difficult, however', you say, 'to bring the mind to a point where it can scorn life.' But do you not see what trifling reasons impel men to scorn life? One hangs himself before the door of his mistress; another hurls himself from the house-top that he may no longer be compelled to bear the taunts of a bad-tempered master; a third, to be saved from arrest after running away, drives a sword into his vitals. Do you not suppose that virtue will be as efficacious as excessive fear? No man can have a peaceful life who thinks too much about lengthening it, or believes that living through many consulships is a great blessing.

Rehearse this thought every day, that you may be able to depart from life contentedly; for many men clutch and cling to life, even as those who are carried down a rushing stream clutch and cling to briars and sharp rocks.

Most men ebb and flow in wretchedness between the fear of death and the hardships of life; they are unwilling to live, and yet they do not know how to die.

For this reason, make life as a whole agreeable to yourself by banishing all worry about it. No good thing renders its possessor happy, unless his mind is reconciled to the possibility of loss; nothing, however, is lost with less discomfort than that which, when lost, cannot be missed. Therefore, encourage and toughen your spirit against the mishaps that afflict even the most powerful.

For example, the fate of Pompey was settled by a boy and a eunuch, that of Crassus by a cruel and insolent Parthian. Gaius Caesar ordered Lepidus to bare his neck for the axe of the tribune Dexter; and he himself offered his own throat to Chaerea.[1] No man has ever been so far advanced by Fortune that she did not threaten him as greatly as she had previously indulged him. Do not trust her seeming calm; in a moment the sea is moved to its depths. The very day the ships have made a brave show in the games, they are engulfed.

---

[1]A reference to the murder of Caligula, on the Palatine, 41 CE.

Reflect that a highwayman or an enemy may cut your throat; and, though he is not your master, every slave wields the power of life and death over you. Therefore I declare to you: he is lord of your life that scorns his own. Think of those who have perished through plots in their own homes, slain either openly or by guile; you will then understand that just as many have been killed by angry slaves as by angry kings. What matter, therefore, how powerful he be whom you fear, when everyone possesses the power which inspires your fear?

'But', you will say, 'if you should chance to fall into the hands of the enemy, the conqueror will command that you be led away' – yes, whither you are already being led.[2] Why do you voluntarily deceive yourself and require to be told now for the first time what fate it is that you have long been labouring under? Take my word for it: since the day you were born you are being led thither. We must ponder this thought, and thoughts of the like nature, if we desire to be calm as we await that last hour, the fear of which makes all previous hours uneasy.

But I must end my letter. Let me share with you the saying which pleased me today. It, too, is culled from another man's Garden:[3] 'Poverty brought into

---

[2]i.e. to death.

[3]The Garden of Epicurus.

conformity with the law of nature, is great wealth.' Do you know what limits that law of nature ordains for us? Merely to avert hunger, thirst, and cold. In order to banish hunger and thirst, it is not necessary for you to pay court at the doors of the purse-proud, or to submit to the stern frown, or to the kindness that humiliates; nor is it necessary for you to scour the seas, or go campaigning; nature's needs are easily provided and ready to hand.

It is the superfluous things for which men sweat – the superfluous things that wear our togas threadbare, that force us to grow old in camp, that dash us upon foreign shores. That which is enough is ready to our hands. He who has made a fair compact with poverty is rich. Farewell.

ON THE PHILOSOPHER'S MEAN

I commend you and rejoice in the fact that you are persistent in your studies, and that, putting all else aside, you make it each day your endeavour to become a better man. I do not merely exhort you to keep at it; I actually beg you to do so. I warn you, however, not to act after the fashion of those who desire to be conspicuous rather than to improve, by doing things which will rouse comment as regards your dress or general way of living.

Repellent attire, unkempt hair, slovenly beard, open scorn of silver dishes, a couch on the bare earth, and any other perverted forms of self-display are to be avoided. The mere name of philosophy, however quietly pursued, is an object of sufficient scorn; and what would happen if we should begin to separate ourselves from the customs of our fellow-men? Inwardly, we ought to be different in all respects, but our exterior should conform to society.

Do not wear too fine, nor yet too frowzy, a toga. One needs no silver plate, encrusted and embossed in solid gold; but we should not believe the lack of silver and gold to be proof of the simple life. Let us try to maintain a higher standard of life than that of the multitude, but not a contrary standard; otherwise, we shall frighten away and repel the very persons whom we are trying to improve. We also bring it about that they are unwilling to imitate us in anything, because they are afraid lest they might be compelled to imitate us in everything.

The first thing which philosophy undertakes to give is fellow-feeling with all men; in other words, sympathy and sociability. We part company with our promise if we are unlike other men. We must see to it that the means by which we wish to draw admiration be not absurd and odious. Our motto,[1] as you know, is 'Live according to Nature', but it is quite contrary to nature to torture the body, to hate unlaboured elegance, to be dirty on purpose, to eat food that is not only plain, but disgusting and forbidding.

Just as it is a sign of luxury to seek out dainties, so it is madness to avoid that which is customary and

---

[1] i.e. of the Stoic school.

can be purchased at no great price. Philosophy calls for plain living, but not for penance; and we may perfectly well be plain and neat at the same time. This is the mean of which I approve; our life should observe a happy medium between the ways of a sage and the ways of the world at large; all men should admire it, but they should understand it also.

'Well then, shall we act like other men? Shall there be no distinction between ourselves and the world?' Yes, a very great one; let men find that we are unlike the common herd, if they look closely. If they visit us at home, they should admire us, rather than our household appointments. He is a great man who uses earthenware dishes as if they were silver, but he is equally great who uses silver as if it were earthenware. It is the sign of an unstable mind not to be able to endure riches.

But I wish to share with you today's profit also. I find in the writings of our Hecato that the limiting of desires helps also to cure fears: 'Cease to hope', he says, 'and you will cease to fear.' 'But how', you will reply, 'can things so different go side by side?' In this way, my dear Lucilius: though they do seem at variance, yet they are really united. Just as the same chain fastens the prisoner and the soldier who guards him, so hope and fear, dissimilar as they are, keep step together; fear follows hope.

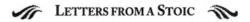

I am not surprised that they proceed in this way; each alike belongs to a mind that is in suspense, a mind that is fretted by looking forward to the future. But the chief cause of both these ills is that we do not adapt ourselves to the present, but send our thoughts a long way ahead. And so foresight, the noblest blessing of the human race, becomes perverted.

Beasts avoid the dangers which they see, and when they have escaped them are free from care; but we men torment ourselves over that which is to come as well as over that which is past. Many of our blessings bring bane to us; for memory recalls the tortures of fear, while foresight anticipates them. The present alone can make no man wretched. Farewell.

CHAPTER SIX

ON SHARING KNOWLEDGE

I feel, my dear Lucilius, that I am being not only reformed, but transformed. I do not yet, however, assure myself, or indulge the hope, that there are no elements left in me which need to be changed. Of course there are many that should be made more compact, or made thinner, or be brought into greater prominence. And indeed this very fact is proof that my spirit is altered into something better – that it can see its own faults, of which it was previously ignorant. In certain cases sick men are congratulated because they themselves have perceived that they are sick.

I therefore wish to impart to you this sudden change in myself; I should then begin to place a surer trust in our friendship – the true friendship which hope and fear and self-interest cannot sever, the friendship in which and for the sake of which men meet death.

I can show you many who have lacked, not a friend, but a friendship; this, however, cannot possibly happen when souls are drawn together by identical inclinations into an alliance of honourable desires. And why can it not happen? Because in such cases men know that they have all things in common, especially their troubles.

You cannot conceive what distinct progress I notice that each day brings to me.

And when you say: 'Give me also a share in these gifts which you have found so helpful,' I reply that I am anxious to heap all these privileges upon you, and that I am glad to learn in order that I may teach. Nothing will ever please me, no matter how excellent or beneficial, if I must retain the knowledge of it to myself. And if wisdom were given me under the express condition that it must be kept hidden and not uttered, I should refuse it. No good thing is pleasant to possess, without friends to share it.

I shall therefore send to you the actual books; and in order that you may not waste time in searching here and there for profitable topics, I shall mark certain passages, so that you can turn at once to those which I approve and admire. Of course, however, the living voice and the intimacy of a common life will help you more than the written word. You must go to the scene of action, first, because men put more faith in their eyes than in their ears, and second, because the way is long if one follows precepts, but short and helpful, if one follows patterns.

Cleanthes could not have been the express image of Zeno, if he had merely heard his lectures; he shared in his life, saw into his hidden purposes, and watched him to see whether he lived according to his own rules. Plato, Aristotle, and the whole throng of sages who were destined to go each his different way, derived more benefit from the character than from the words of Socrates. It was not the classroom of Epicurus, but living together under the same roof, that made great men of Metrodorus, Hermarchus, and Polyaenus. Therefore I summon you, not merely that you may derive benefit, but that you may confer benefit; for we can assist each other greatly.

Meanwhile, I owe you my little daily contribution; you shall be told what pleased me today in the writings of Hecato; it is these words: 'What progress, you ask, have I made? I have begun to be a friend to myself.' That was indeed a great benefit; such a person can never be alone. You may be sure that such a man is a friend to all mankind. Farewell.

ON CROWDS

Do you ask me what you should regard as especially to be avoided? I say, crowds; for as yet you cannot trust yourself to them with safety. I shall admit my own weakness, at any rate; for I never bring back home the same character that I took abroad with me. Something of that which I have forced to be calm within me is disturbed; some of the foes that I have routed return again. Just as the sick man, who has been weak for a long time, is in such a condition that he cannot be taken out of the house without suffering a relapse, so we ourselves are affected when our souls are recovering from a lingering disease.

To consort with the crowd is harmful; there is no person who does not make some vice attractive to us, or stamp it upon us, or taint us unconsciously therewith. Certainly, the greater the mob with which we mingle, the greater the danger.

But nothing is so damaging to good character as the habit of lounging at the games; for then it is that vice steals subtly upon one through the avenue of pleasure.

What do you think I mean? I mean that I come home more greedy, more ambitious, more voluptuous, and even more cruel and inhuman – because I have been among human beings. By chance I attended a midday exhibition, expecting some fun, wit, and relaxation – an exhibition at which men's eyes have respite from the slaughter of their fellow-men. But it was quite the reverse. The previous combats were the essence of compassion; but now all the trifling is put aside and it is pure murder.[1] The men have no defensive armour. They are exposed to blows at all points, and no one ever strikes in vain.

Many persons prefer this programme to the usual pairs and to the bouts 'by request'. Of course they do; there is no helmet or shield to deflect the weapon. What is the need of defensive armour, or of skill? All these mean delaying death. In the morning they throw men to the lions and the bears; at noon, they

---

[1] During the luncheon interval condemned criminals were often driven into the arena and compelled to fight, for the amusement of those spectators who remained throughout the day.

throw them to the spectators. The spectators demand that the slayer shall face the man who is to slay him in his turn; and they always reserve the latest conqueror for another butchering. The outcome of every fight is death, and the means are fire and sword. This sort of thing goes on while the arena is empty.

You may retort: 'But he was a highway robber; he killed a man!' And what of it? Granted that, as a murderer, he deserved this punishment, what crime have you committed, poor fellow, that you should deserve to sit and see this show? In the morning they cried: 'Kill him! Lash him! Burn him! Why does he meet the sword in so cowardly a way? Why does he strike so feebly? Why doesn't he die game? Whip him to meet his wounds! Let them receive blow for blow, with chests bare and exposed to the stroke!' And when the games stop for the intermission, they announce: 'A little throat-cutting in the meantime, so that there may still be something going on!'

Come now; do you[2] not understand even this truth, that a bad example reacts on the agent? Thank the immortal gods that you are teaching cruelty to a person who cannot learn to be cruel.

The young character, which cannot hold fast to righteousness, must be rescued from the mob; it is

---

[2]The remark is addressed to the brutalized spectators.

too easy to side with the majority. Even Socrates, Cato, and Laelius might have been shaken in their moral strength by a crowd that was unlike them; so true it is that none of us, no matter how much he cultivates his abilities, can withstand the shock of faults that approach, as it were, with so great a retinue.

Much harm is done by a single case of indulgence or greed; the familiar friend, if he be luxurious, weakens and softens us imperceptibly; the neighbour, if he be rich, rouses our covetousness; the companion, if he be slanderous, rubs off some of his rust upon us, even though we be spotless and sincere. What then do you think the effect will be on character, when the world at large assaults it? You must either imitate or loathe the world.

But both courses are to be avoided; you should not copy the bad simply because they are many, nor should you hate the many because they are unlike you. Withdraw into yourself, as far as you can. Associate with those who will make a better man of you. Welcome those whom you yourself can improve. The process is mutual; for men learn while they teach.

There is no reason why pride in advertising your abilities should lure you into publicity, so that you should desire to recite or harangue before the general public. Of course I should be willing for you to do so if you had a stock-in-trade that suited such a mob; as it is, there is not a man of them who can understand you. One or two individuals will perhaps come in your way, but even these will have to be moulded and trained by you so that they will understand you. You may say: 'For what purpose did I learn all these things?' But you need not fear that you have wasted your efforts; it was for yourself that you learned them.

In order, however, that I may not today have learned exclusively for myself, I shall share with you three excellent sayings, of the same general purport, which have come to my attention. This letter will give you one of them as payment of my debt; the other two you may accept as a contribution in advance. Democritus says: 'One man means as much to me as a multitude, and a multitude only as much as one man.'

The following also was nobly spoken by someone or other, for it is doubtful who the author was; they asked him what was the object of all this study applied to an art that would reach but very few. He replied: 'I am content with few, content with one, content with none at all.' The third saying – and a noteworthy one, too – is by Epicurus[3] written to one of the partners of his studies: 'I write this not for the many, but for you; each of us is enough of an audience for the other.'

---

[3]Fragment 208, Usener.

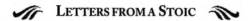

Lay these words to heart, Lucilius, that you may scorn the pleasure which comes from the applause of the majority. Many men praise you; but have you any reason for being pleased with yourself, if you are a person whom the many can understand? Your good qualities should face inwards. Farewell.

ON THE PHILOSOPHER'S SECLUSION

'Do you bid me', you say, 'shun the throng, and withdraw from men, and be content with my own conscience? Where are the counsels of your school, which order a man to die in the midst of active work?' As to the course[1] which I seem to you to be urging on you now and then, my object in shutting myself up and locking the door is to be able to help a greater number. I never spend a day in idleness; I appropriate even a part of the night for study. I do not allow time for sleep but yield to it when I must, and when my eyes are wearied with waking and ready to fall shut, I keep them at their task.

---

[1]As contrasted with the general Stoic doctrine of taking part in the world's work.

I have withdrawn not only from men, but from affairs, especially from my own affairs; I am working for later generations, writing down some ideas that may be of assistance to them. There are certain wholesome counsels, which may be compared to prescriptions of useful drugs; these I am putting into writing; for I have found them helpful in ministering to my own sores, which, if not wholly cured, have at any rate ceased to spread.

I point other men to the right path, which I have found late in life, when wearied with wandering. I cry out to them: 'Avoid whatever pleases the throng: avoid the gifts of Chance! Halt before every good which Chance brings to you, in a spirit of doubt and fear; for it is the dumb animals and fish that are deceived by tempting hopes. Do you call these things the "gifts" of Fortune? They are snares. And any man among you who wishes to live a life of safety will avoid, to the utmost of his power, these limed twigs of her favour, by which we mortals, most wretched in this respect also, are deceived; for we think that we hold them in our grasp, but they hold us in theirs.

'Such a career leads us into precipitous ways, and life on such heights ends in a fall. Moreover, we cannot even stand up against prosperity when she begins to drive us to leeward; nor can we go down, either, "with the ship at least on her course", or once for all;[2] Fortune does not capsize us – she plunges our bows under and dashes us on the rocks.

'Hold fast, then, to this sound and wholesome rule of life; that you indulge the body only so far as is needful for good health. The body should be treated more rigorously, that it may not be disobedient to the mind. Eat merely to relieve your hunger; drink merely to quench your thirst; dress merely to keep out the cold; house yourself merely as a protection against personal discomfort. It matters little whether the house be built of turf, or of variously coloured imported marble; understand that a man is sheltered just as well by a thatch as by a roof of gold. Despise everything that useless toil creates as an ornament and an object of beauty. And reflect that nothing except the soul is worthy of wonder; for to the soul, if it be great, naught is great.'

When I commune in such terms with myself and with future generations, do you not think that I am doing more good than when I appear as counsel in court, or stamp my seal upon a will, or lend my assistance in the senate, by word or action, to a candidate? Believe me, those who seem to be busied with nothing are busied with the greater tasks; they are

_____

[2]From Epicurus (lxxxv, 33), the famous saying of the Rhodian pilot.

dealing at the same time with things mortal and things immortal.

But I must stop, and pay my customary contribution, to balance this letter. The payment shall not be made from my own property; for I am still conning Epicurus. I read today, in his works, the following sentence: 'If you would enjoy real freedom, you must be the slave of Philosophy.' The man who submits and surrenders himself to her is not kept waiting; he is emancipated[3] on the spot. For the very service of Philosophy is freedom.

It is likely that you will ask me why I quote so many of Epicurus's noble words instead of words taken from our own school. But is there any reason why you should regard them as sayings of Epicurus and not common property? How many poets give forth ideas that have been uttered, or may be uttered, by philosophers! I need not touch upon the tragedians and our writers of national drama; for these last are also somewhat serious, and stand half-way between comedy and tragedy. What a quantity of sagacious verses lie buried in the mime! How many of Publilius's lines are worthy of being spoken by buskin-clad actors, as well as by wearers of the slipper![4]

---

[3]Literally 'spun around' by the master and dismissed to freedom.
[4]i.e. comedians or mimes.

I shall quote one verse of his, which concerns philosophy, and particularly that phase of it which we were discussing a moment ago, wherein he says that the gifts of Chance are not to be regarded as part of our possessions:

> Still alien is whatever you have gained
> By coveting.[5]

I recall that you yourself expressed this idea much more happily and concisely:

> What Chance has made yours is not really yours.

And a third, spoken by you still more happily, shall not be omitted:

> The good that could be given, can be removed.

I shall not charge this up to the expense account, because I have given it to you from your own stock. Farewell.

---

[5]Publilius Syrius, *Sententiae.*

ON PHILOSOPHY AND FRIENDSHIP

You desire to know whether Epicurus is right when, in one of his letters,[1] he rebukes those who hold that the wise man is self-sufficient and for that reason does not stand in need of friendships. This is the objection raised by Epicurus against Stilbo and those who believe[2] that the Supreme Good is a soul which is insensible to feeling.

We are bound to meet with a double meaning if we try to express the Greek term 'lack of feeling' summarily, in a single word, rendering it by the Latin word *impatientia*. For it may be understood in the meaning the opposite to that which we wish it to have.

---

[1]Fragment 174, Usener.

[2]i.e. the Cynics.

What we mean to express is a soul which rejects any sensation of evil, but people will interpret the idea as that of a soul which can endure no evil. Consider, therefore, whether it is not better to say 'a soul that cannot be harmed', or 'a soul entirely beyond the realm of suffering'.

There is this difference between ourselves and the other school:[3] our ideal wise man feels his troubles, but overcomes them; their wise man does not even feel them. But we and they alike hold this idea – that the wise man is self-sufficient. Nevertheless, he desires friends, neighbours, and associates, no matter how much he is sufficient unto himself.

And mark how self-sufficient he is; for on occasion he can be content with a part of himself. If he lose a hand through disease or war, or if some accident puts out one or both of his eyes, he will be satisfied with what is left, taking as much pleasure in his impaired and maimed body as he took when it was sound. But while he does not pine for these parts if they are missing, he prefers not to lose them.

In this sense the wise man is self-sufficient, that he can do without friends, not that he desires to do without them. When I say 'can', I mean this: he endures the loss of a friend with equanimity.

---

[3]i.e. the Cynics.

But he need never lack friends, for it lies in his own control how soon he shall make good a loss. Just as Phidias, if he lose a statue, can straightway carve another, even so our master in the art of making friendships can fill the place of a friend he has lost.

If you ask how one can make oneself a friend quickly, I will tell you, provided we are agreed that I may pay my debt at once and square the account, so far as this letter is concerned. Hecato says: 'I can show you a philtre, compounded without drugs, herbs, or any witch's incantation: "If you would be loved, love."' Now there is great pleasure, not only in maintaining old and established friendships, but also in beginning and acquiring new ones.

There is the same difference between winning a new friend and having already won him, as there is between the farmer who sows and the farmer who reaps. The philosopher Attalus used to say: 'It is more pleasant to make than to keep a friend, as it is more pleasant to the artist to paint than to have finished painting.' When one is busy and absorbed in one's work, the very absorption affords great delight; but when one has withdrawn one's hand from the completed masterpiece, the pleasure is not so keen. Henceforth it is the fruits of his art that he enjoys; it was the art itself that he enjoyed while he was painting. In the case of our children, their young manhood yields the more abundant fruits, but their infancy was sweeter.

Let us now return to the question. The wise man, I say, self-sufficient though he be, nevertheless desires friends if only for the purpose of practising friend-ship, in order that his noble qualities may not lie dormant. Not, however, for the purpose mentioned by Epicurus in the letter quoted above: 'That there may be someone to sit by him when he is ill, to help him when he is in prison or in want'; but that he may have someone by whose sick-bed he himself may sit, someone a prisoner in hostile hands whom he himself may set free. He who regards himself only, and enters upon friendships for this reason, reckons wrongly. The end will be like the beginning: he has made friends with one who might assist him out of bondage; at the first rattle of the chain such a friend will desert him.

These are the so-called 'fair-weather' friendships; one who is chosen for the sake of utility will be satis-factory only so long as he is useful. Hence prosperous men are blockaded by troops of friends; but those who have failed stand amid vast loneliness, their friends fleeing from the very crisis which is to test their worth. Hence, also, we notice those many shameful cases of persons who, through fear, desert or betray. The be-ginning and the end cannot but harmonize. He who begins to be your friend because it pays will also cease because it pays. A man will be attracted by some reward offered in exchange for his friendship, if he be attracted by aught in friendship other than friendship itself.

For what purpose, then, do I make a man my friend? In order to have someone for whom I may die, whom I may follow into exile, against whose death I may stake my own life, and pay the pledge, too. The friendship which you portray is a bargain and not a friendship; it regards convenience only, and looks to the results.

Beyond question the feeling of a lover has in it something akin to friendship; one might call it friendship run mad. But, though this is true, does anyone love for the sake of gain, or promotion, or renown? Pure love, careless of all other things, kindles the soul with desire for the beautiful object, not without the hope of a return of the affection. What then? Can a cause which is more honourable produce a passion that is base?

You may retort: 'We are not now discussing the question whether friendship is to be cultivated for its own sake.' On the contrary, nothing more urgently requires demonstration; for if friendship is to be sought for its own sake, he may seek it who is self-sufficient. 'How, then', you ask, 'does he seek it?'

Precisely as he seeks an object of great beauty, not attracted to it by desire for gain, nor yet frightened by the instability of Fortune. One who seeks friendship for favourable occasions strips it of all its nobility.

'The wise man is self-sufficient.' This phrase, my dear Lucilius, is incorrectly explained by many; for they withdraw the wise man from the world, and force him to dwell within his own skin. But we must mark with care what this sentence signifies and how far it applies; the wise man is sufficient unto himself for a happy existence, but not for mere existence. For he needs many helps towards mere existence; but for a happy existence he needs only a sound and upright soul, one that despises Fortune.

I should like also to state to you one of the distinctions of Chrysippus, who declares that the wise man is in want of nothing, and yet needs many things. 'On the other hand', he says, 'nothing is needed by the fool, for he does not understand how to use anything, but he is in want of everything.' The wise man needs hands, eyes, and many things that are necessary for his daily use; but he is in want of nothing. For want implies a necessity, and nothing is necessary to the wise man.

Therefore, although he is self-sufficient, yet he has need of friends. He craves as many friends as possible, not, however, that he may live happily; for he will live happily even without friends. The Supreme Good calls for no practical aids from outside; it is developed at home, and arises entirely within itself. If the good seeks any portion of itself from without, it begins to be subject to the play of Fortune.

People may say: 'But what sort of existence will the wise man have, if he be left friendless when thrown into prison, or when stranded in some foreign nation, or when delayed on a long voyage, or when cast upon a lonely shore?' His life will be like that of Jupiter, who, amid the dissolution of the world, when the gods are confounded together and Nature rests for a space from her work, can retire into himself and give himself over to his own thoughts. In some such way as this the sage will act; he will retreat into himself, and live with himself.

As long as he is allowed to order his affairs according to his judgment, he is self-sufficient – and marries a wife; he is self-sufficient – and brings up children; he is self-sufficient – and yet could not live if he had to live without the society of man. Natural promptings, and not his own selfish needs, draw him into friendships. For just as other things have for us an inherent attractiveness, so has friendship. As we hate solitude and crave society, as nature draws men to each other, so in this matter also there is an attraction which makes us desirous of friendship.

Nevertheless, though the sage may love his friends dearly, often comparing them with himself, and putting them ahead of himself, yet all the good will be limited to his own being, and he will speak the words which were spoken by the very Stilbo whom Epicurus criticizes in his letter. For Stilbo, after his country was captured and his children and his wife lost, as he emerged from the general desolation alone and yet happy, spoke as follows to Demetrius, called Sacker of Cities because of the destruction he brought upon them, in answer to the question whether he had lost anything: 'I have all my goods with me!'

There is a brave and stout-hearted man for you! The enemy conquered, but Stilbo conquered his conqueror. 'I have lost nothing!' Aye, he forced Demetrius to wonder whether he himself had conquered after all. 'My goods are all with me!' In other words, he deemed nothing that might be taken from him to be a good.

We marvel at certain animals because they can pass through fire and suffer no bodily harm; but how much more marvellous is a man who has marched forth unhurt and unscathed through fire and sword and devastation! Do you understand now how much easier it is to conquer a whole tribe than to conquer one *man*? This saying of Stilbo makes common ground with Stoicism; the Stoic also can carry his goods unimpaired through cities that have been burned to ashes; for he is self-sufficient. Such are the bounds which he sets to his own happiness.

But you must not think that our school alone can utter noble words; Epicurus himself, the reviler of Stilbo, spoke similar language; put it down to my credit, though I have already wiped out my debt for the present day. He says: 'Whoever does not regard what he has as most ample wealth, is unhappy, though he be master of the whole world.' Or, if the following seems to you a more suitable phrase – for we must try to render the meaning and not the mere words: 'A man may rule the world and still be unhappy if he does not feel that he is supremely happy.'

In order, however, that you may know that these sentiments are universal, suggested, of course, by Nature, you will find in one of the comic poets this verse:

Unblest is he who thinks himself unblest.[4]

For what does your condition matter, if it is bad in your own eyes?

You may say: 'What then? If yonder man, rich by base means, and yonder man, lord of many but slave of more, shall call themselves happy, will their own opinion make them happy?' It matters not what one

---

[4]Author unknown.

says, but what one feels; also, not how one feels on one particular day, but how one feels at all times. There is no reason, however, why you should fear that this great privilege will fall into unworthy hands; only the wise man is pleased with his own. Folly is ever troubled with weariness of itself. Farewell.

ON LIVING TO ONESELF

Yes, I do not change my opinion: avoid the many, avoid the few, avoid even the individual. I know of no one with whom I should be willing to have you shared. And see what an opinion of you I have; for I dare to trust you with your own self. Crates, they say, the disciple of the very Stilbo whom I mentioned in a former letter, noticed a young man walking by himself, and asked him what he was doing all alone. 'I am communing with myself', replied the youth. 'Pray be careful, then', said Crates, 'and take good heed; you are communing with a bad man!'

When persons are in mourning, or fearful about something, we are accustomed to watch them that we may prevent them from making a wrong use of their loneliness. No thoughtless person ought to be left alone; in such cases he only plans folly, and heaps up future dangers for himself or for others; he brings into play his base desires; the mind displays what fear or shame used to repress; it whets his boldness, stirs his passions, and goads his anger. And finally, the only benefit that solitude confers – the habit of trusting no man, and of fearing no witnesses – is lost to the fool; for he betrays himself.

Mark, therefore, what my hopes are for you – nay, rather, what I am promising myself, inasmuch as hope is merely the title of an uncertain blessing: I do not know any person with whom I should prefer you to associate rather than yourself.

I remember in what a great-souled way you hurled forth certain phrases, and how full of strength they were! I immediately congratulated myself and said: 'These words did not come from the edge of the lips; these utterances have a solid foundation. This man is not one of the many; he has regard for his real welfare.'

Speak, and live, in this way; see to it that nothing keeps you down. As for your former prayers, you may dispense the gods from answering them; offer new prayers; pray for a sound mind and for good health, first of soul and then of body. And of course you should offer those prayers frequently. Call boldly upon God; you will not be asking Him for that which belongs to another.

But I must, as is my custom, send a little gift along with this letter. It is a true saying which I have found in Athenodorus: 'Know that thou art freed from all desires when thou hast reached such a point that thou prayest to God for nothing except what thou canst pray for openly.' But how foolish men are now! They whisper the basest of prayers to heaven; but if anyone listens, they are silent at once. That which they are unwilling for men to know, they communicate to God. Do you not think, then, that some such wholesome advice as this could be given you: 'Live among men as if God beheld you; speak with God as if men were listening'? Farewell.

ON THE BLUSH OF MODESTY

Your friend and I have had a conversation. He is a man of ability; his very first words showed what spirit and understanding he possesses, and what progress he has already made. He gave me a foretaste, and he will not fail to answer thereto. For he spoke not from forethought, but was suddenly caught off his guard. When he tried to collect himself, he could scarcely banish that hue of modesty, which is a good sign in a young man; the blush that spread over his face seemed so to rise from the depths. And I feel sure that his habit of blushing will stay with him after he has strengthened his character, stripped off all his faults, and become wise. For by no wisdom can natural weaknesses of the body be removed. That which is implanted and inborn can be toned down by training, but not overcome.

The steadiest speaker, when before the public, often breaks into a perspiration, as if he had wearied or overheated himself; some tremble in the knees when they rise to speak; I know of some whose teeth chatter, whose tongues falter, whose lips quiver. Training and experience can never shake off this habit; Nature exerts her own power and through such a weakness makes her presence known even to the strongest.

I know that the blush, too, is a habit of this sort, spreading suddenly over the faces of the most dignified men. It is, indeed more prevalent in youth, because of the warmer blood and the sensitive countenance; nevertheless, both seasoned men and aged men are affected by it. Some are most dangerous when they redden, as if they were letting all their sense of shame escape.

Sulla, when the blood mantled his cheeks, was in his fiercest mood. Pompey had the most sensitive cast of countenance; he always blushed in the presence of a gathering, and especially at a public assembly. Fabianus also, I remember, reddened when he appeared as a witness before the senate; and his embarrassment became him to a remarkable degree.

Such a habit is not due to mental weakness, but to the novelty of a situation; an inexperienced person is not necessarily confused, but is usually affected, because he slips into this habit by natural tendency of the body. Just as certain men are full-blooded, so others are of a quick and mobile blood that rushes to the face at once.

As I remarked, Wisdom can never remove this habit; for if she could rub out all our faults, she would be mistress of the universe. Whatever is assigned to us by the terms of our birth and the blend in our constitutions, will stick with us, no matter how hard or how long the soul may have tried to master itself. And we cannot forbid these feelings any more than we can summon them.

Actors in the theatre, who imitate the emotions, who portray fear and nervousness, who depict sorrow, imitate bashfulness by hanging their heads, lowering their voices, and keeping their eyes fixed and rooted upon the ground. They cannot, however, muster a blush; for the blush cannot be prevented or acquired. Wisdom will not assure us of a remedy, or give us help against it; it comes or goes unbidden, and is a law unto itself.

But my letter calls for its closing sentence. Hear and take to heart this useful and wholesome motto:[1] 'Cherish some man of high character, and keep him ever before your eyes, living as if he were watching you, and ordering all your actions as if he beheld them.'

---

[1]Epicurus, Fragment 210, Usener.

Such, my dear Lucilius, is the counsel of Epicurus; he has quite properly given us a guardian and an attendant. We can get rid of most sins, if we have a witness who stands near us when we are likely to go wrong. The soul should have someone whom it can respect – one by whose authority it may make even its inner shrine more hallowed. Happy is the man who can make others better, not merely when he is in their company, but even when he is in their thoughts! And happy also is he who can so revere a man as to calm and regulate himself by calling him to mind! One who can so revere another, will soon be himself worthy of reverence.

Choose, therefore, a Cato; or, if Cato seems too severe a model, choose some Laelius, a gentler spirit. Choose a master whose life, conversation, and soul-expressing face have satisfied you; picture him always to yourself as your protector or your pattern. For we must indeed have someone according to whom we may regulate our characters; you can never straighten that which is crooked unless you use a ruler. Farewell.

ON OLD AGE

Wherever I turn, I see evidences of my advancing years. I visited lately my country-place, and protested against the money which was spent on the tumble-down building. My bailiff maintained that the flaws were not due to his own carelessness; he was doing everything possible, but the house was old. And this was the house which grew under my own hands! What has the future in store for me, if stones of my own age are already crumbling?

I was angry, and I embraced the first opportunity to vent my spleen in the bailiff's presence. 'It is clear', I cried, 'that these plane-trees are neglected; they have no leaves. Their branches are so gnarled and shrivelled; the boles are so rough and unkempt! This would not happen, if someone loosened the earth at their feet, and watered them.' The bailiff swore by my protecting deity that he was doing everything possible, and never relaxed his efforts, but those trees were old. Between you and me, I had planted those trees myself; I had seen them in their first leaf.

Then I turned to the door and asked: 'Who is that broken-down dotard? You have done well to place him at the entrance; for he is outward bound.[1] Where did you get him? What pleasure did it give you to take up for burial some other man's dead?'[2] But the slave said: 'Don't you know me, sir? I am Felicio; you used to bring me little images.[3] My father was Philositus the steward, and I am your pet slave.' 'The man is clean crazy', I remarked. 'Has my pet slave become a little boy again? But it is quite possible; his teeth are just dropping out.'[4]

I owe it to my country-place that my old age became apparent whithersoever I turned. Let us cherish and love old age; for it is full of pleasure if one knows how

---

[1] A jesting allusion to the Roman funeral; the corpse's feet pointing towards the door.

[2] His former owner should have kept him and buried him.

[3] Small figures, generally of terracotta, were frequently given to children as presents at the Saturnalia.

[4] i.e. the old slave resembles a child in that he is losing his teeth (but for the second time).

to use it. Fruits are most welcome when almost over; youth is most charming at its close; the last drink delights the toper – the glass which souses him and puts the finishing touch on his drunkenness.

Each pleasure reserves to the end the greatest delights which it contains. Life is most delightful when it is on the downward slope, but has not yet reached the abrupt decline. And I myself believe that the period which stands, so to speak, on the edge of the roof, possesses pleasures of its own. Or else the very fact of our not wanting pleasures has taken the place of the pleasures themselves. How comforting it is to have tired out one's appetites, and to have done with them!

'But', you say, 'it is a nuisance to be looking death in the face!' Death, however, should be looked in the face by young and old alike. We are not summoned according to our rating on the censor's list.[5] Moreover, no one is so old that it would be improper for him to hope for another day of existence. And one day, mind you, is a stage on life's journey.

Our span of life is divided into parts; it consists of large circles enclosing smaller. One circle embraces and bounds the rest; it reaches from birth to the last day of existence. The next circle limits the period

---

[5] i.e. *seniores*, as contrasted with *iuniores*.

of our young manhood. The third confines all of childhood in its circumference. Again, there is, in a class by itself, the year; it contains within itself all the divisions of time by the multiplication of which we get the total of life. The month is bounded by a narrower ring. The smallest circle of all is the day; but even a day has its beginning and its ending, its sunrise and its sunset.

Hence Heraclitus, whose obscure style gave him his surname,[6] remarked: 'One day is equal to every day.' Different persons have interpreted the saying in different ways. Some hold that days are equal in number of hours, and this is true; for if by 'day' we mean twenty-four hours' time, all days must be equal, inasmuch as the night acquires what the day loses. But others maintain that one day is equal to all days through resemblance, because the very longest space of time possesses no element which cannot be found in a single day – namely, light and darkness – and even to eternity day makes these alternations[7] more numerous, not different when it is shorter and different again when it is longer.

Hence, every day ought to be regulated as if it closed the series, as if it rounded out and completed our existence.

---

[6] ὁσκοτεινός, 'the Obscure'.

[7] i.e. of light and darkness.

Pacuvius, who by long occupancy made Syria his own,[8] used to hold a regular burial sacrifice in his own honour, with wine and the usual funeral feasting, and then would have himself carried from the dining-room to his chamber, while eunuchs applauded and sang in Greek to a musical accompaniment: 'He has lived his life, he has lived his life!'

Thus Pacuvius had himself carried out to burial every day. Let us, however, do from a good motive what he used to do from a debased motive; let us go to our sleep with joy and gladness; let us say:

> I have lived; the course which Fortune set for me
> Is finished.[9]

And if God is pleased to add another day, we should welcome it with glad hearts. That man is happiest, and is secure in his own possession of himself, who can await the morrow without apprehension. When a man has said: 'I have lived!', every morning he arises he receives a bonus.

But now I ought to close my letter. 'What?' you say, 'shall it come to me without any little offering?'

---

[8] *Usus* was the mere enjoyment of a piece of property; *dominium* was the exclusive right to its control. Possession for one, or two, years conferred ownership. Although Pacuvius was governor so long that the province seemed to belong to him, he knew he might die any day.

[9] Virgil, *Aeneid*, iv. 653.

Be not afraid; it brings something – nay, more than something, a great deal. For what is more noble than the following saying[10] of which I make this letter the bearer: 'It is wrong to live under constraint, but no man is constrained to live under constraint.' Of course not. On all sides lie many short and simple paths to freedom; and let us thank God that no man can be kept in life. We may spurn the very constraints that hold us.

'Epicurus', you reply, 'uttered these words; what are you doing with another's property?' Any truth, I maintain, is my own property. And I shall continue to heap quotations from Epicurus upon you, so that all persons who swear by the words of another, and put a value upon the speaker and not upon the thing spoken, may understand that the best ideas are common property. Farewell.

---

[10]Epicurus.

ON GROUNDLESS FEARS

I know that you have plenty of spirit; for even before you began to equip yourself with maxims which were wholesome and potent to overcome obstacles, you were taking pride in your contest with Fortune; and this is all the more true, now that you have grappled with Fortune and tested your powers. For our powers can never inspire in us implicit faith in ourselves except when many difficulties have confronted us on this side and on that, and have occasionally even come to close quarters with us. It is only in this way that the true spirit can be tested – the spirit that will never consent to come under the jurisdiction of things external to ourselves.

This is the touchstone of such a spirit; no prize-fighter can go with high spirits into the strife if he has never been beaten black and blue; the only contestant who can confidently enter the lists is the man who has seen his own blood, who has felt his teeth rattle beneath his opponent's fist, who has been tripped and felt the full force of his adversary's charge, who has been downed in body but not in spirit, one who, as often as he falls, rises again with greater defiance than ever.

So then, to keep up my figure, Fortune has often in the past got the upper hand of you, and yet you have not surrendered, but have leaped up and stood your ground still more eagerly. For manliness gains much strength by being challenged; nevertheless, if you approve, allow me to offer some additional safeguards by which you may fortify yourself.

There are more things, Lucilius, likely to frighten us than there are to crush us; we suffer more often in imagination than in reality. I am not speaking with you in the Stoic strain but in my milder style. For it is our Stoic fashion to speak of all those things, which provoke cries and groans, as unimportant and beneath notice; but you and I must drop such great-sounding words, although, Heaven knows, they are true enough. What I advise you to do is, not to be unhappy before the crisis comes; since it may be that the dangers before which you paled as if they were threatening you will never come upon you; they certainly have not yet come.

CHAPTER THIRTEEN

Accordingly, some things torment us more than they ought; some torment us before they ought; and some torment us when they ought not to torment us at all. We are in the habit of exaggerating, or imagining, or anticipating, sorrow.

The first of these three faults[1] may be postponed for the present, because the subject is under discussion and the case is still in court, so to speak. That which I should call trifling, you will maintain to be most serious; for of course I know that some men laugh while being flogged, and that others wince at a box on the ear. We shall consider later whether these evils derive their power from their own strength, or from our own weakness.

Do me the favour, when men surround you and try to talk you into believing that you are unhappy, to consider not what you hear but what you yourself feel, and to take counsel with your feelings and question yourself independently, because you know your own affairs better than anyone else does. Ask: 'Is there any reason why these persons should condole with me? Why should they be worried or even fear some infection

---

[1] Seneca dismisses the topic of 'exaggerated ills', because judgements will differ concerning present troubles; the Stoics, for example, would not admit that torture was an evil at all. He then passes on to the topic of 'imaginary ills' and afterwards to 'anticipated ills'.

from me, as if troubles could be transmitted? Is there any evil involved, or is it a matter merely of ill report, rather than an evil?' Put the question voluntarily to yourself: 'Am I tormented without sufficient reason, am I morose, and do I convert what is not an evil into what is an evil?'

You may retort with the question: 'How am I to know whether my sufferings are real or imaginary?' Here is the rule for such matters: We are tormented either by things present, or by things to come, or by both. As to things present, the decision is easy. Suppose that your person enjoys freedom and health, and that you do not suffer from any external injury. As to what may happen to it in the future, we shall see later on. Today there is nothing wrong with it.

'But', you say, 'something will happen to it.' First of all, consider whether your proofs of future trouble are sure. For it is more often the case that we are troubled by our apprehensions, and that we are mocked by that mocker, rumour, which is wont to settle wars, but much more often settles individuals. Yes, my dear Lucilius; we agree too quickly with what people say. We do not put to the test those things which cause our fear; we do not examine into them; we blench and retreat just like soldiers who are forced to abandon their camp because of a dust-cloud raised by stampeding cattle, or are thrown into a panic by the spreading of some unauthenticated rumour.

And somehow or other it is the idle report that disturbs us most. For truth has its own definite boundaries, but that which arises from uncertainty is delivered over to guesswork and the irresponsible license of a frightened mind. That is why no fear is so ruinous and so uncontrollable as panic fear. For other fears are groundless, but this fear is witless.

Let us, then, look carefully into the matter. It is likely that some troubles will befall us; but it is not a present fact. How often has the unexpected happened! How often has the expected never come to pass! And even though it is ordained to be, what does it avail to run out to meet your suffering? You will suffer soon enough, when it arrives; so look forward meanwhile to better things.

What shall you gain by doing this? Time. There will be many happenings meanwhile which will serve to postpone, or end, or pass on to another person, the trials which are near or even in your very presence. A fire has opened the way to flight. Men have been let down softly by a catastrophe. Sometimes the sword has been checked even at the victim's throat. Men have survived their own executioners. Even bad fortune is fickle. Perhaps it will come, perhaps not; in the meantime it is not. So look forward to better things.

The mind at times fashions for itself false shapes of evil when there are no signs that point to any evil; it

twists into the worst construction some word of doubtful meaning; or it fancies some personal grudge to
be more serious than it really is, considering not how
angry the enemy is, but to what lengths he may go
if he is angry. But life is not worth living, and there
is no limit to our sorrows, if we indulge our fears to
the greatest possible extent; in this matter, let pru-
dence help you, and contemn with a resolute spirit
even when it is in plain sight. If you cannot do this,
counter one weakness with another, and temper your
fear with hope. There is nothing so certain among
these objects of fear that it is not more certain still that
things we dread sink into nothing and that things we
hope for mock us.

Accordingly, weigh carefully your hopes as well
as your fears, and whenever all the elements are
in doubt, decide in your own favour; believe what
you prefer. And if fear wins a majority of the votes,
incline in the other direction anyhow, and cease to
harass your soul, reflecting continually that most
mortals, even when no troubles are actually at
hand or are certainly to be expected in the future,
become excited and disquieted. No one calls a halt
on himself, when he begins to be urged ahead; nor
does he regulate his alarm according to the truth.
No one says: 'The author of the story is a fool, and
he who has believed it is a fool, as well as he who
fabricated it.' We let ourselves drift with every breeze;

we are frightened at uncertainties, just as if they were certain. We observe no moderation. The slightest thing turns the scales and throws us forthwith into a panic.

But I am ashamed either to admonish you sternly or to try to beguile you with such mild remedies. Let another say: 'Perhaps the worst will not happen.' You yourself must say: 'Well, what if it does happen? Let us see who wins! Perhaps it happens for my best interests; it may be that such a death will shed credit upon my life.' Socrates was ennobled by the hemlock draught. Wrench from Cato's hand his sword, the vindicator of liberty, and you deprive him of the greatest share of his glory.

I am exhorting you far too long, since you need reminding rather than exhortation. The path on which I am leading you is not different from that on which your nature leads you; you were born to such conduct as I describe. Hence there is all the more reason why you should increase and beautify the good that is in you.

But now, to close my letter, I have only to stamp the usual seal upon it, in other words, to commit thereto some noble message to be delivered to you: 'The fool,

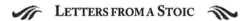

with all his other faults, has this also – he is always getting ready to live.'[2] Reflect, my esteemed Lucilius, on what this saying means, and you will see how revolting is the fickleness of men who lay down every day new foundations of life, and begin to build up fresh hopes even at the brink of the grave.

Look within your own mind for individual instances; you will think of old men who are preparing themselves at that very hour for a political career, or for travel, or for business. And what is baser than getting ready to live when you are already old? I should not name the author of this motto, except that it is somewhat unknown to fame and is not one of those popular sayings of Epicurus which I have allowed myself to praise and to appropriate. Farewell.

---

[2]Epicurus, Fragment 494, Usener.

ON THE REASONS FOR WITHDRAWING FROM THE WORLD

I confess that we all have an inborn affection for our body; I confess that we are entrusted with its guardianship. I do not maintain that the body is not to be indulged at all; but I maintain that we must not be slaves to it. He will have many masters who makes his body his master, who is over-fearful on its behalf, who judges everything according to the body. We should conduct ourselves not as if we ought to live for the body, but as if we could not live without it. Our too great love for it makes us restless with fears, burdens us with cares, and exposes us to insults. Virtue is held too cheap by the man who counts his body too dear. We should cherish the body with the greatest care; but we should also be prepared, when reason, self-respect, and duty demand the sacrifice, to deliver it even to the flames.

Let us, however, in so far as we can, avoid discom-
forts as well as dangers, and withdraw to safe ground,
by thinking continually how we may repel all objects
of fear. If I am not mistaken, there are three main
classes of these: we fear want, we fear sickness, and
we fear the troubles which result from the violence
of the stronger. And of all these, that which shakes
us most is the dread which hangs over us from our
neighbour's ascendancy; for it is accompanied by
great outcry and uproar. But the natural evils which I
have mentioned – want and sickness – steal upon us
silently with no shock of terror to the eye or to the
ear. The other kind of evil comes, so to speak, in the
form of a huge parade. Surrounding it is a retinue
of swords and fire and chains and a mob of beasts
to be let loose upon the disembowelled entrails of
men. Picture to yourself under this head the prison,
the cross, the rack, the hook, and the stake which
they drive straight through a man until it protrudes
from his throat. Think of human limbs torn apart by
chariots driven in opposite directions, of the terrible
shirt smeared and interwoven with inflammable
materials, and of all the other contrivances devised by
cruelty, in addition to those which I have mentioned![1]
It is not surprising, then, if our greatest terror is of

---

[1]Tacitus, *Annals*, xv. 44, describing the tortures practised upon
the Christians.

such a fate; for it comes in many shapes and its paraphernalia are terrifying. For just as the torturer accomplishes more in proportion to the number of instruments which he displays – indeed, the spectacle overcomes those who would have patiently withstood the suffering – similarly, of all the agencies which coerce and master our minds, the most effective are those which can make a display. Those other troubles are of course not less serious; I mean hunger, thirst, ulcers of the stomach, and fever that parches our very bowels. They are, however, secret; they have no bluster and no heralding; but these, like huge arrays of war, prevail by virtue of their display and their equipment.

Let us, therefore, see to it that we abstain from giving offence. It is sometimes the people that we ought to fear; or sometimes a body of influential oligarchs in the senate, if the method of governing the State is such that most of the business is done by that body; and sometimes individuals equipped with power by the people and against the people. It is burdensome to keep the friendship of all such persons; it is enough not to make enemies of them. So the wise man will never provoke the anger of those in power; nay, he will even turn his course, precisely as he would turn from a storm if he were steering a ship. When you travelled to Sicily, you crossed the Straits. The reckless pilot scorned the blustering

South Wind – the wind which roughens the Sicilian Sea and forces it into choppy currents; he sought not the shore on the left,[2] but the strand hard by the place where Charybdis throws the seas into confusion. Your more careful pilot, however, questions those who know the locality as to the tides and the meaning of the clouds; he holds his course far from that region notorious for its swirling waters. Our wise man does the same; he shuns a strong man who may be injurious to him, making a point of not seeming to avoid him, because an important part of one's safety lies in not seeking safety openly; for what one avoids, one condemns.

We should, therefore, look about us, and see how we may protect ourselves from the mob. And first of all, we should have no cravings like theirs; for rivalry results in strife. Again, let us possess nothing that can be snatched from us to the great profit of a plotting foe. Let there be as little booty as possible on your person. No one sets out to shed the blood of his fellow-men for the sake of bloodshed – at any rate very few. More murderers speculate on their profits than give vent to hatred. If you are

---

[2]Scylla was a rock on the Italian side of the Straits. Charybdis was a whirlpool on the Sicillian side. Servius on Virgil, *Aeneid*, iii, 420 defines the *dextrum* as the shore 'to the right of those coming from the Ionian sea'.

empty-handed, the highwayman passes you by; even along an infested road, the poor may travel in peace. Next, we must follow the old adage and avoid three things with special care: hatred, jealousy, and scorn. And wisdom alone can show you how this may be done. It is hard to observe a mean; we must be chary of letting the fear of jealousy lead us into becoming objects of scorn, lest, when we choose not to stamp others down, we let them think that they can stamp us down. The power to inspire fear has caused many men to be in fear. Let us withdraw ourselves in every way; for it is as harmful to be scorned as to be admired.

One must therefore take refuge in philosophy; this pursuit, not only in the eyes of good men, but also in the eyes of those who are even moderately bad, is a sort of protecting emblem. For speechmaking at the bar, or any other pursuit that claims the people's attention, wins enemies for a man; but Philosophy is peaceful and minds her own business. Men cannot scorn her; she is honoured by every profession, even the vilest among them. Evil can never grow so strong, and nobility of character can never be so plotted against, that the name of philosophy shall cease to be worshipful and sacred.

Philosophy itself, however, should be practised with calmness and moderation. 'Very well, then', you retort, 'do you regard the philosophy of Marcus Cato as moderate? Cato's voice strove to check a civil war. Cato parted the swords of maddened chieftains. When some fell foul of Pompey and others fell foul of Caesar, Cato defied both parties at once!' Nevertheless, one may well question whether, in those days, a wise man ought to have taken any part in public affairs, and ask: 'What do you mean, Marcus Cato? It is not now a question of freedom; long since has freedom gone to rack and ruin. The question is, whether it is Caesar or Pompey who controls the State. Why, Cato, should you take sides in that dispute? It is no business of yours; a tyrant is being selected. What does it concern you who conquers? The better man may win; but the winner is bound to be the worse man.' I have referred to Cato's final role. But even in previous years the wise man was not permitted to intervene in such plundering of the state; for what could Cato do but raise his voice and utter unavailing words? At one time he was 'hustled' by the mob and spat upon and forcibly removed from the forum and marked for exile; at another, he was taken straight to prison from the senate-chamber.

However, we shall consider later whether the wise man ought to give his attention to politics; meanwhile, I beg you to consider those Stoics who, shut out from public life, have withdrawn into privacy for the purpose of improving men's existence and framing laws for the human race without incurring the displeasure of those in power. The wise man will not upset the customs of the people, nor will he invite the attention of the populace by any novel ways of living.

'What then? Can one who follows out this plan be safe in any case?' I cannot guarantee you this any more than I can guarantee good health in the case of a man who observes moderation; although, as a matter of fact, good health results from such moderation. Sometimes a vessel perishes in harbour, but what do you think happens on the open sea? And how much more beset with danger that man would be, who even in his leisure is not secure, if he were busily working at many things! Innocent persons sometimes perish; who would deny that? But the guilty perish more frequently. A soldier's skill is not at fault if he receives the death-blow through his armour. And finally, the wise man regards the reason for all his actions, but not the results. The beginning is in our own power; Fortune decides the issue, but I do not allow her to pass sentence upon myself. You may say: 'But she can inflict a measure of suffering and of trouble.' The highwayman does not pass sentence when he slays.

Now you are stretching forth your hand for the daily gift. Golden indeed will be the gift with which I shall

load you; and, inasmuch as we have mentioned gold, let me tell you how its use and enjoyment may bring you greater pleasure. 'He who needs riches least, enjoys riches most.'[3] 'Author's name, please!' you say. Now, to show you how generous I am, it is my intent to praise the dicta of other schools. The phrase belongs to Epicurus, or Metrodorus, or someone of that particular thinking-shop. But what difference does it make who spoke the words? They were uttered for the world. He who craves riches feels fear on their account. No man, however, enjoys a blessing that brings anxiety; he is always trying to add a little more. While he puzzles over increasing his wealth, he forgets how to use it. He collects his accounts, he wears out the pavement in the forum, he turns over his ledger[4] – in short, he ceases to be master and becomes a steward. Farewell.

---

[3]Epicurus iii. p. 63. 19, Usener.

[4]*Kalendarium* in Latin because interest was reckoned according to the Kalends of each month.

ON BRAWN AND BRAINS

The old Romans had a custom which survived even into my lifetime. They would add to the opening words of a letter: 'If you are well, it is well; I also am well.' Persons like ourselves would do well to say: 'If you are studying philosophy, it is well.' For this is just what 'being well' means. Without philosophy the mind is sickly, and the body, too, though it may be very powerful, is strong only as that of a madman or a lunatic is strong.

This, then, is the sort of health you should primarily cultivate; the other kind of health comes second, and will involve little effort, if you wish to be well physically. It is indeed foolish, my dear Lucilius, and very unsuitable for a cultivated man, to work hard over developing the muscles and broadening the shoulders and strengthening the lungs. For although your heavy feeding produce good results and your sinews grow solid, you can never be a match, either in strength or in weight, for a first-class bull. Besides, by overloading the body with food you strangle the soul and render it less active. Accordingly, limit the flesh as much as possible, and allow free play to the spirit.

Many inconveniences beset those who devote themselves to such pursuits. In the first place, they have their exercises, at which they must work and waste their life-force and render it less fit to bear a strain or the severer studies. Second, their keen edge is dulled by heavy eating. Besides, they must take orders from slaves of the vilest stamp – men who alternate between the oil-flask[1] and the flagon, whose day passes satisfactorily if they have got up a good perspiration and quaffed, to make good what they have lost in sweat, huge draughts of liquor which will sink deeper because of their fasting. Drinking and sweating – it's the life of a dyspeptic!

Now there are short and simple exercises which tire the body rapidly, and so save our time; and time is something of which we ought to keep strict account. These exercises are running, brandishing weights, and jumping – high-jumping or broad-jumping, or

---

[1] i.e. the prize-ring; the contestants were rubbed with oil before the fight began.

the kind which I may call, 'the Priest's dance',[2] or, in slighting terms, 'the clothes-cleaner's jump'.[3] Select for practice any one of these, and you will find it plain and easy.

But whatever you do, come back soon from body to mind. The mind must be exercised both day and night, for it is nourished by moderate labour; and this form of exercise need not be hampered by cold or hot weather, or even by old age. Cultivate that good which improves with the years.

Of course I do not command you to be always bending over your books and your writing materials; the mind must have a change – but a change of such a kind that it is not unnerved, but merely unbent. Riding in a litter shakes up the body, and does not interfere with study; one may read, dictate, converse, or listen to another; nor does walking prevent any of these things.

You need not scorn voice-culture; but I forbid you to practise raising and lowering your voice by scales and specific intonations. What if you should next propose to take lessons in walking! If you consult the sort of person whom starvation has taught new tricks, you will have someone to regulate your steps, watch every

---

[2]Named from the Salii, or leaping priests of Mars.

[3]The fuller, or washerman, cleansed the clothes by leaping and stamping upon them in the tub.

mouthful as you eat, and go to such lengths as you yourself, by enduring him and believing in him, have encouraged his effrontery to go. 'What, then?' you will ask, 'is my voice to begin at the outset with shouting and straining the lungs to the utmost?' No; the natural thing is that it be aroused to such a pitch by easy stages, just as persons who are wrangling begin with ordinary conversational tones and then pass to shouting at the top of their lungs. No speaker cries 'Help me, citizens!' at the outset of his speech.

Therefore, whenever your spirit's impulse prompts you, raise a hubbub, now in louder now in milder tones, according as your voice, as well as your spirit, shall suggest to you, when you are moved to such a performance. Then let your voice, when you rein it in and call it back to earth, come down gently, not collapse; it should trail off in tones halfway between high and low, and should not abruptly drop from its raving in the uncouth manner of countrymen. For our purpose is, not to give the voice exercise, but to make it give us exercise.

You see, I have relieved you of no slight bother; and I shall throw in a little complementary present – it is Greek, too. Here is the proverb; it is an excellent one: 'The fool's life is empty of gratitude and full of fears; its course lies wholly toward the future.' 'Who uttered these words?' you say. The same writer whom I mentioned before.[4] And what sort of life do you think is meant by the fool's life? That of Baba and Isio?[5] No; he means our own, for we are plunged by our blind desires into ventures which will harm us, but certainly will never satisfy us; for if we could be satisfied with anything, we should have been satisfied long ago; nor do we reflect how pleasant it is to demand nothing, how noble it is to be contented and not to be dependent upon Fortune.

Therefore continually remind yourself, Lucilius, how many ambitions you have attained. When you see many ahead of you, think how many are behind! If you would thank the gods, and be grateful for your past life, you should contemplate how many men you have outstripped. But what have you to do with the others? You have outstripped yourself.

Fix a limit which you will not even desire to pass, should you have the power. At last, then, away with all these treacherous goods! They look better to those who hope for them than to those who have attained them. If there were anything substantial in them, they would sooner or later satisfy you; as it is, they merely rouse the drinkers' thirst. Away with fripperies which only serve for show! As to what the future's uncertain

---

[4]Epicurus, Fragment 491, Usener.

[5]Court fools of the period.

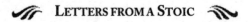

lot has in store, why should I demand of Fortune that she give, rather than demand of myself that I should not crave? And why should l crave? Shall I heap up my winnings, and forget that man's lot is unsubstantial? For what end should I toil? Lo, today is the last; if not, it is near the last. Farewell.

ON PHILOSOPHY, THE GUIDE OF LIFE

It is clear to you, I am sure, Lucilius, that no man can live a happy life, or even a supportable life, without the study of wisdom; you know also that a happy life is reached when our wisdom is brought to completion, but that life is at least endurable even when our wisdom is only begun. This idea, however, clear though it is, must be strengthened and implanted more deeply by daily reflection; it is more important for you to keep the resolutions you have already made than to go on and make noble ones. You must persevere, must develop new strength by continuous study, until that which is only a good inclination becomes a good settled purpose.

Hence you no longer need to come to me with much talk and protestations; I know that you have made great progress. I understand the feelings which prompt your words; they are not feigned or specious words. Nevertheless I shall tell you what I think – that at present I have hopes for you, but not yet perfect trust. And I wish that you would adopt the same attitude towards yourself; there is no reason why you should put confidence in yourself too quickly and readily. Examine yourself; scrutinize and observe yourself in diverse ways; but mark, before all else, whether it is in philosophy or merely in life itself that you have made progress.

Philosophy is no trick to catch the public; it is not devised for show. It is a matter, not of words, but of facts. It is not pursued in order that the day may yield some amusement before it is spent, or that our leisure may be relieved of a tedium that irks us. It moulds and constructs the soul; it orders our life, guides our conduct, shows us what we should do and what we should leave undone; it sits at the helm and directs our course as we waver amid uncertainties. Without it, no one can live fearlessly or in peace of mind. Countless things that happen every hour call for advice, and such advice is to be sought in philosophy.

Perhaps someone will say: 'How can philosophy help me, if Fate exists? Of what avail is philosophy, if God rules the universe? Of what avail is it, if Chance governs everything? For not only is it impossible to change things that are determined, but it is also impossible to plan beforehand against what is undetermined; either God has forestalled my plans, and decided what I am to do, or else Fortune gives no free play to my plans.'

Whether the truth, Lucilius, lies in one or in all of these views, we must be philosophers; whether Fate binds us down by an inexorable law, or whether God as arbiter of the universe has arranged everything, or whether Chance drives and tosses human affairs without method, philosophy ought to be our defence. She will encourage us to obey God cheerfully, but Fortune defiantly; she will teach us to follow God and endure Chance.

But it is not my purpose now to be led into a discussion as to what is within our own control – if foreknowledge is supreme, or if a chain of fated events drags us along in its clutches, or if the sudden and the unexpected play the tyrant over us; I return now to my warning and my exhortation, that you should not allow the impulse of your spirit to weaken and grow cold. Hold fast to it and establish it firmly, in order that what is now impulse may become a habit of the mind.

If I know you well, you have already been trying to find out, from the very beginning of my letter, what little contribution it brings to you. Sift the letter, and you will find it. You need not wonder at any genius of mine; for as yet I am lavish only with other men's property. But why did I say 'other men'? Whatever is well said by anyone is mine. This also is a saying of Epicurus:[1] 'If you live according to nature, you will never be poor; if you live according to opinion, you will never be rich.'

Nature's wants are slight; the demands of opinion are boundless. Suppose that the property of many millionaires is heaped up in your possession. Assume that fortune carries you far beyond the limits of a private income, decks you with gold, clothes you in purple, and brings you to such a degree of luxury and wealth that you can bury the earth under your marble floors; that you may not only possess, but tread upon, riches. Add statues, paintings, and whatever any art has devised for the satisfaction of luxury; you will only learn from such things to crave still greater.

Natural desires are limited, but those which spring from false opinion can have no stopping-point. The false has no limits. When you are travelling on a road, there must be an end, but when astray, your wanderings are limitless. Recall your steps, therefore, from idle things, and when you would know whether that which you seek is based upon a natural or upon a

---

[1]Fragment 201, Usener.

misleading desire, consider whether it can stop at any definite point. If you find, after having travelled far, that there is a more distant goal always in view, you may be sure that this condition is contrary to nature. Farewell.

ON PHILOSOPHY
AND RICHES

Cast away everything of that sort, if you are wise; nay, rather that you may be wise; strive towards a sound mind at top speed and with your whole strength. If any bond holds you back, untie it, or sever it. 'But', you say, 'my estate delays me; I wish to make such disposition of it that it may suffice for me when I have nothing to do, lest either poverty be a burden to me, or I myself a burden to others.'

You do not seem, when you say this, to know the strength and power of that good which you are considering. You do indeed grasp the all-important thing, the great benefit which philosophy confers, but you do not yet discern accurately its various functions, nor do you yet know how great is the help we receive from philosophy in everything, everywhere – how (to use

Cicero's language) it not only succours us in the greatest matters but also descends to the smallest. Take my advice; call Wisdom into consultation; she will advise you not to sit for ever at your ledger.

Doubtless, your object, what you wish to attain by such postponement of your studies, is that poverty may not have to be feared by you. But what if it is something to be desired? Riches have shut off many a man from the attainment of wisdom; poverty is unburdened and free from care. When the trumpet sounds, the poor man knows that he is not being attacked; when there is a cry of 'Fire', he only seeks a way of escape, and does not ask what he can save; if the poor man must go to sea, the harbour does not resound, nor do the wharves bustle with the retinue of one individual. No throng of slaves surrounds the poor man – slaves for whose mouths the master must covet the fertile crops of regions beyond the sea.

It is easy to fill a few stomachs, when they are well trained and crave nothing else but to be filled. Hunger costs but little; squeamishness costs much. Poverty is contented with fulfilling pressing needs.

Why, then, should you reject Philosophy as a comrade?

Even the rich man copies her ways when he is in his senses. If you wish to have leisure for your mind, either be a poor man, or resemble a poor man. Study cannot be helpful unless you take pains to live simply, and living simply is voluntary poverty. Away, then, with all excuses like: 'I have not yet enough; when I have gained the desired amount, then I shall devote myself wholly to philosophy.' And yet this ideal, which you are putting off and placing second to other interests, should be secured first of all; you should begin with it. You retort: 'I wish to acquire something to live on.' Yes, but learn while you are acquiring it; for if anything forbids you to live nobly, nothing forbids you to die nobly.

There is no reason why poverty should call us away from philosophy – no, nor even actual want. For when hastening after wisdom, we must endure even hunger. Men have endured hunger when their towns were besieged, and what other reward for their endurance did they obtain than that they did not fall under the conqueror's power? How much greater is the promise of the prize of everlasting liberty, and the assurance that we need fear neither God nor man! Even though we starve, we must reach that goal.

Armies have endured all manner of want, have lived on roots, and have resisted hunger by means of food too revolting to mention. All this they have suffered to gain a kingdom, and – what is more marvellous – to gain a kingdom that will be another's. Will any man hesitate to endure poverty, in order that he may free his mind from madness?

Therefore one should not seek to lay up riches first; one may attain to philosophy, however, even without money for the journey.

It is indeed so. After you have come to possess all other things, shall you then wish to possess wisdom also? Is philosophy to be the last requisite in life – a sort of supplement? Nay, your plan should be this: be a philosopher now, whether you have anything or not – for if you have anything, how do you know that you have not too much already? – but if you have nothing, seek understanding first, before anything else.

'But', you say, 'I shall lack the necessities of life.' In the first place, you cannot lack them; because nature demands but little, and the wise man suits his needs to nature. But if the utmost pinch of need arrives, he will quickly take leave of life and cease being a trouble to himself. If, however, his means of existence are meagre and scanty, he will make the best of them, without being anxious or worried about anything more than the bare necessities; he will do justice to his belly and his shoulders; with free and happy spirit he will laugh at the bustling of rich men, and the flurried ways of those who are hastening after wealth,

And say: 'Why of your own accord postpone your real life to the distant future? Shall you wait for some interest to fall due, or for some income on your merchandise, or for a place in the will of some wealthy old man, when you can be rich here and now. Wisdom offers wealth in ready money, and pays it over to those in whose eyes she has made wealth superfluous.' These remarks refer to other men; you are nearer the rich class. Change the age in which you live, and you have too much. But in every age, what is enough remains the same.

I might close my letter at this point, if I had not got you into bad habits. One cannot greet Parthian royalty without bringing a gift; and in your case I cannot say farewell without paying a price. But what of it? I shall borrow from Epicurus:[1] 'The acquisition of riches has been for many men, not an end, but a change, of troubles.'

I do not wonder. For the fault is not in the wealth, but in the mind itself. That which had made poverty a burden to us has made riches also a burden. Just as it matters little whether you lay a sick man on a wooden or on a golden bed, for whithersoever he be moved he will carry his malady with him, so one need not care whether the diseased mind is bestowed upon riches or upon poverty. His malady goes with the man. Farewell.

---

[1]Fragment 479, Usener.

CHAPTER EIGHTEEN

ON FESTIVALS AND FASTING

It is the month of December, and yet the city is at this very moment in a sweat. Licence is given to the general merrymaking. Everything resounds with mighty preparations – as if the Saturnalia differed at all from the usual business day! So true it is that the difference is nil, that I regard as correct the remark of the man who said: 'Once December was a month; now it is a year.'[1]

If I had you with me, I should be glad to consult you and find out what you think should be done – whether we ought to make no change in our daily routine, or whether, in order not to be out of sympathy with the ways of the public, we should dine

---

[1]i.e. the whole year is a Saturnalia.

in gayer fashion and doff the toga. As it is now, we Romans have changed our dress for the sake of pleasure and holiday-making, though in former times that was only customary when the State was disturbed and had fallen on evil days.

I am sure that, if I know you aright, playing the part of an umpire you would have wished that we should be neither like the liberty-capped[2] throng in all ways, nor in all ways unlike them; unless, perhaps, this is just the season when we ought to lay down the law to the soul, and bid it be alone in refraining from pleasures just when the whole mob has let itself go in pleasures; for this is the surest proof which a man can get of his own constancy, if he neither seeks the things which are seductive and allure him to luxury, nor is led into them.

It shows much more courage to remain dry and sober when the mob is drunk and vomiting, but it shows greater self-control to refuse to withdraw oneself and to do what the crowd does, but in a different way – thus neither making oneself conspicuous nor becoming one of the crowd. For one may keep holiday without extravagance.

I am so firmly determined, however, to test the constancy of your mind that, drawing from the

---

[2]The *pilleus* was worn by newly freed slaves and by the Roman populace on festal occasions.

teachings of great men, I shall give you also a lesson: set aside a certain number of days, during which you shall be content with the scantiest and cheapest fare, with coarse and rough dress, saying to yourself the while: 'Is this the condition that I feared?'

It is precisely in times of immunity from care that the soul should toughen itself beforehand for occasions of greater stress, and it is while Fortune is kind that it should fortify itself against her violence. In days of peace the soldier performs manoeuvres, throws up earthworks with no enemy in sight, and wearies himself by gratuitous toil, in order that he may be equal to unavoidable toil. If you would not have a man flinch when the crisis comes, train him before it comes. Such is the course which those men[3] have followed who, in their imitation of poverty, have every month come almost to want, that they might never recoil from what they had so often rehearsed.

You need not suppose that I mean meals like Timon's, or 'paupers' huts', or any other device which luxurious millionaires use to beguile the tedium of their lives. Let the pallet be a real one, and the coarse cloak; let the bread be hard and grimy. Endure all this for three or four days at a time, sometimes for more, so that it may be a test of

---

[3]The Epicurians.

yourself instead of a mere hobby. Then, I assure you, my dear Lucilius, you will leap for joy when filled with a pennyworth of food, and you will understand that a man's peace of mind does not depend upon Fortune; for, even when angry she grants enough for our needs.

There is no reason, however, why you should think that you are doing anything great; for you will merely be doing what many thousands of slaves and many thousands of poor men are doing every day. But you may credit yourself with this item – that you will not be doing it under compulsion, and that it will be as easy for you to endure it permanently as to make the experiment from time to time. Let us practise our strokes on the 'dummy';[4] let us become intimate with poverty, so that Fortune may not catch us off our guard. We shall be rich with all the more comfort, if we once learn how far poverty is from being a burden.

Even Epicurus, the teacher of pleasure, used to observe stated intervals, during which he satisfied his hunger in niggardly fashion; he wished to see whether he thereby fell short of full and complete happiness, and, if so, by what amount he fell short, and whether this amount was worth purchasing

---

[4]The post that gladiators used when preparing themselves for combats in the arena.

at the price of great effort. At any rate, he makes such a statement in the well-known letter written to Polyaenus in the archonship of Charinus. Indeed, he boasts that he himself lived on less than a penny, but that Metrodorus, whose progress was not yet so great, needed a whole penny.

Do you think that there can be fullness on such fare? Yes, and there is pleasure also – not that shifty and fleeting pleasure which needs a fillip now and then, but a pleasure that is steadfast and sure. For though water, barley-meal, and crusts of barley-bread are not a cheerful diet, yet it is the highest kind of pleasure to be able to derive pleasure from this sort of food, and to have reduced one's needs to that modicum which no unfairness of Fortune can snatch away.

Even prison fare is more generous, and those who have been set apart for capital punishment are not so meanly fed by the man who is to execute them. Therefore, what a noble soul must one have, to descend of one's own free will to a diet which even those who have been sentenced to death have not to fear! This is indeed forestalling the spear-thrusts of Fortune.

So begin, my dear Lucilius, to follow the custom of these men, and set apart certain days on which you shall withdraw from your business and make yourself at home with the scantiest fare. Establish business relations with poverty.

Dare, O my friend, to scorn the sight of wealth,
And mould thyself to kinship with thy God.[5]

For he alone is in kinship with God who has scorned wealth. Of course I do not forbid you to possess it, but I would have you reach the point at which you possess it dauntlessly; this can be accomplished only by persuading yourself that you can live happily without it as well as with it, and by regarding riches always as likely to elude you.

But now I must begin to fold up my letter. 'Settle your debts first', you cry. Here is a draft on Epicurus; he will pay down the sum: 'Ungoverned anger begets madness.'[6] You cannot help knowing the truth of these words, since you have had not only slaves, but also enemies.

But indeed this emotion blazes out against all sorts of persons; it springs from love as much as from hate, and shows itself not less in serious matters than in jest and sport. And it makes no difference how important the provocation may be, but into what kind of soul it penetrates. Similarly with fire; it does not matter

---

[5]Virgil, *Aeneid* viii. 364 f.
[6]Fragment 484, Usener.

how great is the flame, but what it falls upon. For solid timbers have repelled a very great fire; conversely, dry and easily inflammable stuff nourishes the slightest spark into a conflagration. So it is with anger, my dear Lucilius; the outcome of a mighty anger is madness, and hence anger should be avoided, not merely that we may escape excess, but that we may have a healthy mind. Farewell.

ON WORLDLINESS AND RETIREMENT

I leap for joy whenever I receive letters from you. For they fill me with hope; they are now not mere assurances concerning you, but guarantees. And I beg and pray you to proceed in this course; for what better request could I make of a friend than one which is to be made for his own sake? If possible, withdraw yourself from all the business of which you speak, and if you cannot do this, tear yourself away. We have dissipated enough of our time already; let us in old age begin to pack up our baggage.

Surely there is nothing in this that men can begrudge us. We have spent our lives on the high seas; let us die in harbour. Not that I would advise you to try to win fame by your retirement; one's retirement should neither be paraded nor concealed. Not concealed, I say, for I shall not go so far in urging you as to expect you to condemn all men as mad and then seek out for yourself a hiding-place and oblivion; rather make this your business, that your retirement be not conspicuous, though it should be obvious.

In the second place, while those whose choice is un-hampered from the start will deliberate on that other question, whether they wish to pass their lives in ob-scurity, in your case there is not a free choice. Your ability and energy have thrust you into the work of the world; so have the charm of your writings and the friendships you have made with famous and notable men. Renown has already taken you by storm. You may sink yourself into the depths of obscurity and ut-terly hide yourself; yet your earlier acts will reveal you.

You cannot keep lurking in the dark; much of the old gleam will follow you wherever you fly.

Peace you can claim for yourself without being dis-liked by anyone, without any sense of loss, and without any pangs of spirit. For what will you leave behind you that you can imagine yourself reluctant to leave? Your clients? But none of these men courts you for yourself; they merely court something from you. Peo-ple used to hunt friends, but now they hunt pelf; if a lonely old man changes his will, the morning-caller transfers himself to another door. Great things cannot be bought for small sums; so reckon up whether it is preferable to leave your own true self, or merely some of your belongings.

Would that you had had the privilege of growing old amid the limited circumstances of your origin, and that fortune had not raised you to such heights! You were removed far from the sight of wholesome living by your swift rise to prosperity, by your province, by your position as procurator,[1] and by all that such things promise; you will next acquire more important duties and after them still more. And what will be the result?

Why wait until there is nothing left for you to crave? That time will never come. We hold that there is a succession of causes, from which fate is woven; similarly, you may be sure, there is a succession in our desires; for one begins where its predecessor ends. You have been thrust into an existence which will never of itself put an end to your wretchedness and your slavery. Withdraw your chafed neck from the yoke; it is better that it should be cut off once for all, than galled forever.

If you retreat to privacy, everything will be on a smaller scale, but you will be satisfied abundantly;

---

[1] Lucilius was prominent in the civil service and had filled many important positions. At the time when the *Letters* were written, he was procurator in Sicily.

in your present condition, however, there is no satisfaction in the plenty which is heaped upon you on all sides. Would you rather be poor and sated, or rich and hungry? Prosperity is not only greedy, but it also lies exposed to the greed of others. And as long as nothing satisfies you, you yourself cannot satisfy others.

'But', you say, 'how can I take my leave?' Any way you please. Reflect how many hazards you have ventured for the sake of money, and how much toil you have undertaken for a title! You must dare something to gain leisure, also – or else grow old amid the worries of procuratorships[2] abroad and subsequently of civil duties at home, living in turmoil and in ever fresh floods of responsibilities, which no man has ever succeeded in avoiding by unobtrusiveness or by seclusion of life. For what bearing on the case has your personal desire for a secluded life? Your position in the world desires the opposite! What if, even now, you allow that position to grow greater? But all that is added to your successes will be added to your fears.

---

[2]The procurator did the work of a quaestor in an imperial province. Positions at Rome to which Lucilius might succeed included *praefectus annonae*, in charge of the grain supply, or *praefectus urbi*, Director of Public Safety, and others.

CHAPTER NINETEEN

At this point I should like to quote a saying of Maecenas, who spoke the truth when he stood on the very summit:[3] 'There's thunder even on the loftiest peaks.' If you ask me in what book these words are found, they occur in the volume entitled *Prometheus*.[4] He simply meant to say that these lofty peaks have their tops surrounded with thunderstorms. But is any power worth so high a price that a man like you would ever, in order to obtain it, adopt a style so debauched as that?[5] Maecenas was indeed a man of parts, who would have left a great pattern for Roman oratory to follow, had his good fortune not made him effeminate – nay, had it not emasculated him! An end like his awaits you also, unless you forthwith shorten sail and – as Maecenas was not willing to do until it was too late – hug the shore!

This saying of Maecenas's might have squared my account with you; but I feel sure, knowing you, that you will get out an injunction against me, and that you will be unwilling to accept payment of my debt in such crude and debased currency. However that

---

[3] And therefore could speak with authority on this point.

[4] Perhaps a tragedy. Maecenas wrote a *Symposium*, a work *De cultu suo, Octavia*, some stray verse, and perhaps some history.

[5] Seneca whimsically pretends to assume that eccentric literary style and high political position go hand in hand. See also the following sentence.

may be, I shall draw on the account of Epicurus.[6] He says: 'You must reflect carefully beforehand with whom you are to eat and drink, rather than what you are to eat and drink. For a dinner of meats without the company of a friend is like the life of a lion or a wolf.'

This privilege will not be yours unless you withdraw from the world; otherwise, you will have as guests only those whom your slave-secretary[7] sorts out from the throng of callers. It is, however, a mistake to select your friend in the reception hall or to test him at the dinner table. The most serious misfortune for a busy man who is overwhelmed by his possessions is, that he believes men to be his friends when he himself is not a friend to them, and that he deems his favours to be effective in winning friends, although, in the case of certain men, the more they owe, the more they hate. A trifling debt makes a man your debtor; a large one makes him an enemy.

'What', you say, 'do not kindnesses establish friendships?' They do, if one has had the privilege of choosing those who are to receive them, and if they are placed judiciously, instead of being scattered broadcast.

---

[6]Fragment 542, Usener.

[7]A slave kept by every prominent Roman to identify the master's friends and dependants.

Therefore, while you are beginning to call your mind your own, meantime apply this maxim of the wise: consider that it is more important who receives a thing, than what it is he receives. Farewell.

ON PRACTISING WHAT YOU PREACH

If you are in good health and if you think yourself worthy of becoming at last your own master, I am glad. For the credit will be mine, if I can drag you from the floods in which you are being buffeted without hope of emerging. This, however, my dear Lucilius, I ask and beg of you, on your part, that you let wisdom sink into your soul, and test your progress, not by mere speech or writings, but by stoutness of heart and decrease of desire. Prove your words by your deeds.

Far different is the purpose of those who are speech-making and trying to win the approbation of a throng of hearers, far different that of those who allure the ears of young men and idlers by many-sided or fluent argumentation; philosophy teaches us to act, not to speak; it exacts of every man that he should live according to his own standards, that his life should not be out of harmony with his words, and that, further, his inner life should be of one hue and not out of harmony with all his activities. This, I say, is the highest duty and the highest proof of wisdom – that deed and word should be in accord, that a man should be equal to himself under all conditions, and always the same.

'But', you reply, 'can maintain this standard?' Very few, to be sure, but there are some. It is indeed a hard undertaking, and I do not say that the philosopher can always keep the same pace. But he can always travel the same path.

Observe yourself, then, and see whether your dress and your house are inconsistent, whether you treat yourself lavishly and your family meanly, whether you eat frugal dinners and yet build luxurious houses. You should lay hold, once for all, upon a single norm to live by, and should regulate your whole life according to this norm. Some men restrict themselves at home, but strut with swelling port before the public; such discordance is a fault, and it indicates a wavering mind which cannot yet keep its balance.

And I can tell you, further, whence arise this unsteadiness and disagreement of action and purpose; it is because no man resolves upon what he wishes, and, even if he has done so, he does not persist in it, but jumps the track; not only does he change, but he returns and slips back to the conduct which he has abandoned and abjured.

Therefore, to omit the ancient definitions of wisdom and to include the whole manner of human life, I can be satisfied with the following: 'What is wisdom? Always desiring the same things, and always refusing the same things.' You may be excused from adding the little proviso – that what you wish, should be right; since no man can always be satisfied with the same thing, unless it is right.

For this reason men do not know what they wish, except at the actual moment of wishing; no man ever decided once and for all to desire or to refuse. Judgment varies from day to day, and changes to the opposite, making many a man pass his life in a kind of game. Press on, therefore, as you have begun; perhaps you will be led to perfection, or to a point which you alone understand is still short of perfection.

'But what', you say, 'will become of my crowded household without a household income?' If you stop supporting that crowd, it will support itself; or perhaps you will learn by the bounty of poverty what you cannot learn by your own bounty. Poverty will keep for you your true and tried friends; you will be rid of the men who were not seeking you for yourself, but for something which you have. Is it not true, however, that you should love poverty, if only for this single reason – that it will show you those by whom you are loved? O when will that time come, when no one shall tell lies to compliment you!

Accordingly, let your thoughts, your efforts, your desires, help to make you content with your own self and with the goods that spring from yourself; and commit all your other prayers to God's keeping! What happiness could come closer home to you? Bring yourself down to humble conditions, from which you cannot be ejected; and in order that you may do so with greater alacrity, the contribution contained in this letter shall refer to that subject; I shall bestow it upon you forthwith.

Although you may look askance, Epicurus will once again be glad to settle my indebtedness: 'Believe me, your words will be more imposing if you sleep on a cot and wear rags. For in that case you will not be merely saying them; you will be demonstrating their truth.' I, at any rate, listen in a different spirit to the utterances of our friend Demetrius, after I have seen him reclining without even a cloak to cover him, and, more than this, without rugs to lie upon. He is not only a teacher of the truth, but a witness to the truth.

'May not a man, however, despise wealth when it lies in his very pocket?' Of course; he also is great-souled, who sees riches heaped up round him and, after wondering long and deeply because they have come into his possession, smiles, and hears rather than feels that they are his. It means much not to be spoiled by intimacy with riches; and he is truly great who is poor amidst riches.

'Yes, but I do not know', you say, 'how the man you speak of will endure poverty, if he falls into it suddenly.' Nor do I, Epicurus, know whether the poor man you speak of will despise riches, should he suddenly fall into them; accordingly, in the case of both, it is the mind that must be appraised, and we must investigate whether your man is pleased with his poverty, and whether my man is displeased with his riches. Otherwise, the cot-bed and the rags are slight proof of his good intentions if it has not been made clear that the person concerned endures these trials not from necessity but from preference.

It is the mark, however, of a noble spirit not to pre-cipitate oneself into such things on the ground that they are better, but to practise for them on the ground that they are thus easy to endure. And they are easy to endure, Lucilius; when, however, you come to them after long rehearsal, they are even pleasant; for they contain a sense of freedom from care – and without this nothing is pleasant.

I hold it essential, therefore, to do as I have told you in a letter that great men have often done: to

reserve a few days in which we may prepare ourselves for real poverty by means of fancied poverty. There is all the more reason for doing this, because we have been steeped in luxury and regard all duties as hard and onerous. Rather let the soul be roused from its sleep and be prodded, and let it be reminded that Nature has prescribed very little for us. No man is born rich. Every man, when he first sees light, is commanded to be content with milk and rags. Such is our beginning, and yet kingdoms are all too small for us! Farewell.

CHAPTER TWENTY ONE

ON THE RENOWN WHICH MY WRITINGS MAY BRING YOU

Do you conclude that you are having difficulties with those men about whom you wrote to me? Your greatest difficulty is with yourself; for you are your own stumbling block. You do not know what you want. You are better at approving the right course than at following it out. You see where the true happiness lies, but you have not the courage to attain it. Let me tell you what it is that hinders you, inasmuch as you do not of yourself discern it.

You think that this condition, which you are to abandon, is one of importance, and after resolving upon that ideal state of calm into which you hope to pass, you are held back by the lustre of your present life, from which it is your intention to depart, just as if you were about to fall into a state of filth and darkness. This is a mistake, Lucilius; to go from your present life into the other is a promotion. There is the same difference between these two lives as there is between mere brightness and real light; the latter has a definite source within itself, the other borrows its radiance; the one is called forth by an illumination coming from the outside, and anyone who stands between the source and the object immediately turns the latter into a dense shadow; but the other has a glow that comes from within.

It is your own studies that will make you shine and will render you eminent. Allow me to mention the case of Epicurus.

He was writing[1] to Idomeneus and trying to recall him from a showy existence to sure and steadfast renown. Idomeneus was at that time a minister of state who exercised a rigorous authority and had important affairs in hand. 'If', said Epicurus, 'you are attracted by fame, my letters will make you more renowned than all the things which you cherish and which make you cherished.'

Did Epicurus speak falsely? Who would have known of Idomeneus had not the philosopher thus engraved his name in those letters of his? All the grandees and satraps, even the king himself, who was petitioned for the title which Idomeneus sought, are

---

[1]Fragment 132, Usener.

sunk in deep oblivion. Cicero's letters keep the name of Atticus from perishing. It would have profited Atticus nothing to have an Agrippa for a son-in-law, a Tiberius for the husband of his grand-daughter, and a Drusus Caesar for a great-grandson; amid these mighty names his name would never be spoken, had not Cicero bound him to himself.[2]

The deep flood of time will roll over us; some few great men will raise their heads above it, and, though destined at the last to depart into the same realms of silence, will battle against oblivion and maintain their ground for long.

That which Epicurus could promise his friend, this I promise you, Lucilius. I shall find favour among later generations; I can take with me names that will endure as long as mine. Our poet Virgil promised an eternal name to two heroes, and is keeping his promise:[3]

> Blest heroes twain! If power my song possess,
> The record of your names shall never be
> Erased from out the book of Time, while yet
> Aeneas' tribe shall keep the Capitol,
> That rock immovable, and Roman sire
> Shall empire hold.

---

[2] i.e. Cicero's letters did more to preserve the name of Atticus than such a connection with the imperial house would have done.

[3] *Aeneid*, ix. 446 ff.

Whenever men have been thrust forward by fortune, whenever they have become part and parcel of another's influence, they have found abundant favour, their houses have been thronged, only so long as they themselves have kept their position; when they themselves have left it, they have slipped at once from the memory of men. But in the case of innate ability, the respect in which it is held increases, and not only does honour accrue to the man himself, but whatever has attached itself to his memory is passed on from one to another.[4]

In order that Idomeneus may not be introduced free of charge into my letter, he shall make up the indebtedness from his own account. It was to him that Epicurus addressed the well-known saying[5] urging him to make Pythocles rich, but not rich in the vulgar and equivocal way. 'If you wish', said he, 'to make Pythocles rich, do not add to his store of money, but subtract from his desires.'

This idea is too clear to need explanation, and too clever to need reinforcement. There is, however, one point on which I would warn you – not to consider that this statement applies only to riches; its value will be the same, no matter how you apply it. 'If you

---

[4]As in the case of Epicurus and Idomeneus, Cicero and Atticus, Virgil and Euryalus and Nisus ... and Seneca and Lucilius!

[5]Fragment 135, Usener.

wish to make Pythocles honourable, do not add to his honours, but subtract from his desires'; 'If you wish Pythocles to have pleasure forever, do not add to his pleasures, but subtract from his desires'; 'If you wish to make Pythocles an old man, filling his life to the full, do not add to his years, but subtract from his desires.'

There is no reason why you should hold that these words belong to Epicurus alone; they are public property. I think we ought to do in philosophy as they are wont to do in the Senate: when someone has made a motion, of which I approve to a certain extent, I ask him to make his motion in two parts, and I vote for the part which I approve. So I am all the more glad to repeat the distinguished words of Epicurus, in order that I may prove to those who have recourse to him through a bad motive, thinking that they will have in him a screen for their own vices, that they must live honourably, no matter what school they follow.

Go to his Garden and read the motto carved there: 'Stranger, here you will do well to tarry; here our highest good is pleasure.' The caretaker of that abode, a kindly host, will be ready for you; he will welcome you with barley-meal and serve you water also in abundance, with these words: 'Have you not been well entertained?' 'This garden', he says, 'does not whet your appetite; it quenches it. Nor does it make you more thirsty with every drink; it slakes the thirst by a natural cure – a cure that demands no fee. This is the "pleasure" in which I have grown old.'

In speaking with you, however, I refer to those desires which refuse alleviation, which must be bribed to cease. For in regard to the exceptional desires, which may be postponed, which may be chastened and checked, I have this one thought to share with you: a pleasure of that sort is according to our nature, but it is not according to our needs; one owes nothing to it; whatever is expended upon it is a free gift. The belly will not listen to advice; it makes demands, it importunes. And yet it is not a troublesome creditor; you can send it away at small cost, provided only that you give it what you owe, not merely all you are able to give. Farewell.

CHAPTER TWENTY TWO

ON THE FUTILITY OF HALF-WAY MEASURES

You understand by this time that you must withdraw yourself from those showy and depraved pursuits, but you still wish to know how this may be accomplished. There are certain things which can be pointed out only by someone who is present. The physician cannot prescribe by letter the proper time for eating or bathing; he must feel the pulse. There is an old adage about gladiators – that they plan their fight in the ring; as they intently watch, something in the adversary's glance, some movement of his hand, even some slight bending of his body, gives a warning.

We can formulate general rules and commit them to writing, as to what is usually done, or ought to be done; such advice may be given, not only to our absent friends, but also to succeeding generations. In regard, however, to that second[1] question – when or how your plan is to be carried out – no one will advise at long range; we must take counsel in the presence of the actual situation.

You must be not only present in the body, but watchful in mind, if you would avail yourself of the fleeting opportunity. Accordingly, look about you for the opportunity; if you see it, grasp it, and with all your energy and with all your strength devote yourself to this task – to rid yourself of those business duties.

Now listen carefully to the opinion which I shall offer; it is my opinion that you should withdraw either from that kind of existence, or else from existence altogether. But I likewise maintain that you should take a gentle path, that you may loosen rather than cut the knot which you have bungled so badly in tying – provided that if there shall be no other way of loosening it, you may actually cut it. No man is so faint-hearted that he would rather hang in suspense forever than drop once for all.

Meanwhile – and this is of first importance – do not hamper yourself; be content with the business into

---

[1]The first question, 'Shall I withdraw from the world?' has been answered, apparently by Lucilius himself. The second was, 'How can I accomplish this?' Seneca pretends to answer it, although he feels that this should be done in personal conference rather than by writing.

which you have lowered yourself, or, as you prefer to have people think, have tumbled. There is no reason why you should be struggling on to something further; if you do, you will lose all grounds of excuse, and men will see that it was not a tumble. The usual explanation which men offer is wrong: 'I was compelled to do it. Suppose it was against my will; I had to do it.' But no one is compelled to pursue prosperity at top speed; it means something to call a halt – even if one does not offer resistance – instead of pressing eagerly after favouring fortune.

Shall you then be put out with me, if I not only come to advise you, but also call in others to advise you – wiser heads than my own, men before whom I am wont to lay any problem upon which I am pondering? Read the letter of Epicurus[2] which bears on this matter; it is addressed to Idomeneus. The writer asks him to hasten as fast as he can, and beat a retreat before some stronger influence comes between and takes from him the liberty to withdraw.

But he also adds that one should attempt nothing except at the time when it can be attempted suitably and seasonably. Then, when the long-sought occasion comes, let him be up and doing. Epicurus forbids[3] us to doze when we are meditating escape; he bids us

---

[2]See the preceding letter of Seneca.

[3]Fragment 133, Usener.

hope for a safe release from even the hardest trials, provided that we are not in too great a hurry before the time, nor too dilatory when the time arrives.

Now, I suppose, you are looking for a Stoic motto also. There is really no reason why anyone should slander that school to you on the ground of its rashness; as a matter of fact, its caution is greater than its courage. You are perhaps expecting the sect to utter such words as these: 'It is base to flinch under a burden. Wrestle with the duties which you have once undertaken. No man is brave and earnest if he avoids danger, if his spirit does not grow with the very difficulty of his task.'

Words like these will indeed be spoken to you, if only your perseverance shall have an object that is worthwhile, if only you will not have to do or to suffer anything unworthy of a good man; besides, a good man will not waste himself upon mean and discreditable work or be busy merely for the sake of being busy. Neither will he, as you imagine, become so involved in ambitious schemes that he will have continually to endure their ebb and flow. Nay, when he sees the dangers, uncertainties, and hazards in which he was formerly tossed about, he will withdraw – not turning his back to the foe, but falling back little by little to a safe position.

From business, however, my dear Lucilius, it is easy to escape, if only you will despise the rewards of business. We are held back and kept from escaping by thoughts like these: 'What then? Shall I leave behind me these great prospects? Shall I depart at the very time of harvest? Shall I have no slaves at my side? No retinue for my litter? No crowd in my reception-room?'

Hence men leave such advantages as these with reluctance; they love the reward of their hardships, but curse the hardships themselves.

Men complain about their ambitions as they complain about their mistresses; in other words, if you penetrate their real feelings, you will find, not hatred, but bickering. Search the minds of those who cry down what they have desired, who talk about escaping from things which they are unable to do without; you will comprehend that they are lingering of their own free will in a situation which they declare they find it hard and wretched to endure.

It is so, my dear Lucilius; there are a few men whom slavery holds fast, but there are many more who hold fast to slavery.

If, however, you intend to be rid of this slavery; if freedom is genuinely pleasing in your eyes; and if you seek counsel for this one purpose – that you may have the good fortune to accomplish this purpose without perpetual annoyance – how can the whole company of Stoic thinkers fail to approve your course? Zeno, Chrysippus, and all their kind will give you advice that is temperate, honourable, and suitable.

But if you keep turning round and looking about, in order to see how much you may carry away with you, and how much money you may keep to equip yourself for the life of leisure, you will never find a way out. No man can swim ashore and take his baggage with him. Rise to a higher life, with the favour of the gods, but let it not be favour of such a kind as the gods give to men when with kind and genial faces they bestow magnificent ills, justified in so doing by the one fact that the things which irritate and torture have been bestowed in answer to prayer.

I was just putting the seal upon this letter, but it must be broken again, in order that it may go to you with its customary contribution, bearing with it some noble word. And lo, here is one that occurs to my mind; I do not know whether its truth or its nobility of utterance is the greater. 'Spoken by whom?' you ask. By Epicurus;[4] for I am still appropriating other men's belongings.

The words are: 'Everyone goes out of life just as if he had but lately entered it.' Take anyone off his guard – young, old, or middle-aged; you will find that all are equally afraid of death, and equally ignorant of life. No one has anything finished, because we have kept putting off into the future all our undertakings.[5]

---

[4]Fragment 495, Usener.

[5]i.e. the old man is like the infant in this, also – that he can look back upon nothing which he has finished, because he has always put off finishing things.

No thought in the quotation given above pleases me more than that it taunts old men with being infants.

'No one', he says, 'leaves this world in a different manner from one who has just been born.' That is not true, for we are worse when we die than when we were born; but it is our fault, and not that of Nature. Nature should scold us, saying: 'What does this mean? I brought you into the world without desires or fears, free from superstition, treachery and the other curses. Go forth as you were when you entered!'

A man has caught the message of wisdom, if he can die as free from care as he was at birth; but as it is, we are all a-flutter at the approach of the dreaded end. Our courage fails us, our cheeks blanch; our tears fall, though they are unavailing. But what is baser than to fret at the very threshold of peace?

The reason, however, is, that we are stripped of all our goods, we have jettisoned our cargo of life and are in distress; for no part of it has been packed in the hold; it has all been heaved overboard and has drifted away. Men do not care how nobly they live, but only how long, although it is within the reach of every man to live nobly, but within no man's power to live long. Farewell.

CHAPTER TWENTY THREE

ON THE TRUE JOY WHICH COMES FROM PHILOSOPHY

Do you suppose that I shall write you how kindly the winter season has dealt with us – a short season and a mild one – or what a nasty spring we are having – cold weather out of season – and all the other trivialities which people write when they are at a loss for topics of conversation? No; I shall communicate something which may help both you and myself. And what shall this 'something' be, if not an exhortation to soundness of mind? Do you ask what is the foundation of a sound mind? It is, not to find joy in useless things. I said that it was the foundation; it is really the pinnacle.

We have reached the heights if we know what it is that we find joy in and if we have not placed our happiness in the control of externals. The man who is goaded ahead by hope of anything, though it be within reach, though it be easy of access, and though his ambitions have never played him false, is troubled and unsure of himself.

Above all, my dear Lucilius, make this your business: learn how to feel joy.

Do you think that I am now robbing you of many pleasures when I try to do away with the gifts of chance, when I counsel the avoidance of hope, the sweetest thing that gladdens our hearts? Quite the contrary; I do not wish you ever to be deprived of gladness. I would have it born in your house; and it is born there, if only it be inside of you. Other objects of cheer do not fill a man's bosom; they merely smooth his brow and are inconstant – unless perhaps you believe that he who laughs has joy. The very soul must be happy and confident, lifted above every circumstance.

Real joy, believe me, is a stern matter. Can one, do you think, despise death with a carefree countenance, or with a 'blithe and gay' expression, as our young dandies are accustomed to say? Or can one thus open his door to poverty, or hold the curb on his pleasures, or contemplate the endurance of pain? He who ponders these things[1] in his heart is indeed full of joy, but

---

[1]Death, poverty, temptation, and suffering.

it is not a cheerful joy. It is just this joy, however, of which I would have you become the owner; for it will never fail you when once you have found its source.

The yield of poor mines is on the surface; those are really rich whose veins lurk deep, and they will make more bountiful returns to him who delves unceasingly. So too those baubles which delight the common crowd afford but a thin pleasure, laid on as a coating, and every joy that is only plated lacks a real basis. But the joy of which I speak, that to which I am endeavouring to lead you, is something solid, disclosing itself the more fully as you penetrate into it.

Therefore I pray you, my dearest Lucilius, do the one thing that can render you really happy: cast aside and trample under foot all those things that glitter outwardly and are held out to you[2] by another or as obtainable from another; look toward the true good, and rejoice only in that which comes from your own store. And what do I mean by 'from your own store'? I mean from your very self, that which is the best part of you. The frail body, also, even though we can accomplish nothing without it, is to be regarded as necessary rather than as important; it involves us in vain pleasures, short-lived, and soon

---

[2]By the various sects that professed to teach how happiness is to be obtained.

to be regretted, which, unless they are reined in by extreme self-control, will be transformed into the opposite. This is what I mean: pleasure, unless it has been kept within bounds, tends to rush headlong into the abyss of sorrow.

But it is hard to keep within bounds that which you believe to be good. The real good may be coveted with safety.

Do you ask me what this real good is, and whence it derives? I will tell you: it comes from a good conscience, from honourable purposes, from right actions, from contempt of the gifts of chance, from an even and calm way of living which treads but one path. For men who leap from one purpose to another, or do not even leap but are carried over by a sort of hazard – how can such wavering and unstable persons possess any good that is fixed and lasting?

There are only a few who control themselves and their affairs by a guiding purpose; the rest do not proceed; they are merely swept along, like objects afloat in a river. And of these objects, some are held back by sluggish waters and are transported gently; others are torn along by a more violent current; some, which are nearest the bank, are left there as the current slackens; and others are carried out to sea by the onrush of the stream. Therefore, we should decide what we wish, and abide by the decision.

Now is the time for me to pay my debt. I can give you a saying of your friend Epicurus[3] and thus clear this letter of its obligation: 'It is bothersome always to be beginning life.' Or another, which will perhaps express the meaning better: 'They live ill who are always beginning to live.'

You are right in asking why; the saying certainly stands in need of a commentary. It is because the life of such persons is always incomplete. But a man cannot stand prepared for the approach of death if he has just begun to live. We must make it our aim already to have lived long enough. No one deems that he has done so, if he is just on the point of planning his life.

You need not think that there are few of this kind; practically everyone is of such a stamp. Some men, indeed, only begin to live when it is time for them to leave off living. And if this seems surprising to you, I shall add that which will surprise you still more: some men have left off living before they have begun. Farewell.

---

[3]Fragment 493, Usener.

CHAPTER TWENTY FOUR

ON DESPISING DEATH[1]

You write me that you are anxious about the result of a lawsuit, with which an angry opponent is threatening you; and you expect me to advise you to picture to yourself a happier issue, and to rest in the allurements of hope. Why, indeed, is it necessary to summon trouble – which must be endured soon enough when it has once arrived – or to anticipate trouble and ruin the present through fear of the future? It is indeed foolish to be unhappy now because you may be unhappy at some future time.

But I shall conduct you to peace of mind by another route: if you would put off all worry, assume that

---

[1]Seneca's theme is suggested by the fear that possesses Lucilius as to the issue of a lawsuit. This fear is taken as typical of all fears, and Seneca devotes most of his letter to the greatest fear of all – fear of death.

what you fear may happen will certainly happen in any event; whatever the trouble may be, measure it in your own mind, and estimate the amount of your fear. You will thus understand that what you fear is either insignificant or short-lived.

And you need not spend a long time in gathering illustrations which will strengthen you; every epoch has produced them. Let your thoughts travel into any era of Roman or foreign history, and there will throng before you notable examples of high achievement or of high endeavour.

If you lose this case, can anything more severe happen to you than being sent into exile or led to prison? Is there a worse fate that any man may fear than being burned or being killed? Name such penalties one by one, and mention the men who have scorned them; one does not need to hunt for them – it is simply a matter of selection.

Sentence of conviction was borne by Rutilius as if the injustice of the decision were the only thing which annoyed him. Exile was endured by Metellus with courage, by Rutilius even with gladness; for the former consented to come back only because his country called him; the latter refused to return when Sulla summoned him – and nobody in those days said 'No' to Sulla! Socrates in prison discoursed, and declined to flee when certain persons gave him the

140

opportunity; he remained there, in order to free mankind from the fear of two most grievous things, death and imprisonment.

Mucius put his hand into the fire. It is painful to be burned, but how much more painful to inflict such suffering upon oneself! Here was a man of no learning, not primed to face death and pain by any words of wisdom, and equipped only with the courage of a soldier, who punished himself for his fruitless daring; he stood and watched his own right hand falling away piecemeal on the enemy's brazier,[2] nor did he withdraw the dissolving limb, with its uncovered bones, until his foe removed the fire. He might have accomplished something more successful in that camp, but never anything more brave. See how much keener a brave man is to lay hold of danger than a cruel man is to inflict it: Porsenna was more ready to pardon Mucius for wishing to slay him than Mucius to pardon himself for failing to slay Porsenna!

'Oh', say you, 'those stories have been droned to death in all the schools; pretty soon, when you reach the topic "On Despising Death", you will be telling me about Cato.' But why should I not tell you about Cato, how he read Plato's[3] book on that last glorious night,

---

[2] The *foculus* in this version of the story was evidently a movable fire, a brazier.

[3] The *Phaedo* on the immortality of the soul.

with a sword laid at his pillow? He had provided these two requisites for his last moments – the first, that he might have the will to die, and the second, that he might have the means. So he put his affairs in order – as well as one could put in order that which was ruined and near its end – and thought that he ought to see to it that no one should have the power to slay or the good fortune to save[4] Cato.

Drawing the sword – which he had kept unstained from all bloodshed against the final day – he cried: 'Fortune, you have accomplished nothing by resisting all my endeavours. I have fought, till now, for my country's freedom, and not for my own, I did not strive so doggedly to be free, but only to live among the free. Now, since the affairs of mankind are beyond hope, let Cato be withdrawn to safety.'

So saying, he inflicted a mortal wound upon his body. After the physicians had bound it up, Cato had less blood and less strength, but no less courage; angered now not only at Caesar but also at himself, he rallied his unarmed hands against his wound, and expelled, rather than dismissed, that noble soul which had been so defiant of all worldly power.

I am not now heaping up these illustrations for the purpose of exercising my wit, but for the purpose of encouraging you to face that which is thought to

---

[4]i.e. to save and bring back to Rome as prisoner.

be most terrible. And I shall encourage you all the more easily by showing that not only resolute men have despised that moment when the soul breathes its last, but that certain persons, who were craven in other respects, have equalled in this regard the courage of the bravest. Take, for example, Scipio, the father-in-law of Gnaeus Pompeius: he was driven back upon the African coast by a headwind and saw his ship in the power of the enemy. He therefore pierced his body with a sword, and when they asked where the commander was, he replied: 'All is well with the commander.'

These words brought him up to the level of his ancestors and suffered not the glory which fate gave to the Scipios in Africa[5] to lose its continuity. It was a great deed to conquer Carthage, but a greater deed to conquer death. 'All is well with the commander!' Ought a general to die otherwise, especially one of Cato's generals?

I shall not refer you to history, or collect examples of those men who throughout the ages have despised death; for they are very many. Consider these times of ours, whose enervation and over-refinement call

---

[5]Scipio Africanus defeated Hannibal at Zama in 202 BCE. Scipio Aemilianus, also surnamed Africanus, was by adoption the grandson of Hannibal's conqueror. He captured Carthage in the Third Punic War, 146 BCE. The Scipio mentioned by Seneca died in 46 BCE.

forth our complaints; they nevertheless will include men of every rank, of every lot in life, and of every age, who have cut short their misfortunes by death.

Believe me, Lucilius; death is so little to be feared that through its good offices nothing is to be feared.

Therefore, when your enemy threatens, listen unconcernedly. Although your conscience makes you confident, yet, since many things have weight which are outside your case,[6] both hope for that which is utterly just, and prepare yourself against that which is utterly unjust. Remember, however, before all else, to strip things of all that disturbs and confuses, and to see what each is at bottom; you will then comprehend that they contain nothing fearful except the actual fear.

What you see happening to boys happens also to ourselves, who are only slightly bigger boys: when those whom they love, with whom they daily associate, with whom they play, appear with masks on, the boys are frightened out of their wits. We should strip the mask, not only from men, but from things, and restore to each object its own aspect.

'Why dost thou[7] hold up before my eyes swords, fires, and a throng of executioners raging about

---

[6]He refers to the lawsuit Lucilius is involved with.

[7]Seneca here inserts an 'apostrophe', a literary device common in Greek drama and literary works where the narrator speaks directly to an idea (here Death and Pain) in order to personify it and bring it to life.

thee? Take away all that vain show, behind which thou lurkest and scarest fools! Ah! Thou art naught but Death, whom only yesterday a manservant of mine and a maidservant did despise! Why dost thou again unfold and spread before me, with all that great display, the whip and the rack? Why are those engines of torture made ready, one for each several member of the body, and all the other innumerable machines for tearing a man apart piecemeal? Away with all such stuff, which makes us numb with terror! And thou, silence the groans, the cries, and the bitter shrieks ground out of the victim as he is torn on the rack! Forsooth thou are naught but Pain, scorned by yonder gout-ridden wretch, endured by yonder dyspeptic in the midst of his dainties, borne bravely by the girl in travail. Slight thou art, if I can bear thee; short thou art if I cannot bear thee!'

Ponder these words which you have often heard and often uttered. Moreover, prove by the result whether that which you have heard and uttered is true. For there is a very disgraceful charge often brought against our school – that we deal with the words, and not with the deeds, of philosophy.

What, have you only at this moment learned that death is hanging over your head, at this moment exile, at this moment grief? You were born to these perils. Let us think of everything that can happen as something which will happen.

I know that you have really done what I advised you to do; I now warn you not to drown your soul in these petty anxieties of yours; if you do, the soul will be dulled and will have too little vigour left when the time comes for it to arise. Remove the mind from this case of yours to the case of men in general. Say to yourself that our petty bodies are mortal and frail; pain can reach them from other sources than from wrong or the might of the stronger. Our pleasures themselves become torments; banquets bring indigestion, carousals paralysis of the muscles and palsy, sensual habits affect the feet, the hands, and every joint of the body.

I may become a poor man; I shall then be one among many. I may be exiled; I shall then regard myself as born in the place to which I shall be sent. They may put me in chains. What then? Am I free from bonds now? Behold this clogging burden of a body, to which nature has fettered me! 'I shall die,' you say; you mean to say 'I shall cease to run the risk of sickness; I shall cease to run the risk of imprisonment; I shall cease to run the risk of death.'

I am not so foolish as to go through at this juncture the arguments which Epicurus harps upon, and say that the terrors of the world below are idle – that Ixion does not whirl round on his wheel, that Sisyphus does not shoulder his stone uphill, that a man's entrails cannot be restored and devoured every day;[8] no one is so childish as to fear Cerberus, or the shadows, or the spectral garb of those who are held together by naught but their unfleshed bones. Death either annihilates us or strips us bare. If we are then released, there remains the better part, after the burden has been withdrawn; if we are annihilated, nothing remains; good and bad are alike removed.

Allow me at this point to quote a verse of yours, first suggesting that, when you wrote it, you meant it for yourself no less than for others. It is ignoble to say one thing and mean another; and how much more ignoble to write one thing and mean another! I remember one day you were handling the well-known commonplace – that we do not suddenly fall on death, but advance towards it by slight degrees; we die every day.

For every day a little of our life is taken from us; even when we are growing, our life is on the wane. We lose our childhood, then our boyhood, and then our youth. Counting even yesterday, all past time is lost time; the very day which we are now spending is shared between ourselves and death. It is not the last drop that empties the water-clock, but all that which previously has flowed out; similarly, the final hour when we cease to exist does not of itself bring death;

---

[8]As mythology describes the treatment of Tityus or of Prometheus.

it merely of itself completes the death process. We reach death at that moment, but we have been a long time on the way.

In describing this situation, you said in your customary, style (for you are always impressive, but never more pungent than when you are putting the truth in appropriate words):

Not single is the death which comes; the death
Which takes us off is but the last of all.

I prefer that you should read your own words rather than my letter; for then it will be clear to you that this death, of which we are afraid, is the last but not the only death.

I see what you are looking for; you are asking what I have packed into my letter, what inspiriting saying from some master-mind, what useful precept. So I shall send you something dealing with this very subject which has been under discussion. Epicurus[9] upbraids those who crave, as much as those who shrink from, death: 'It is absurd' he says, 'to run towards death because you are tired of life, when it is your manner of life that has made you run towards death.'

And in another passage:[10] 'What is so absurd as to seek death, when it is through fear of death that you

---

[9]Fragment 496, Usener.

[10]Fragment 498, Usener.

have robbed your life of peace?' And you may add a third statement, of the same stamp:[11] 'Men are so thoughtless, nay, so mad, that some, through fear of death, force themselves to die.'

Whichever of these ideas you ponder, you will strengthen your mind for the endurance alike of death and of life. For we need to be warned and strengthened in both directions – not to love or to hate life overmuch; even when reason advises us to make an end of it, the impulse is not to be adopted without reflection or at headlong speed.

The brave and wise man should not beat a hasty retreat from life; he should make a becoming exit. And above all, he should avoid the weakness which has taken possession of so many – the lust for death. For just as there is an unreflecting tendency of the mind towards other things, so, my dear Lucilius, there is an unreflecting tendency towards death; this often seizes upon the noblest and most spirited men, as well as upon the craven and the abject. The former despise life; the latter find it irksome.

Others also are moved by a satiety of doing and see-ing the same things, and not so much by a hatred of life as because they are cloyed with it. We slip into this condition, while philosophy itself pushes us on, and

---

[11]Fragment 497, Usener.

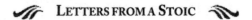

we say: 'How long must I endure the same things? Shall I continue to wake and sleep, be hungry and be cloyed, shiver and perspire? There is an end to nothing; all things are connected in a sort of circle; they flee and they are pursued. Night is close at the heels of day, day at the heels of night; summer ends in autumn, winter rushes after autumn, and winter softens into spring; all nature in this way passes, only to return. I do nothing new; I see nothing new; sooner or later one sickens of this, also.' There are many who think that living is not painful, but superfluous. Farewell.

CHAPTER TWENTY FIVE

ON REFORMATION

With regard to these two friends of ours, we must proceed along different lines; the faults of the one are to be corrected, the other's are to be crushed out. I shall take every liberty; for I do not love this one[1] if I am unwilling to hurt his feelings. 'What', you say, 'do you expect to keep a forty-year-old ward under your tutelage? Consider his age, how hardened it now is, and past handling! Such a man cannot be reshaped; only young minds are moulded.' I do not know whether I shall make progress, but I should prefer to lack success rather than to lack faith. You need not despair of curing sick men even when the disease is chronic, if only you hold out against excess and force

---

[1]The second friend, whose faults are to be crushed out. He proves to be some forty years old; the other is a youth.

them to do and submit to many things against their will. As regards our other friend I am not sufficiently confident, either, except for the fact that he still has sense of shame enough to blush for his sins. This modesty should be fostered; so long as it endures in his soul, there is some room for hope. But as for this veteran of yours, I think we should deal more carefully with him, that he may not become desperate about himself.

There is no better time to approach him than now, when he has an interval of rest and seems like one who has corrected his faults. Others have been cheated by this interval of virtue on his part, but he does not cheat me. I feel sure that these faults will return, as it were, with compound interest, for just now, I am certain, they are in abeyance but not absent. I shall devote some time to the matter, and try to see whether or not something can be done.

But do you yourself, as indeed you are doing, show me that you are stout-hearted? lighten your baggage for the march. None of our possessions is essential. Let us return to the law of nature; for then riches are laid up for us. The things which we actually need are free for all, or else cheap; nature craves only bread and water. No one is poor according to this standard; when a man has limited his desires within these bounds, he can challenge the happiness of Jove himself, as Epicurus says. I must insert in this letter one or two more of his sayings:[2]

'Do everything as if Epicurus were watching you.' There is no real doubt that it is good for one to have appointed a guardian over oneself, and to have someone whom you may look up to, someone whom you may regard as a witness of your thoughts. It is, indeed, nobler by far to live as you would live under the eyes of some good man, always at your side; but nevertheless I am content if you only act, in whatever you do, as you would act if anyone at all were looking on; because solitude prompts us to all kinds of evil.

And when you have progressed so far that you have also respect for yourself, you may send away your attendant; but until then, set as a guard over yourself the authority of some man, whether your choice be the great Cato or Scipio, or Laelius – or any man in whose presence even abandoned wretches would check their bad impulses. Meantime, you are engaged in making of yourself the sort of person in whose company you would not dare to sin. When this aim has been accomplished and you begin to hold yourself in some esteem, I shall gradually allow you to do what Epicurus, in another passage, suggests:[3] 'The time when you should most of all

---

[2]Fragment 211, Usener.

[3]Fragment 209, Usener.

withdraw into yourself is when you are forced to be in a crowd.'

You ought to make yourself of a different stamp from the multitude. Therefore, while it is not yet safe to withdraw into solitude,[4] seek out certain individuals; for everyone is better off in the company of somebody or other – no matter who – than in his own company alone. 'The time when you should most of all withdraw into yourself is when you are forced to be in a crowd.' Yes, provided that you are a good, tranquil, and self-restrained man; otherwise, you had better withdraw into a crowd in order to get away from yourself. Alone, you are too close to a rascal. Farewell.

---

[4]Because solitude is a prompt to evil.

CHAPTER TWENTY SIX

ON OLD AGE AND DEATH

I was just lately telling you that I was within sight of old age.[1] I am now afraid that I have left old age behind me. For some other word would now apply to my years, or at any rate to my body; since old age means a time of life that is weary rather than crushed. You may rate me in the worn-out class – of those who are nearing the end.

Nevertheless, I offer thanks to myself, with you as witness; for I feel that age has done no damage to my mind, though I feel its effects on my constitution. Only my vices, and the outward aids to these vices, have reached senility; my mind is strong and rejoices that it has but slight connection with the body. It has

---

[1]Seneca was by this time at least sixty-five years old, and probably older.

laid aside the greater part of its load. It is alert; it takes issue with me on the subject of old age; it declares that old age is its time of bloom.

Let me take it at its word, and let it make the most of the advantages it possesses. The mind bids me do some thinking and consider how much of this peace of spirit and moderation of character I owe to wisdom and how much to my time of life; it bids me distinguish carefully what I cannot do and what I do not want to do...[2] For why should one complain or regard it as a disadvantage, if powers which ought to come to an end have failed?

'But', you say, 'it is the greatest possible disadvantage to be worn out and to die off, or rather, if I may speak literally, to melt away! For we are not suddenly smitten and laid low; we are worn away, and every day reduces our powers to a certain extent.'

But is there any better end to it all than to glide off to one's proper haven, when nature slips the cable? Not that there is anything painful in a shock and a sudden departure from existence; it is merely because this other way of departure is easy – a gradual withdrawal. I, at any rate, as if the test were at hand and

---

[2]This text for this passage is corrupt. The course of the argument requires something like this: for it is just as much to my advantage not to be able to do what I do not want to do, as it is to be able to do whatever gives me pleasure.

the day were come which is to pronounce its decision concerning all the years of my life, watch over myself and commune thus with myself:

'The showing which we have made up to the present time, in word or deed, counts for nothing. All this is but a trifling and deceitful pledge of our spirit, and is wrapped in much charlatanism. I shall leave it to Death to determine what progress I have made. Therefore with no faint heart I am making ready for the day when, putting aside all stage artifice and actor's rouge, I am to pass judgment upon myself – whether I am merely declaiming brave sentiments, or whether I really feel them; whether all the bold threats I have uttered against fortune are a pretence and a farce.

'Put aside the opinion of the world; it is always wavering and always takes both sides. Put aside the studies which you have pursued throughout your life; Death will deliver the final judgment in your case. This is what I mean: your debates and learned talks, your maxims gathered from the teachings of the wise, your cultured conversation – all these afford no proof of the real strength of your soul. Even the most timid man can deliver a bold speech. What you have done in the past will be manifest only at the time when you draw your last breath. I accept the terms; I do not shrink from the decision.'

This is what I say to myself, but I would have you think that I have said it to you also. You are younger, but what does that matter? There is no fixed count of our years. You do not know where death awaits you, so be ready for it everywhere.

I was just intending to stop, and my hand was making ready for the closing sentence, but the rites are still to be performed and the travelling money for the letter disbursed. And just assume that I am not telling where I intend to borrow the necessary sum; you know upon whose coffers I depend. Wait for me but a moment, and I will pay you from my own account; meanwhile, Epicurus will oblige me with these words:[3] 'Think on death', or rather, if you prefer the phrase, on 'migration to heaven'.

The meaning is clear – that it is a wonderful thing to learn thoroughly how to die. You may deem it superfluous to learn a text that can be used only once, but that is just the reason why we ought to think on a thing. When we can never prove whether we really know a thing, we must always be learning it.

'Think on death.' In saying this, he bids us think on freedom. He who has learned to die has unlearned slavery; he is above any external power, or, at any rate, he is beyond it. What terrors have prisons and bonds

---

[3]Epicurus, Fragment 205, Usener.

and bars for him? His way out is clear. There is only one chain which binds us to life, and that is the love of life. The chain may not be cast off, but it may be rubbed away, so that, when necessity shall demand, nothing may retard or hinder us from being ready to do at once that which at some time we are bound to do. Farewell.

CHAPTER TWENTY SEVEN

ON THE GOOD
WHICH ABIDES

'What', say you, 'are you giving me advice? Indeed, have you already advised yourself, already corrected your own faults? Is this the reason why you have leisure to reform other men?' No, I am not so shameless as to undertake to cure my fellow-men when I am ill myself. I am, however, discussing with you troubles which concern us both, and sharing the remedy with you, just as if we were lying ill in the same hospital. Listen to me, therefore, as you would if I were talking to myself. I am admitting you to my inmost thoughts, and am having it out with myself, merely making use of you as my pretext.

I keep crying out to myself: 'Count your years, and you will be ashamed to desire and pursue the same things you desired in your boyhood days. Of this one thing make sure against your dying day – let your faults die before you die. Away with those disordered pleasures, which must be dearly paid for; it is not only those which are to come that harm me, but also those which have come and gone. Just as crimes, even if they have not been detected when they were committed, do not allow anxiety to end with them; so with guilty pleasures, regret remains even after the pleasures are over. They are not substantial, they are not trustworthy; even if they do not harm us, they are fleeting.

'Cast about rather for some good which will abide. But there can be no such good except as the soul discovers it for itself within itself. Virtue alone affords everlasting and peace-giving joy; even if some obstacle arise, it is but like an intervening cloud, which floats beneath the sun but never prevails against it.'

When will it be your lot to attain this joy? Thus far, you have indeed not been sluggish, but you must quicken your pace. Much toil remains; to confront it, you must yourself lavish all your waking hours, and all your efforts, if you wish the result to be accomplished. This matter cannot be delegated to someone else.

The other kind of literary activity[1] admits of outside assistance. Within our own time there was a

---

[1] i.e. ordinary studies, or literature, as contrasted with philosophy.

162

certain rich man named Calvisius Sabinus; he had the bank account and the brains of a freedman.[2] I never saw a man whose good fortune was a greater offence against propriety. His memory was so faulty that he would sometimes forget the name of Ulysses, or Achilles, or Priam – names which we know as well as we know those of our own attendants. No major-domo in his dotage, who cannot give men their right names, but is compelled to invent names for them – no such man, I say, calls off the names[3] of his master's tribesmen so atrociously as Sabinus used to call off the Trojan and Achaean heroes. But none the less did he desire to appear learned.

So he devised this short cut to learning: he paid fabulous prices for slaves – one to know Homer by heart and another to know Hesiod; he also delegated a special slave to each of the nine lyric poets. You need not wonder that he paid high prices for these slaves; if he did not find them ready to hand he had them made to order. After collecting this retinue, he began to make life miserable for his guests; he would keep these fellows at the foot of his couch, and ask them from time

---

[2]Compare with the following the vulgarities of Trimalchio in the Satire of Petronius, and the bad taste of Nasidienus in Horace.

[3]At the *salutatio*, or morning call. The position of *nomenclator*, 'caller-of-names', was originally devoted more strictly to political purposes. Here it is primarily social.

to time for verses which he might repeat, and then frequently break down in the middle of a word.

Satellius Quadratus, a feeder, and consequently a fawner, upon addle-pated millionaires, and also (for this quality goes with the other two) a flouter of them, suggested to Sabinus that he should have philologists to gather up the bits.[4] Sabinus remarked that each slave cost him one hundred thousand sesterces; Satellius replied: 'You might have bought as many book-cases for a smaller sum.' But Sabinus held to the opinion that what any member of his household knew, he himself knew also.

This same Satellius began to advise Sabinus to take wrestling lessons – sickly, pale, and thin as he was, Sabinus answered: 'How can I? I can scarcely stay alive now.' 'Don't say that, I implore you,' replied the other, 'consider how many perfectly healthy slaves you have!' No man is able to borrow or buy a sound mind; in fact, as it seems to me, even though sound minds were for sale, they would not find buyers. Depraved minds, however, are bought and sold every day.

But let me pay off my debt and say farewell: 'Real wealth is poverty adjusted to the law of Nature.'[5]

---

[4]i.e. all the ideas that dropped out of the head of Sabinus. The slave who picked up the crumbs was called *analecta*.

[5]Epicurus, Fragment 477, Usener.

CHAPTER TWENTY SEVEN

Epicurus has this saying in various ways and contexts, but it can never be repeated too often, since it can never be learned too well. For some persons the remedy should be merely prescribed; in the case of others, it should be forced down their throats. Farewell.

CHAPTER TWENTY EIGHT

ON TRAVEL AS A CURE FOR DISCONTENT

Do you suppose that you alone have had this experience? Are you surprised, as if it were a novelty, that after such long travel and so many changes of scene you have not been able to shake off the gloom and heaviness of your mind? You need a change of soul rather than a change of climate. Though you may cross vast spaces of sea, and though, as our Virgil[1] remarks:

> Lands and cities are left astern, your faults will follow you whithersoever you travel.

Socrates made the same remark to one who complained; he said: 'Why do you wonder that globe-trotting does not help you, seeing that you

---

[1] *Aeneid*, iii. 72.

always take yourself with you? The reason which set you wandering is ever at your heels.' What pleasure is there in seeing new lands? Or in surveying cities and spots of interest? All your bustle is useless. Do you ask why such flight does not help you? It is because you flee along with yourself. You must lay aside the burdens of the mind; until you do this, no place will satisfy you.

Reflect that your present behaviour is like that of the prophetess whom Virgil describes:[2] she is excited and goaded into fury, and contains within herself much inspiration that is not her own:

> The priestess raves, if haply she may shake
> The great god from her heart.

You wander hither and yon, to rid yourself of the burden that rests upon you, though it becomes more troublesome by reason of your very restlessness, just as in a ship the cargo when stationary makes no trouble, but when it shifts to this side or that, it causes the vessel to heel more quickly in the direction where it has settled. Anything you do tells against you, and you hurt yourself by your very unrest; for you are shaking up a sick man.

That trouble once removed, all change of scene will become pleasant; though you may be driven to the

---

[2] *Aeneid*, vi. 78

uttermost ends of the earth, in whatever corner of a savage land you may find yourself, that place, however forbidding, will be to you a hospitable abode. The person you are matters more than the place to which you go; for that reason we should not make the mind a bondsman to any one place. Live in this belief: 'I am not born for any one corner of the universe; this whole world is my country.'

If you saw this fact clearly, you would not be surprised at getting no benefit from the fresh scenes to which you roam each time through weariness of the old scenes. For the first would have pleased you in each case, had you believed it wholly yours. As it is, however, you are not journeying; you are drifting and being driven, only exchanging one place for another, although that which you seek – to live well – is found everywhere.

Can there be any spot so full of confusion as the Forum? Yet you can live quietly even there, if necessary. Of course, if one were allowed to make one's own arrangements, I should flee far from the very sight and neighbourhood of the Forum. For just as pestilential places assail even the strongest constitution, so there are some places which are also unwholesome for a healthy mind which is not yet quite sound, though recovering from its ailment.

I disagree with those who strike out into the midst of the billows and, welcoming a stormy existence, wrestle daily in hardihood of soul with life's problems. The wise man will endure all that, but will not choose it; he will prefer to be at peace rather than at war. It helps little to have cast out your own faults if you must quarrel with those of others.

Says one: 'There were thirty tyrants surrounding Socrates, and yet they could not break his spirit'; but what does it matter how many masters a man has? 'Slavery' has no plural; and he who has scorned it is free – no matter amid how large a mob of overlords he stands.

It is time to stop, but not before I have paid duty. 'The knowledge of sin is the beginning of salvation.' This saying of Epicurus[3] seems to me to be a noble one. For he who does not know that he has sinned does not desire correction; you must discover yourself in the wrong before you can reform yourself.

Some boast of their faults. Do you think that the man has any thought of mending his ways who counts over his vices as if they were virtues? Therefore, as far as possible, prove yourself guilty, hunt up charges against yourself; play the part, first of accuser, then of judge, last of intercessor. At times be harsh with yourself. Farewell.

---

[3]Fragment 522, Usener.

CHAPTER TWENTY NINE

ON THE CRITICAL CONDITION OF MARCELLINUS

You have been inquiring about our friend Marcellinus and you desire to know how he is getting along. He seldom comes to see me, for no other reason than that he is afraid to hear the truth, and at present he is removed from any danger of hearing it; for one must not talk to a man unless he is willing to listen. That is why it is often doubted whether Diogenes and the other Cynics, who employed an undiscriminating freedom of speech and offered advice to any who came in their way, ought to have pursued such a plan.

For what if one should chide the deaf or those who are speechless from birth or by illness? But you answer: 'Why should I spare words? They cost nothing. I cannot know whether I shall help the man to whom I give advice; but I know well that I shall help someone if I advise many. I must scatter this advice by the handful. It is impossible that one who tries often should not sometime succeed.'

This very thing, my dear Lucilius, is, I believe, exactly what a great-souled man ought not to do; his influence is weakened; it has too little effect upon those whom it might have set right if it had not grown so stale. The archer ought not to hit the mark only sometimes; he ought to miss it only sometimes. That which takes effect by chance is not an art. Now wisdom is an art; it should have a definite aim, choosing only those who will make progress, but withdrawing from those whom it has come to regard as hopeless – yet not abandoning them too soon, and just when the case is becoming hopeless trying drastic remedies.

As to our friend Marcellinus, I have not yet lost hope. He can still be saved, but the helping hand must be offered soon. There is indeed danger that he may pull his helper down; for there is in him a native character of great vigour, though it is already inclining to wickedness. Nevertheless I shall brave this danger and be bold enough to show him his faults.

He will act in his usual way; he will have recourse to his wit – the wit that can call forth smiles even from mourners. He will turn the jest, first against himself, and then against me. He will forestall every word which I am about to utter. He will quiz our philosophic systems; he will accuse philosophers of accepting doles, keeping mistresses, and indulging their appetites. He will point out to me one philosopher who has been caught in adultery, another who haunts the cafes, and another who appears at court.

He will bring to my notice Aristo, the philosopher of Marcus Lepidus, who used to hold discussions in his carriage; for that was the time which he had taken for editing his researches, so that Scaurus said of him when asked to what school he belonged: 'At any rate, he isn't one of the Walking Philosophers.' Julius Graecinus, too, a man of distinction, when asked for an opinion on the same point, replied: 'I cannot tell you; for I don't know what he does when dismounted,' as if the query referred to a chariot-gladiator.[1]

It is mountebanks of that sort, for whom it would be more creditable to have left philosophy alone than to traffic in her, whom Marcellinus will throw in my teeth. But I have decided to put up with taunts; he may stir my laughter, but I perchance shall stir him to tears; or, if he persist in his jokes, I shall rejoice, so to speak, in the midst of sorrow, because he is blessed with such

---

[1] The *essedarius* fought from a car. When his adversary forced him out of the car, he was compelled to continue the fight on foot, like an unhorsed knight.

a merry sort of lunacy. But that kind of merriment does not last long. Observe such men, and you will note that within a short space of time they laugh to excess and rage to excess.

It is my plan to approach him and to show him how much greater was his worth when many thought it less. Even though I shall not root out his faults, I shall put a check upon them; they will not cease, but they will stop for a time; and perhaps they will even cease, if they get the habit of stopping. This is a thing not to be despised, since to men who are seriously stricken the blessing of relief is a substitute for health.

So while I prepare myself to deal with Marcellinus, do you in the meantime, who are able, and who understand whence and whither you have made your way, and who for that reason have an inkling of the distance yet to go, regulate your character, rouse your courage, and stand firm in the face of things which have terrified you. Do not count the number of those who inspire fear in you. Would you not regard as foolish one who was afraid of a multitude in a place where only one at a time could pass? Just so, there are not many who have access to you to slay you, though there are many who threaten you with death. Nature has so ordered it that, as only one has given you life, so only one will take it away.

If you had any shame, you would have let me off from paying the last instalment. Still, I shall not be niggardly either, but shall discharge my debts to the last penny and force upon you what I still owe: 'I have never wished to cater to the crowd; for what I know, they do not approve, and what they approve, I do not know.'[2]

'Who said this?' you ask, as if you were ignorant whom I am pressing into service; it is Epicurus. But this same watchword rings in your ears from every sect – Peripatetic, Academic, Stoic, Cynic. For who that is pleased by virtue can please the crowd? It takes trickery to win popular approval; and you must needs make yourself like unto them; they will withhold their approval if they do not recognize you as one of themselves. However, what you think of yourself is much more to the point than what others think of you. The favour of ignoble men can be won only by ignoble means.

What benefit, then, will that vaunted philosophy confer, whose praises we sing, and which, we are told, is to be preferred to every art and every possession? Assuredly, it will make you prefer to please yourself rather than the populace, it will make you weigh, and not merely count, men's judgments, it will make

---

[2]Epicurus, Fragment 187, Usener.

you live without fear of gods or men, it will make you either overcome evils or end them. Otherwise, if I see you applauded by popular acclamation, if your entrance upon the scene is greeted by a roar of cheering and clapping – marks of distinction meet only for actors – if the whole state, even the women and children, sing your praises, how can I help pitying you? For I know what pathway leads to such popularity. Farewell.

ON CONQUERING THE CONQUEROR

I have beheld Aufidius Bassus, that noble man, shattered in health and wrestling with his years. But they already bear upon him so heavily that he cannot be raised up; old age has settled down upon him with great – yes, with its entire, weight. You know that his body was always delicate and sapless. For a long time he has kept it in hand, or, to speak more correctly, has kept it together; of a sudden it has collapsed.

Just as in a ship that springs a leak, you can always stop the first or the second fissure, but when many holes begin to open and let in water, the gaping hull cannot be saved; similarly, in an old man's body, there is a certain limit up to which you can sustain and prop its weakness. But when it comes to resemble a decrepit building – when every joint begins to spread and while one is being repaired another falls apart – then it is time for a man to look about him and consider how he may get out.[1]

But the mind of our friend Bassus is active. Philosophy bestows this boon upon us; it makes us joyful in the very sight of death, strong and brave no matter in what state the body may be, cheerful and never failing though the body fail us. A great pilot can sail even when his canvas is rent; if his ship be dismantled, he can yet put in trim what remains of her hull and hold her to her course. This is what our friend Bassus is doing; and he contemplates his own end with the courage and countenance which you would regard as undue indifference in a man who so contemplated another's.

This is a great accomplishment, Lucilius, and one which needs long practice to learn – to depart calmly when the inevitable hour arrives. Other kinds of death contain an ingredient of hope: a disease comes to an end; a fire is quenched; falling houses have set down in safety those whom they seemed certain to crush; the sea has cast ashore unharmed those whom it had engulfed, by the same force through which it drew them down; the soldier has drawn back his sword from the very neck of his doomed foe. But those whom old age

---

[1] i.e. *exeas e vita*, 'depart from life'.

is leading away to death have nothing to hope for; old age alone grants no reprieve. No ending, to be sure, is more painless; but there is none more lingering.

Our friend Bassus seemed to me to be attending his own funeral, and laying out his own body for burial, and living almost as if he had survived his own death, and bearing with wise resignation his grief at his own departure. For he talks freely about death, trying hard to persuade us that if this process contains any element of discomfort or of fear, it is the fault of the dying person, and not of death itself; also, that there is no more inconvenience at the actual moment than there is after it is over.

'And it is just as insane', he adds, 'for a man to fear what will not happen to him, as to fear what he will not feel if it does happen.' Or does anyone imagine it to be possible that the agency by which feeling is removed can be itself felt? 'Therefore', says Bassus, 'death stands so far beyond all evil that it is beyond all fear of evils.'

I know that all this has often been said and should be often repeated; but neither when I read them were such precepts so effective with me, nor when I heard them from the lips of those who were at a safe distance from the fear of the things which they declared were not to be feared. But this old man had the greatest weight with me when he discussed death and death was near.

For I must tell you what I myself think: I hold that one is braver at the very moment of death than when one is approaching death. For death, when it stands near us, gives even to inexperienced men the courage not to seek to avoid the inevitable. So the gladiator, who throughout the fight has been no matter how faint-hearted, offers his throat to his opponent and directs the wavering blade to the vital spot.[2] But an end that is near at hand, and is bound to come, calls for tenacious courage of soul; this is a rarer thing, and none but the wise man can manifest it.

Accordingly, I listened to Bassus with the deepest pleasure; he was casting his vote concerning death and pointing out what sort of a thing it is when it is observed, so to speak, nearer at hand. I suppose that a man would have your confidence in a larger degree, and would have more weight with you, if he had come back to life and should declare from experience that there is no evil in death; and so, regarding the approach of death, those will tell you best what disquiet it brings who have stood in its path, who have seen it coming and have welcomed it.

Bassus may be included among these men; and he had no wish to deceive us. He says that it is as foolish

---

[2]The defeated gladiator is supposed to be on his back, his opponent standing over him and about to deliver the final blow. As the blade wavers at the throat, searching for the jugular vein, the victim directs the point.

to fear death as to fear old age; for death follows old age precisely as old age follows youth. He who does not wish to die cannot have wished to live. For life is granted to us with the reservation that we shall die; to this end our path leads. Therefore, how foolish it is to fear it, since men simply await that which is sure, but fear only that which is uncertain!

Death has its fixed rule – equitable and unavoidable. Who can complain when he is governed by terms which include everyone? The chief part of equity, however, is equality.

But it is superfluous at the present time to plead Nature's cause; for she wishes our laws to be identical with her own; she but resolves that which she has compounded, and compounds again that which she has resolved.

Moreover, if it falls to the lot of any man to be set gently adrift by old age – not suddenly torn from life, but withdrawn bit by bit – oh, verily he should thank the gods, one and all, because, after he has had his fill, he is removed to a rest which is ordained for mankind, a rest that is welcome to the weary. You may observe certain men who crave death even more earnestly than others are wont to beg for life. And I do not know which men give us greater courage – those who call for death, or those who meet it cheerfully and tranquilly – for the first attitude is sometimes inspired by madness and sudden anger, the second is the calm which results from fixed judgement. Before now men have gone to meet death in a fit of rage; but when death comes to meet him, no one welcomes it cheerfully, except the man who has long since composed himself for death.

I admit, therefore, that I have visited this dear friend of mine more frequently on many pretexts, but with the purpose of learning whether I should find him always the same, and whether his mental strength was perhaps waning in company with his bodily powers. But it was on the increase, just as the joy of the charioteer is wont to show itself more clearly when he is on the seventh round[3] of the course, and nears the prize.

Indeed, he often said, in accord with the counsels of Epicurus:[4] 'I hope, first of all, that there is no pain at the moment when a man breathes his last; but if there is, one will find an element of comfort in its very shortness. For no great pain lasts long. And at all events, a man will find relief at the very time when soul and body are being torn asunder, even though the process be accompanied by excruciating pain, in the thought that after this pain is over he can feel no more pain. I am sure, however, that an old man's

---

[3]i.e. when on the home stretch.
[4]Fragment 503, Usener.

soul is on his very lips, and that only a little force is necessary to disengage it from the body. A fire which has seized upon a substance that sustains it needs water to quench it, or, sometimes, the destruction of the building itself; but the fire which lacks sustaining fuel dies away of its own accord.'

I am glad to hear such words, my dear Lucilius – not as new to me, but as leading me into the presence of an actual fact. And what then? Have I not seen many men break the thread of life? I have indeed seen such men; but those have more weight with me who approach death without any loathing for life, letting death in, so to speak, and not pulling it towards them.

Bassus kept saying: 'It is due to our own fault that we feel this torture, because we shrink from dying only when we believe that our end is near at hand.' But who is not near death? It is ready for us in all places and at all times. 'Let us consider', he went on to say, 'when some agency of death seems imminent, how much nearer are other varieties of dying which are not feared by us.'

A man is threatened with death by an enemy, but this form of death is anticipated by an attack of indigestion. And if we are willing to examine critically the various causes of our fear, we shall find that some exist, and others only seem to be. We do not fear death; we fear the thought of death. For death itself is always the same distance from us; wherefore, if it is to be

feared at all, it is to be feared always. For what season of our life is exempt from death?

But what I really ought to fear is that you will hate this long letter worse than death itself; so I shall stop. Do you, however, always think on death in order that you may never fear it? Farewell.

CHAPTER THIRTY ONE

ON SIREN SONGS

Now I recognize my Lucilius! He is beginning to reveal the character of which he gave promise. Follow up the impulse which prompted you to make for all that is best, treading under your feet that which is approved by the crowd. I would not have you greater or better than you planned; for in your case the mere foundations have covered a large extent of ground; only finish all that you have laid out, and take in hand the plans which you have had in mind.

In short, you will be a wise man, if you stop up your ears; nor is it enough to close them with wax; you need a denser stopple than that which they say Ulysses used for his comrades. The song which he feared was alluring, but came not from every side; the song, however, which you have to fear, echoes round you not from a single headland, but from every quarter of the world. Sail, therefore, not past one region which you mistrust because of its treacherous delights, but past every city. Be deaf to those who love you most of all; they pray for bad things with good intentions. And, if you would be happy, entreat the gods that none of their fond desires for you may be brought to pass.

What they wish to have heaped upon you are not really good things; there is only one good, the cause and the support of a happy life – trust in oneself. But this cannot be attained, unless one has learned to despise toil and to reckon it among the things which are neither good nor bad. For it is not possible that a single thing should be bad at one time and good at another, at times light and to be endured, and at times a cause of dread.

Work is not a good.[1] Then what is a good? I say, the scorning of work. That is why I should rebuke men who toil to no purpose. But when, on the other hand, a man is struggling towards honourable things, in proportion as he applies himself more and more, and allows himself less and less to be beaten or to halt, I shall recommend his conduct and shout my

---

[1]The argument is that work is not, in itself, a good; if it were, it would not be praiseworthy at one time and to be deprecated at another. It belongs, therefore, to the class of things which the Stoics call ἀδιάφορα, *indifferentia, res mediae.*

encouragement, saying: 'By so much you are better! Rise, draw a fresh breath, and surmount that hill, if possible, at a single spurt!'

Work is the sustenance of noble minds. There is, then, no reason why, in accordance with that old vow of your parents, you should pick and choose what fortune you wish should fall to your lot, or what you should pray for; besides, it is base for a man who has already travelled the whole round of highest honours to be still importuning the gods. What need is there of vows? Make yourself happy through your own efforts; you can do this, if once you comprehend that whatever is blended with virtue is good, and that whatever is joined to vice is bad. Just as nothing gleams if it has no light blended with it, and nothing is black unless it contains darkness or draws to itself something of dimness, and as nothing is hot without the aid of fire, and nothing cold without air; so it is the association of virtue and vice that makes things honourable or base.

What then is good? The knowledge of things. What is evil? The lack of knowledge of things. Your wise man, who is also a craftsman, will reject or choose in each case as it suits the occasion; but he does not fear that which he rejects, nor does he admire that which he chooses, if only he has a stout and unconquerable soul. I forbid you to be cast down or depressed. It is not enough if you do not shrink from work; ask for it.

'But', you say, 'is not trifling and superfluous work, and work that has been inspired by ignoble causes, a bad sort of work?' No; no more than that which is expended upon noble endeavours, since the very quality that endures toil and rouses itself to hard and uphill effort, is of the spirit, which says: 'Why do you grow slack? It is not the part of a man to fear sweat.'

And besides this, in order that virtue may be perfect, there should be an even temperament and a scheme of life that is consistent with itself throughout; and this result cannot be attained without knowledge of things, and without the art[2] which enables us to understand things human and things divine. That is the greatest good. If you seize this good, you begin to be the associate of the gods, and not their suppliant.

'But how', you ask, 'does one attain that goal?' You do not need to cross the Pennine or Graian[3] hills, or traverse the Candavian[4] waste, or face the Syrtes,[5] or Scylla, or Charybdis, although you have travelled through all these places for the bribe of a petty governorship; the journey for which nature has equipped you is safe and pleasant. She has given you such gifts

---

[2]i.e. philosophy.

[3]The Great St. Bernard and Little St. Bernard routes over the Alps.

[4]A mountain in Illyria, over which the Via Egnatia ran.

[5]Dangerous quicksands along the north coast of Africa.

that you may, if you do not prove false to them, rise level with God.

Your money, however, will not place you on a level with God; for God has no property. Your bordered robe[6] will not do this; for God is not clad in raiment; nor will your reputation, nor a display of self, nor a knowledge of your name widespread throughout the world; for no one has knowledge of God; many even hold him in low esteem, and do not suffer for so doing. The throng of slaves which carries your litter along the city streets and in foreign places will not help you; for this God of whom I speak, though the highest and most powerful of beings, carries all things on his own shoulders. Neither can beauty or strength make you blessed, for none of these qualities can withstand old age.

What we have to seek for, then, is that which does not each day pass more and more under the control of some power which cannot be withstood.[7] And what is this? It is the soul – but the soul that is upright, good, and great. What else could you call such a soul than a god dwelling as a guest in a human body? A soul like this may descend into a Roman knight just as well as into a freedman's son or a slave. For what is a Roman knight, or a freedman's son, or a slave? They are mere

---

[6]The *toga praetexta*, badge of the official position of Lucilius.

[7]For example, Time or Chance.

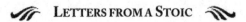

titles, born of ambition or of wrong. One may leap to heaven from the very slums. Only rise

And mould thyself to kinship with thy God.[8]

This moulding will not be done in gold or silver; an image that is to be in the likeness of God cannot be fashioned of such materials; remember that the gods, when they were kind unto men,[9] were moulded in clay. Farewell.

---

[8]Virgil, *Aeneid*, viii. 364 f.

[9]In the Golden Age, as described in Epicurus, when men were nearest to nature and 'fresh from the gods'.

CHAPTER THIRTY TWO

ON PROGRESS

I have been asking about you, and inquiring of everyone who comes from your part of the country, what you are doing, and where you are spending your time, and with whom. You cannot deceive me; for I am with you. Live just as if I were sure to get news of your doings, nay, as if I were sure to behold them. And if you wonder what particularly pleases me that I hear concerning you, it is that I hear nothing, that most of those whom I ask do not know what you are doing.

This is sound practice – to refrain from associating with men of different stamp and different aims. And I am indeed confident that you cannot be warped, that you will stick to your purpose, even though the crowd may surround and seek to distract you. What, then, is on my mind? I am not afraid lest they work a change in you, but I am afraid lest they may hinder your progress. And much harm is done even by one who holds you back, especially since life is so short; and we make it still shorter by our unsteadiness, by making ever fresh beginnings at life, now one and immediately another. We break up life into little bits, and fritter it away.

Hasten ahead, then, dearest Lucilius, and reflect how greatly you would quicken your speed if an enemy were at your back, or if you suspected the cavalry were approaching and pressing hard upon your steps as you fled. It is true; the enemy is indeed pressing upon you; you should therefore increase your speed and escape away and reach a safe position, remembering continually what a noble thing it is to round out your life before death comes, and then await in peace the remaining portion of your time, claiming nothing for yourself, since you are in possession of the happy life; for such a life is not made happier for being longer.

O when shall you see the time when you shall know that time means nothing to you, when you shall be peaceful and calm, careless of the morrow, because you are enjoying your life to the full?

Would you know what makes men greedy for the future? It is because no one has yet found himself. Your parents, to be sure, asked other blessings for you, but I myself pray rather that you may despise all those things which your parents wished for you in abundance. Their prayers plunder many another person, simply that you may be enriched. Whatever they make over to you must be removed from someone else.

I pray that you may get such control over yourself that your mind, now shaken by wandering thoughts, may at last come to rest and be steadfast, that it may be content with itself and, having attained an understanding of what things are truly good – and they are in our possession as soon as we have this knowledge – that it may have no need of added years. He has at length passed beyond all necessities – he has won his honourable discharge and is free – who still lives after his life has been completed. Farewell.

CHAPTER THIRTY THREE

ON THE FUTILITY OF
LEARNING MAXIMS

You wish me to close these letters also, as I closed my former letters, with certain utterances taken from the chiefs of our school. But they did not interest themselves in choice extracts; the whole texture of their work is full of strength. There is unevenness, you know, when some objects rise conspicuous above others. A single tree is not remarkable if the whole forest rises to the same height.

Poetry is crammed with utterances of this sort, and so is history. For this reason I would not have you think that these utterances belong to Epicurus: they are common property and are emphatically our own.[1] They are, however, more noteworthy in

---

[1] i.e. Stoic as well as Epicurean.

Epicurus, because they appear at infrequent intervals and when you do not expect them, and because it is surprising that brave words should be spoken at any time by a man who made a practice of being effeminate. For that is what most persons maintain. In my own opinion, however, Epicurus is really a brave man, even though he did wear long sleeves.[2] Fortitude, energy, and readiness for battle are to be found among the Persians,[3] just as much as among men who have girded themselves up high.

Therefore, you need not call upon me for extracts and quotations; such thoughts as one may extract here and there in the works of other philosophers run through the whole body of our writings. Hence we have no 'show-window goods', nor do we deceive the purchaser in such a way that, if he enters our shop, he will find nothing except that which is displayed in the window. We allow the purchasers themselves to get their samples from anywhere they please.

Suppose we should desire to sort out each separate motto from the general stock; to whom shall we credit them? To Zeno, Cleanthes, Chrysippus, Panaetius, or

---

[2]The sleeveless and 'girt-up' tunic is the sign of energy. Suetonius, *Caligula*, 52: the effeminate Caligula would 'appear in public with a long-sleeved tunic and bracelets'.

[3]Who wore sleeves.

Posidonius? We Stoics are not subjects of a despot: each of us lays claim to his own freedom. With them,[4] on the other hand, whatever Hermarchus says, or Metrodorus, is ascribed to one source. In that brotherhood, everything that any man utters is spoken under the leadership and commanding authority of one alone. We cannot, I maintain, no matter how we try, pick out anything from so great a multitude of things equally good.

Only the poor man counts his flock.[5]

Wherever you direct your gaze, you will meet with something that might stand out from the rest, if the context in which you read it were not equally notable.

For this reason, give over hoping that you can skim, by means of epitomes, the wisdom of distinguished men. Look into their wisdom as a whole; study it as a whole. They are working out a plan and weaving together, line upon line, a masterpiece, from which nothing can be taken away without injury to the whole. Examine the separate parts, if you like, provided you examine them as parts of the man himself. She is not a beautiful woman whose ankle or arm is praised, but she whose general appearance makes you forget to admire her single attributes.

---

[4]i.e. the Epicureans.

[5]Ovid, *Metamorphosis*, xiii. 824.

If you insist, however, I shall not be niggardly with you, but lavish; for there is a huge multitude of these passages; they are scattered about in profusion – they do not need to be gathered together, but merely to be picked up. They do not drip forth occasionally; they flow continuously. They are unbroken and are closely connected. Doubtless they would be of much benefit to those who are still novices and worshipping outside the shrine; for single maxims sink in more easily when they are marked off and bounded like a line of verse.

That is why we give to children a proverb, or that which the Greeks call *Chria*, to be learned by heart; that sort of thing can be comprehended by the young mind, which cannot as yet hold more. For a man, however, whose progress is definite, to chase after choice extracts and to prop his weakness by the best known and the briefest sayings and to depend upon his memory, is disgraceful; it is time for him to lean on himself. He should make such maxims and not memorize them. For it is disgraceful even for an old man, or one who has sighted old age, to have a notebook knowledge. 'This is what Zeno said.' But what have you yourself said? 'This is the opinion of Cleanthes.' But what is your own opinion? How long shall you march under another man's orders? Take command, and utter some word which posterity will remember. Put forth something from your own stock.

For this reason I hold that there is nothing of eminence in all such men as these, who never create anything themselves, but always lurk in the shadow of others, playing the role of interpreters, never daring to put once into practice what they have been so long in learning. They have exercised their memories on other men's material. But it is one thing to remember, another to know. Remembering is merely safeguarding something entrusted to the memory; knowing, however, means making everything your own; it means not depending upon the copy and not all the time glancing back at the master.

'Thus said Zeno, thus said Cleanthes, indeed!' Let there be a difference between yourself and your book! How long shall you be a learner? From now on be a teacher as well! 'But why', one asks, 'should I have to continue hearing lectures on what I can read?' 'The living voice', one replies, 'is a great help.' Perhaps, but not the voice which merely makes itself the mouth-piece of another's words, and only performs the duty of a reporter.

Consider this fact also. Those who have never attained their mental independence begin, in the first place, by following the leader in cases where everyone has deserted the leader; then, in the second place, they follow him in matters where the truth is still being investigated. However, the truth will never

be discovered if we rest contented with discoveries already made. Besides, he who follows another not only discovers nothing but is not even investigating.

What then? Shall I not follow in the footsteps of my predecessors? I shall indeed use the old road, but if I find one that makes a shorter cut and is smoother to travel, I shall open the new road. Men who have made these discoveries before us are not our masters, but our guides. Truth lies open for all; it has not yet been monopolized. And there is plenty of it left even for posterity to discover. Farewell.

CHAPTER THIRTY FOUR

ON A PROMISING PUPIL

I grow in spirit and leap for joy and shake off my years and my blood runs warm again, whenever I understand, from your actions and your letters, how far you have outdone yourself; for as to the ordinary man, you left him in the rear long ago. If the farmer is pleased when his tree develops so that it bears fruit, if the shepherd takes pleasure in the increase of his flocks, if every man regards his pupil as though he discerned in him his own early manhood – what, then, do you think are the feelings of those who have trained a mind and moulded a young idea, when they see it suddenly grown to maturity?

I claim you for myself; you are my handiwork. When I saw your abilities, I laid my hand upon you,[1] I exhorted you, I applied the goad and did not permit you to march lazily, but roused you continually. And now I do the same, but by this time I am cheering on one who is in the race and so in turn cheers me on.

'What else do you want of me, then?' you ask; 'the will is still mine.' Well, the will in this case is almost everything, and not merely the half, as in the proverb 'A task once begun is half done'. It is more than half, for the matter of which we speak is determined by the soul.[2] Hence it is that the larger part of goodness is the will to become good. You know what I mean by a good man? One who is complete, finished – whom no constraint or need can render bad.

I see such a person in you, if only you go steadily on and bend to your task, and see to it that all your actions and words harmonize and correspond with each other and are stamped in the same mould. If a man's acts are out of harmony, his soul is crooked. Farewell.

---

[1] A reference to the act (*iniectio*) by which a Roman took possession of a thing belonging to him, e.g. a runaway slave – without a decision of the court.

[2] i.e. the proverb may apply to tasks which a man performs with his hands, but it is an understatement when applied to the tasks of the soul.

CHAPTER THIRTY FIVE

ON THE FRIENDSHIP OF KINDRED MINDS

When I urge you so strongly to your studies, it is my own interest which I am consulting; I want your friendship, and it cannot fall to my lot unless you proceed, as you have begun, with the task of developing yourself. For now, although you love me, you are not yet my friend. 'But', you reply, 'are these words of different meaning?' Nay, more, they are totally unlike in meaning. A friend loves you, of course, but one who loves you is not in every case your friend. Friendship, accordingly, is always helpful, but love sometimes even does harm. Try to perfect yourself, if for no other reason, in order that you may learn how to love.

Hasten, therefore, in order that, while thus perfecting yourself for my benefit, you may not have learned perfection for the benefit of another. To be sure, I am already deriving some profit by imagining that we two shall be of one mind, and that whatever portion of my strength has yielded to age will return to me from your strength, although there is not so very much difference in our ages.

But yet I wish to rejoice in the accomplished fact. We feel a joy over those whom we love, even when separated from them, but such a joy is light and fleeting; the sight of a man, and his presence, and communion with him, afford something of living pleasure; this is true, at any rate, if one not only sees the man one desires, but the sort of man one desires. Give yourself to me, therefore, as a gift of great price, and, that you may strive the more, reflect that you yourself are mortal, and that I am old.

Hasten to find me, but hasten to find yourself first. Make progress, and, before all else, endeavour to be consistent with yourself. And when you would find out whether you have accomplished anything, consider whether you desire the same things today that you desired yesterday. A shifting of the will indicates that the mind is at sea, heading in various directions, according to the course of the wind. But that which is settled and solid does not wander from its place. This is the blessed lot of the completely wise man, and also, to a certain extent, of him who is progressing and has made some headway. Now what is the difference between these two classes of men? The one is in motion, to be sure, but does not change its position; it merely tosses up and down where it is; the other is not in motion at all. Farewell.

CHAPTER THIRTY SIX

ON THE VALUE OF RETIREMENT

Encourage your friend to despise stout-heartedly those who upbraid him because he has sought the shade of retirement and has abdicated his career of honours, and, though he might have attained more, has preferred tranquillity to them all. Let him prove daily to these detractors how wisely he has looked out for his own interests. Those whom men envy will continue to march past him; some will be pushed out of the ranks, and others will fall. Prosperity is a turbulent thing; it torments itself. It stirs the brain in more ways than one, goading men on to various aims – some to power, and others to high living. Some it puffs up; others it slackens and wholly enervates.

'But', the retort comes, 'so-and-so carries his prosperity well.' Yes; just as he carries his liquor. So you need not let this class of men persuade you that one who is besieged by the crowd is happy; they run to him as crowds rush for a pool of water, rendering it muddy while they drain it. But you say: 'Men call our friend a trifler and a sluggard.' There are men, you know, whose speech is awry, who use the contrary[1] terms. They called him happy; what of it? Was he happy?

Even the fact that to certain persons he seems a man of a very rough and gloomy cast of mind does not trouble me. Aristo[2] used to say that he preferred a youth of stern disposition to one who was a jolly fellow and agreeable to the crowd. 'For', he added, 'wine which, when new, seemed harsh and sour, becomes good wine; but that which tasted well at the vintage cannot stand age.' So let them call him stern and a foe to his own advancement. It is just this sternness that will go well when it is aged, provided only that he continues to cherish virtue and to absorb thoroughly the studies which make for culture – not those with which it is sufficient for a man to sprinkle himself, but those in which the mind should be steeped.

Now is the time to learn. 'What? Is there any time when a man should not learn?' By no means; but just as it is creditable for every age to study, so it is not

---

[1] i.e. they are no more correct now, when they called him a trifler, than they were before, when they called him happy.

[2] Aristo of Chios.

creditable for every age to be instructed. An old man learning his ABC is a disgraceful and absurd object; the young man must store up, the old man must use. You will therefore be doing a thing most helpful to yourself if you make this friend of yours as good a man as possible; those kindnesses, they tell us, are to be both sought for and bestowed, which benefit the giver no less than the receiver; and they are unquestionably the best kind.

Finally, he has no longer any freedom in the matter; he has pledged his word. And it is less disgraceful to compound with a creditor than to compound with a promising future. To pay his debt of money, the business man must have a prosperous voyage, the farmer must have fruitful fields and kindly weather, but the debt which your friend owes can be completely paid by mere goodwill.

Fortune has no jurisdiction over character. Let him so regulate his character that in perfect peace he may bring to perfection that spirit within him which feels neither loss nor gain, but remains in the same attitude, no matter how things fall out. A spirit like this, if it is heaped with worldly goods, rises superior to its wealth; if, on the other hand, chance has stripped him of a part of his wealth, or even all, it is not impaired.

If your friend had been born in Parthia, he would have begun, when a child, to bend the bow; if in

Germany, he would forthwith have been brandishing his slender spear; if he had been born in the days of our forefathers, he would have learned to ride a horse and smite his enemy hand to hand. These are the occupations which the system of each race recommends to the individual – yes, prescribes for him.

To what, then, shall this friend[3] of yours devote his attention? I say, let him learn that which is helpful against all weapons, against every kind of foe – contempt of death; because no one doubts that death has in it something that inspires terror, so that it shocks even our souls, which nature has so moulded that they love their own existence; for otherwise there would be no need to prepare ourselves, and to whet our courage, to face that towards which we should move with a sort of voluntary instinct, precisely as all men tend to preserve their existence.

No man learns a thing in order that, if necessity arises, he may lie down with composure upon a bed of roses; but he steels his courage to this end – that he may not surrender his plighted faith to torture, and that, if need be, he may some day stay out his watch in the trenches, even though wounded, without even leaning on his spear; because sleep is likely to

---

[3]As a Roman, living in an age when philosophy was recommended and prescribed.

creep over men who support themselves by any prop whatsoever.

In death there is nothing harmful; for there must exist something to which it is harmful.[4]

And yet, if you are possessed by so great a craving for a longer life, reflect that none of the objects which vanish from our gaze and are reabsorbed into the world of things, from which they have come forth and are soon to come forth again, is annihilated; they merely end their course and do not perish. And death, which we fear and shrink from, merely interrupts life, but does not steal it away; the time will return when we shall be restored to the light of day; and many men would object to this, were they not brought back in forgetfulness of the past.

But I mean to show you later,[5] with more care, that everything which seems to perish merely changes. Since you are destined to return, you ought to depart with a tranquil mind. Mark how the round of the

---

[4]And since after death we do not exist, death cannot be harmful to us. Seneca has in mind the argument of Epicurus (Diogenes Laertius, x. 124–5): 'Therefore the most dread-inspiring of all evils, death, is nothing to us; for when we exist; death is not present in us, and when death is present, then we do not exist. Therefore it does not concern either the living or the dead; for to the living it has no existence, and the dead do not themselves exist.'

[5]For example, in Epicurus. lxxvii.

universe repeats its course; you will see that no star in our firmament is extinguished, but that they all set and rise in alternation. Summer has gone, but another year will bring it again; winter lies low, but will be restored by its own proper months; night has overwhelmed the sun, but day will soon rout the night again. The wandering stars retrace their former courses; a part of the sky is rising unceasingly, and a part is sinking.

One word more, and then I shall stop; infants, and boys, and those who have gone mad, have no fear of death, and it is most shameful if reason cannot afford us that peace of mind to which they have been brought by their folly. Farewell.

CHAPTER THIRTY SEVEN

ON ALLEGIANCE TO VIRTUE

You have promised to be a good man; you have enlisted under oath; that is the strongest chain which will hold you to a sound understanding. Any man will be but mocking you, if he declares that this is an effeminate and easy kind of soldiering. I will not have you deceived. The words of this most honourable compact are the same as the words of that most disgraceful one, to wit:[1] 'Through burning, imprisonment, or death by the sword.'

From the men who hire out their strength for the arena, who eat and drink what they must pay for with their blood, security is taken that they will

---

[1]He refers to the famous oath which the gladiator took when he hired himself to the fighting-master; *uri, vinciri, verberari, ferroque necari patior.*

endure such trials even though they be unwilling; from you, that you will endure them willingly and with alacrity. The gladiator may lower his weapon and test the pity of the people;[2] but you will neither lower your weapon nor beg for life. You must die erect and unyielding. Moreover, what profit is it to gain a few days or a few years? There is no discharge for us from the moment we are born.

'Then how can I free myself?' you ask. You cannot escape necessities, but you can overcome them.

By force a way is made.[3]

And this way will be afforded you by philosophy. Betake yourself therefore to philosophy if you would be safe, untroubled, happy, in fine, if you wish to be – and that is most important – free. There is no other way to attain this end.

Folly[4] is low, abject, mean, slavish, and exposed to many of the cruellest passions. These passions, which are heavy taskmasters, sometimes ruling by turns, and sometimes together, can be banished from you

---

[2] Awaiting the signal of 'thumbs up' or 'thumbs down' from the crowd.

[3] Virgil, *Aeneid*, ii. 494.

[4] In the language of Stoicism, ἀμαθία, *stultitia*, 'folly', is the antithesis of σοφία, *sapientia*, 'wisdom'.

by wisdom, which is the only real freedom. There is but one path leading thither, and it is a straight path; you will not go astray. Proceed with steady step, and if you would have all things under your control, put yourself under the control of reason; if reason becomes your ruler, you will become ruler over many. You will learn from her what you should undertake, and how it should be done; you will not blunder into things.

You can show me no man who knows how he began to crave that which he craves. He has not been led to that pass by forethought; he has been driven to it by impulse. Fortune attacks us as often as we attack Fortune. It is disgraceful, instead of proceeding ahead, to be carried along, and then suddenly, amid the whirlpool of events, to ask in a dazed way: 'How did I get into this condition?' Farewell.

CHAPTER THIRTY EIGHT

ON QUIET CONVERSATION

You are right when you urge that we increase our mutual traffic in letters. But the greatest benefit is to be derived from conversation, because it creeps by degrees into the soul. Lectures prepared beforehand and spouted in the presence of a throng have in them more noise but less intimacy. Philosophy is good advice; and no one can give advice at the top of his lungs. Of course we must sometimes also make use of these harangues, if I may so call them, when a doubting member needs to be spurred on; but when the aim is to make a man learn, and not merely to make him wish to learn, we must have recourse to the low-toned words of conversation. They enter more easily, and stick in the memory; for we do not need many words, but, rather, effective words.

Words should be scattered like seed; no matter how small the seed may be, if it has once found favourable ground, it unfolds its strength and from an insignificant thing spreads to its greatest growth. Reason grows in the same way; it is not large to the outward view, but increases as it does its work. Few words are spoken, but if the mind has truly caught them, they come into their strength and spring up. Yes, precepts and seeds have the same quality; they produce much, and yet they are slight things. Only, as I said, let a favourable mind receive and assimilate them. Then of itself the mind also will produce bounteously in its turn, giving back more than it has received. Farewell.

CHAPTER THIRTY NINE

ON NOBLE ASPIRATIONS

I shall indeed arrange for you, in careful order and narrow compass, the notes which you request. But consider whether you may not get more help from the customary method[1] than from that which is now commonly called a 'breviary', though in the good old days, when real Latin was spoken, it was called

---

[1] The regular method of studying philosophy was, as we infer from this letter, a course of reading in the philosophers. Seneca deprecates the use of the 'cram', which is only a memory-help, as a substitute for reading, on the ground that by its use one does not, in the first place, learn the subject, and, in the second place and chiefly, that one loses the inspiration to be derived by direct contact with great thinkers. The request of Lucilius for a cram thus suggests the main topic of the letter, which is taken up in the second paragraph.

a 'summary'.[2] The former is more necessary to one who is learning a subject, the latter to one who knows it. For the one teaches, the other stirs the memory. But I shall give you abundant opportunity for both.[3] A man like you should not ask me for this authority or that; he who furnishes a voucher for his statements argues himself unknown.

I shall therefore write exactly what you wish, but I shall do it in my own way; until then, you have many authors whose works will presumably keep your ideas sufficiently in order. Pick up the list of the philosophers; that very act will compel you to wake up when you see how many men have been working for your benefit. You will desire eagerly to be one of them yourself. For this is the most excellent quality that the noble soul has within itself, that it can be roused to honourable things.

No man of exalted gifts is pleased with that which is low and mean; the vision of great achievement summons him and uplifts him.

Just as the flame springs straight into the air and cannot be cabined or kept down any more than it can

---

[2]i.e. the word *breviarium*, 'abridgment', 'abstract', has displaced the better word *summarium*, 'outline of chief points'.

[3]i.e. to do the proper philosophy reading *and* to review it by means of the summary. The reading will enable Lucilius to identify for himself the authors of the several passages or doctrines.

repose in quiet, so our soul is always in motion, and the more ardent it is, the greater its motion and activity. But happy is the man who has given it this impulse towards better things! He will place himself beyond the jurisdiction of chance; he will wisely control prosperity; he will lessen adversity, and will despise what others hold in admiration.

It is the quality of a great soul to scorn great things and to prefer that which is ordinary rather than that which is too great. For the one condition is useful and life-giving, but the other does harm just because it is excessive. Similarly, too rich a soil makes the grain fall flat, branches break down under too heavy a load, excessive productiveness does not bring fruit to ripeness. This is the case with the soul also; for it is ruined by uncontrolled prosperity, which is used not only to the detriment of others, but also to the detriment of itself.

What enemy was ever so insolent to any opponent as are their pleasures to certain men? The only excuse that we can allow for the incontinence and mad lust of these men is the fact that they suffer the evils which they have inflicted upon others. And they are rightly harassed by this madness, because desire must have unbounded space for its excursions, if it transgresses nature's mean. For this has its bounds, but waywardness and the acts that spring from wilful lust are without boundaries.

Utility measures our needs, but by what standard can you check the superfluous? It is for this reason that men sink themselves in pleasures, and they cannot do without them when once they have become accustomed to them, and for this reason they are most wretched, because they have reached such a pass that what was once superfluous to them has become indispensable. And so they are the slaves of their pleasures instead of enjoying them; they even love their own ills[4] – and that is the worst ill of all! Then it is that the height of unhappiness is reached, when men are not only attracted, but even pleased, by shameful things, and when there is no longer any room for a cure, now that those things which once were vices have become habits. Farewell.

---

[4]i.e. their pleasures. These ills, by being cultivated, become vices.

CHAPTER FORTY

ON THE PROPER STYLE FOR A PHILOSOPHER'S DISCOURSE

I thank you for writing to me so often; for you are revealing your real self to me in the only way you can. I never receive a letter from you without being in your company forthwith. If the pictures of our absent friends are pleasing to us, though they only refresh the memory and lighten our longing by a solace that is unreal and unsubstantial, how much more pleasant is a letter, which brings us real traces, real evidences, of an absent friend! For that which is sweetest when we meet face to face is afforded by the impress of a friend's hand upon his letter – recognition.

You write me that you heard a lecture by the philosopher Serapio, when he landed at your present place of residence. 'He is wont', you say, 'to wrench up his words with a mighty rush, and he does not let them flow forth one by one, but makes them crowd and dash upon each other. For the words come in such quantity that a single voice is inadequate to utter them.' I do not approve of this in a philosopher; his speech, like his life, should be composed; and nothing that rushes headlong and is hurried is well ordered. That is why, in Homer, the rapid style, which sweeps down without a break like a snow-squall, is assigned to the younger speaker; from the old man eloquence flows gently, sweeter than honey.[1]

Therefore, mark my words; that forceful manner of speech, rapid and copious, is more suited to a mountebank than to a man who is discussing and teaching an important and serious subject. But I object just as strongly that he should drip out his words as that he should go at top speed; he should neither keep the ear on the stretch, nor deafen it. For that poverty-stricken and thin-spun style also makes the audience less attentive because they are weary of its stammering slowness; nevertheless, the word which has been long awaited sinks in more easily than the word which flits past us on the wing. Finally, people speak of 'handing down' precepts to their pupils, but one is not 'handing down' that which eludes the grasp.

Besides, speech that deals with the truth should be unadorned and plain. This popular style has

---

[1] *Iliad*, iii. 222 (Odysseus).

nothing to do with the truth; its aim is to impress the common herd, to ravish heedless ears by its speed; it does not offer itself for discussion, but snatches itself away from discussion. But how can that speech govern others which cannot itself be governed? May I not also remark that all speech which is employed for the purpose of healing our minds ought to sink into us? Remedies do not avail unless they remain in the system.

Besides, this sort of speech contains a great deal of sheer emptiness; it has more sound than power. My terrors should be quieted, my irritations soothed, my illusions shaken off, my indulgences checked, my greed rebuked. And which of these cures can be brought about in a hurry? What physician can heal his patient on a flying visit? May I add that such a jargon of confused and ill-chosen words cannot afford pleasure, either?

No; but just as you are well satisfied, in the majority of cases, to have seen through tricks which you did not think could possibly be done,[2] so in the case of these word-gymnasts – to have heard them once is amply sufficient. For what can a man desire to learn or to imitate in them? What is he to think of their souls, when

---

[2]Seneca is comparing with the juggler's tricks the verbal performances of certain lecturers, whose jargon one marvels at but does not care to hear again.

their speech is sent into the charge in utter disorder, and cannot be kept in hand?

Just as, when you run downhill, you cannot stop at the point where you had decided to stop, but your steps are carried along by the momentum of your body and are borne beyond the place where you wished to halt; so this speed of speech has no control over itself, nor is it seemly for philosophy; since Philosophy should carefully place her words, not fling them out, and should proceed step by step.

'What then?' you say; 'should not philosophy some-times take a loftier tone?' Of course she should; but dignity of character should be preserved, and this is stripped away by such violent and excessive force. Let philosophy possess great forces, but kept well under control; let her stream flow unceasingly, but never be-come a torrent. And I should hardly allow even to an orator a rapidity of speech like this, which cannot be called back, which goes lawlessly ahead; for how could it be followed by jurors, who are often inexperienced and untrained? Even when the orator is carried away by his desire to show off his powers, or by uncontrol-lable emotion, even then he should not quicken his pace and heap up words to an extent greater than the ear can endure.

You will be acting rightly, therefore, if you do not regard those men who seek how much they may say, rather than how they shall say it, and if for yourself you choose, provided a choice must be made, to speak as Publius Vinicius the stammerer does. When Asellius was asked how Vinicius spoke, he replied: 'Gradually'! (It was a remark of Geminus Varius, by the way: 'I don't see how you can call that man "eloquent"; why, he can't get out three words together.') Why, then, should you not choose to speak as Vinicius does?

Though of course some wag may cross your path, like the person who said, when Vinicius was dragging out his words one by one, as if he were dictating and not speaking. 'Say, haven't you anything to say?' And yet that were the better choice, for the rapidity of Quintus Haterius, the most famous orator of his age, is, in my opinion, to be avoided by a man of sense. Haterius never hesitated, never paused; he made only one start, and only one stop.

However, I suppose that certain styles of speech are more or less suitable to nations also; in a Greek you can put up with the unrestrained style, but we Romans, even when writing, have become accustomed to separate our words.[3] And our compatriot Cicero, with whom Roman oratory sprang into prominence, was also a slow pacer.[4] The Roman

---

[3] The Greek texts were still written without separation of the words, in contrast with the Roman.

[4] *Gradarius* may be contrasted with *tolutarius*, 'trotter'. The word might also mean one who walks with dignified step, as in a religious procession.

language is more inclined to take stock of itself, to weigh, and to offer something worth weighing.

Fabianus, a man noteworthy because of his life, his knowledge, and, less important than either of these, his eloquence also, used to discuss a subject with dispatch rather than with haste; hence you might call it ease rather than speed. I approve this quality in the wise man; but I do not demand it; only let his speech proceed unhampered, though I prefer that it should be deliberately uttered rather than spouted.

However, I have this further reason for frightening you away from the latter malady, namely, that you could only be successful in practising this style by losing your sense of modesty; you would have to rub all shame from your countenance,[5] and refuse to hear yourself speak. For that heedless flow will carry with it many expressions which you would wish to criticize.

And, I repeat, you could not attain it and at the same time preserve your sense of shame. Moreover, you would need to practise every day, and transfer your attention from subject matter to words. But words, even if they came to you readily and flowed

---

[5]After a violent rubbing, the face would not show blushes.

without any exertion on your part, yet would have to be kept under control. For just as a less ostentatious gait becomes a philosopher, so does a restrained style of speech, far removed from boldness. Therefore, the ultimate kernel of my remarks is this: I bid you be slow of speech. Farewell.

CHAPTER FORTY ONE

ON THE GOD WITHIN US

You are doing an excellent thing, one which will be wholesome for you, if, as you write me, you are persisting in your effort to attain sound understanding; it is foolish to pray for this when you can acquire it from yourself. We do not need to uplift our hands towards heaven, or to beg the keeper of a temple to let us approach his idol's ear, as if in this way our prayers were more likely to be heard. God is near you, He is with you, He is within you.

This is what I mean, Lucilius: a holy spirit indwells within us, one who marks our good and bad deeds, and is our guardian. As we treat this spirit, so are we treated by it. Indeed, no man can be good without the help of God. Can one rise superior to fortune unless

God helps him to rise? He it is that gives noble and upright counsel. In each good man:

A god doth dwell, but what god know we not.[1]

If ever you have come upon a grove that is full of ancient trees which have grown to an unusual height, shutting out a view of the sky by a veil of pleached and intertwining branches, then the loftiness of the forest, the seclusion of the spot, and your marvel at the thick unbroken shade in the midst of the open spaces, will prove to you the presence of deity. Or if a cave, made by the deep crumbling of the rocks, holds up a mountain on its arch, a place not built with hands but hollowed out into such spaciousness by natural causes, your soul will be deeply moved by a certain intimation of the existence of God. We worship the sources of mighty rivers; we erect altars at places where great streams burst suddenly from hidden sources; we adore springs of hot water as divine, and consecrate certain pools because of their dark waters or their immeasurable depth.

If you see a man who is unterrified in the midst of dangers, untouched by desires, happy in adversity, peaceful amid the storm, who looks down upon men from a higher plane, and views the gods on a footing of equality, will not a feeling of reverence for him steal

---

[1]Virgil, *Aeneid*, viii. 352.

over you? Will you not say: 'This quality is too great and too lofty to be regarded as resembling this petty body in which it dwells? A divine power has descended upon that man.'

When a soul rises superior to other souls, when it is under control, when it passes through every experience as if it were of small account, when it smiles at our fears and at our prayers, it is stirred by a force from heaven. A thing like this cannot stand upright unless it be propped by the divine. Therefore, a greater part of it abides in that place from whence it came down to earth. Just as the rays of the sun do indeed touch the earth, but still abide at the source from which they are sent; even so the great and hallowed soul, which has come down in order that we may have a nearer knowledge of divinity, does indeed associate with us, but still cleaves to its origin; on that source it depends, thither it turns its gaze and strives to go, and it concerns itself with our doings only as a being superior to ourselves.

What, then, is such a soul? One which is resplendent with no external good, but only with its own. For what is more foolish than to praise in a man the qualities which come from without? And what is more insane than to marvel at characteristics which may at the next instant be passed on to someone else? A golden bit does not make a better horse.

The lion with gilded mane, in process of being trained and forced by weariness to endure the decoration, is sent into the arena in quite a different way from the wild lion whose spirit is unbroken; the latter, indeed, bold in his attack, as nature wished him to be, impressive because of his wild appearance – and it is his glory that none can look upon him without fear – is favoured[2] in preference to the other lion, that languid and gilded brute.

No man ought to glory except in that which is his own. We praise a vine if it makes the shoots teem with increase, if by its weight it bends to the ground the very poles which hold its fruit; would any man prefer to this vine one from which golden grapes and golden leaves hang down? In a vine the virtue peculiarly its own is fertility; in man also we should praise that which is his own. Suppose that he has a retinue of comely slaves and a beautiful house, that his farm is large and large his income; none of these things is in the man himself; they are all on the outside.

Praise the quality in him which cannot be given or snatched away, that which is the peculiar property of the man. Do you ask what this is? It is soul, and reason brought to perfection in the soul. For man is a reasoning animal. Therefore, man's highest good is

---

[2]The spectators of the fight, which is to take place between the two lions, applaud the wild lion and bet on him.

attained, if he has fulfilled the good for which nature designed him at birth.

And what is it which this reason demands of him? The easiest thing in the world – to live in accordance with his own nature. But this is turned into a hard task by the general madness of mankind; we push one another into vice. And how can a man be recalled to salvation, when he has none to restrain him, and all mankind to urge him on? Farewell.

CHAPTER FORTY TWO

ON VALUES

Has that friend of yours already made you believe that he is a good man? And yet it is impossible in so short a time for one either to become good or be known as such. Do you know what kind of man I now mean when I speak of 'a good man'? I mean one of the second grade, like your friend. For one of the first class perhaps springs into existence, like the phoenix, only once in five hundred years. And it is not surprising, either, that greatness develops only at long intervals; Fortune often brings into being commonplace powers, which are born to please the mob, but she holds up for our approval that which is extraordinary by the very fact that she makes it rare.

This man, however, of whom you spoke, is still far from the state which he professes to have reached.

And if he knew what it meant to be 'a good man', he would not yet believe himself such; perhaps he would even despair of his ability to become good. 'But', you say, 'he thinks ill of evil men.' Well, so do evil men themselves; and there is no worse penalty for vice than the fact that it is dissatisfied with itself and all its fellows.

'But he hates those who make an ungoverned use of great power suddenly acquired.' I retort that he will do the same thing as soon as he acquires the same powers. In the case of many men, their vices, being powerless, escape notice; although, as soon as the persons in question have become satisfied with their own strength, the vices will be no less daring than those which prosperity has already disclosed.

These men simply lack the means whereby they may unfold their wickedness. Similarly, one can handle even a poisonous snake while it is stiff with cold; the poison is not lacking; it is merely numbed into inaction. In the case of many men, their cruelty, ambition, and indulgence only lack the favour of Fortune to make them dare crimes that would match the worst. That their wishes are the same you will in a moment discover, in this way: give them the power equal to their wishes.

Do you remember how, when you declared that a certain person was under your influence, I pronounced him fickle and a bird of passage, and said that you held him not by the foot but merely by a wing? Was I mistaken? You grasped him only by a feather; he left it in your hands and escaped. You know what an exhibition he afterwards made of himself before you, how many of the things he attempted were to recoil upon his own head. He did not see that in endangering others he was tottering to his own downfall. He did not reflect how burdensome were the objects which he was bent upon attaining, even if they were not superfluous.

Therefore, with regard to the objects which we pursue, and for which we strive with great effort, we should note this truth; either there is nothing desirable in them, or the undesirable is preponderant. Some objects are superfluous; others are not worth the price we pay for them. But we do not see this clearly, and we regard things as free gifts when they really cost us very dear.

Our stupidity may be clearly proved by the fact that we hold that 'buying' refers only to the objects for which we pay cash, and we regard as free gifts the things for which we spend our very selves. These we should refuse to buy, if we were compelled to give in payment for them our houses or some attractive and profitable estate; but we are eager to attain them at the cost of anxiety, of danger, and of lost honour, personal freedom, and time; so true it is that each man regards nothing as cheaper than himself.

Let us therefore act, in all our plans and conduct, just as we are accustomed to act whenever we approach a huckster who has certain wares for sale; let us see how much we must pay for that which we crave. Very often the things that cost nothing cost us the most heavily; I can show you many objects the quest and acquisition of which have wrested freedom from our hands. We should belong to ourselves, if only these things did not belong to us.

I would therefore have you reflect thus, not only when it is a question of gain, but also when it is a question of loss. 'This object is bound to perish.' Yes, it was a mere extra; you will live without it just as easily as you have lived before. If you have possessed it for a long time, you lose it after you have had your fill of it; if you have not possessed it long, then you lose it before you have become wedded to it. 'You will have less money.' Yes, and less trouble.

'Less influence.' Yes, and less envy. Look about you and note the things that drive us mad, which we lose with a flood of tears; you will perceive that it is not the loss that troubles us with reference to these things, but a notion of loss. No one feels that they have been lost, but his mind tells him that it has been so. He that owns himself has lost nothing. But how few men are blessed with ownership of self! Farewell.

CHAPTER FORTY THREE

ON THE RELATIVITY OF FAME

Do you ask how the news reached me, and who informed me, that you were entertaining this idea, of which you had said nothing to a single soul? It was that most knowing of persons – gossip. 'What', you say, 'am I such a great personage that I can stir up gossip?' Now there is no reason why you should measure yourself according to this part of the world;[1] have regard only to the place where you are dwelling.

Any point which rises above adjacent points is great, at the spot where it rises. For greatness is not absolute; comparison increases it or lessens it. A ship which looms large in the river seems tiny when on the ocean. A rudder which is large for one vessel is small for another.

---

[1] i.e. Rome.

So you in your province[2] are really of importance, though you scorn yourself. Men are asking what you do, how you dine, and how you sleep, and they find out, too; hence there is all the more reason for your living circumspectly. Do not, however, deem yourself truly happy until you find that you can live before men's eyes, until your walls protect but do not hide you; although we are apt to believe that these walls surround us, not to enable us to live more safely, but that we may sin more secretly.

I shall mention a fact by which you may weigh the worth of a man's character: you will scarcely find any-one who can live with his door wide open. It is our conscience, not our pride, that has put doorkeepers at our doors; we live in such a fashion that being sud-denly disclosed to view is equivalent to being caught in the act. What profits it, however, to hide ourselves away, and to avoid the eyes and ears of men?

A good conscience welcomes the crowd, but a bad conscience, even in solitude, is disturbed and troubled. If your deeds are honourable, let everybody know them; if base, what matters it that no one knows them, as long as you yourself know them? How wretched you are if you despise such a witness! Farewell.

----

[2]Lucilius was at this time the imperial procurator in Sicily.

CHAPTER FORTY FOUR

ON PHILOSOPHY AND PEDIGREES

You are again insisting to me that you are a nobody, and saying that Nature in the first place, and Fortune in the second, have treated you too scurvily, and this in spite of the fact that you have it in your power to separate yourself from the crowd and rise to the highest human happiness! If there is any good in philosophy, it is this – that it never looks into pedigrees. All men, if traced back to their original source, spring from the gods.

You are a Roman knight, and your persistent work promoted you to this class; yet surely there are many to whom the fourteen rows are barred;[1]

---

[1]Alluding to seats reserved for the knights at the theatre. The *equites* class of Romans were originally knights or horseman, but over time became a social class. The *equites* ranked below the Senatorial class.

the senate-chamber is not open to all; the army, too, is scrupulous in choosing those whom it admits to toil and danger. But a noble mind is free to all men; according to this test, we may all gain distinction. Philosophy neither rejects nor selects anyone; its light shines for all.

Socrates was no aristocrat. Cleanthes worked at a well and served as a hired man watering a garden. Philosophy did not find Plato already a nobleman; it made him one. Why then should you despair of becoming able to rank with men like these? They are all your ancestors, if you conduct yourself in a manner worthy of them; and you will do so if you convince yourself at the outset that no man outdoes you in real nobility.

We have all had the same number of forefathers; there is no man whose first beginning does not transcend memory. Plato says: 'Every king springs from a race of slaves, and every slave has had kings among his ancestors.'[2] The flight of time, with its vicissitudes, has jumbled all such things together, and Fortune has turned them upside down.

Then who is well-born? He who is by nature well fitted for virtue. That is the one point to be considered; otherwise, if you hark back to antiquity, every one

---

[2]Plato, *Theaetetus.*

traces back to a date before which there is nothing. From the earliest beginnings of the universe to the present time, we have been led forward out of origins that were alternately illustrious and ignoble. A hall full of smoke-begrimed busts does not make the nobleman. No past life has been lived to lend us glory, and that which has existed before us is not ours; the soul alone renders us noble, and it may rise superior to Fortune out of any earlier condition, no matter what that condition has been.

Suppose, then, that you were not a Roman knight, but a freedman, you might nevertheless by your own efforts come to be the only free man amid a throng of gentlemen. 'How?' you ask. Simply by distinguishing between good and bad things without patterning your opinion from the populace. You should look, not to the source from which these things come, but to the goal towards which they tend. If there is anything that can make life happy, it is good on its own merits; for it cannot degenerate into evil.

Where, then, lies the mistake, since all men crave the happy life? It is that they regard the means for producing happiness as happiness itself, and, while seeking happiness, they are really fleeing from it. For although the sum and substance of the happy life is unalloyed freedom from care, and though the secret of such freedom is unshaken confidence, yet men gather

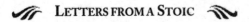

together that which causes worry, and, while travelling life's treacherous road, not only have burdens to bear, but even draw burdens to themselves; hence they recede farther and farther from the achievement of that which they seek, and the more effort they expend, the more they hinder themselves and are set back. This is what happens when you hurry through a maze; the faster you go, the worse you are entangled. Farewell.

CHAPTER FORTY FIVE

ON SOPHISTICAL ARGUMENTATION

You complain that in your part of the world there is a scant supply of books. But it is quality, rather than quantity, that matters; a limited list of reading benefits; a varied assortment serves only for delight. He who would arrive at the appointed end must follow a single road and not wander through many ways. What you suggest is not travelling; it is mere tramping.

'But', you say, 'I should rather have you give me advice than books.' Still, I am ready to send you all the books I have, to ransack the whole storehouse. If it were possible, I should join you there myself; and were it not for the hope that you will soon complete your term of office, I should have imposed upon myself this old man's journey; no Scylla or Charybdis or their storied straits could have frightened me away.

I should not only have crossed over, but should have been willing to swim over those waters, provided that I could greet you and judge in your presence how much you had grown in spirit.

Your desire, however, that I should dispatch to you my own writings does not make me think myself learned, any more than a request for my picture would flatter my beauty. I know that it is due to your charity rather than to your judgment. And even if it is the result of judgment, it was charity that forced the judgment upon you.

But whatever the quality of my works may be, read them as if I were still seeking, and were not aware of, the truth, and were seeking it obstinately, too. For I have sold myself to no man; I bear the name of no master. I give much credit to the judgment of great men, but I claim something also for my own. For these men, too, have left to us, not positive discoveries, but problems whose solution is still to be sought. They might perhaps have discovered the essentials, had they not sought the superfluous also.

They lost much time in quibbling about words and in sophistical argumentation; all that sort of thing exercises the wit to no purpose. We tie knots and bind up words in double meanings, and then try to untie them.

Have we leisure enough for this? Do we already know how to live, or die? We should rather proceed with our whole souls towards the point where it is our duty to take heed lest things, as well as words, deceive us.

Why, pray, do you discriminate between similar words, when nobody is ever deceived by them except during the discussion? It is things that lead us astray: it is between things that you must discriminate. We embrace evil instead of good; we pray for something opposite to that which we have prayed for in the past. Our prayers clash with our prayers, our plans with our plans.

How closely flattery resembles friendship! It not only apes friendship, but outdoes it, passing it in the race; with wide-open and indulgent ears it is welcomed and sinks to the depths of the heart, and it is pleasing precisely wherein it does harm. Show me how I may be able to see through this resemblance! An enemy comes to me full of compliments, in the guise of a friend. Vices creep into our hearts under the name of virtues, rashness lurks beneath the appellation of bravery, moderation is called sluggishness, and the coward is regarded as prudent; there is great danger if we go astray in these matters. So stamp them with special labels.

Then, too, the man who is asked whether he has horns on his head is not such a fool as to feel for them on his forehead, nor again so silly or dense that you can persuade him by means of argumentation, no matter how subtle, that he does not know the facts. Such quibbles are just as harmlessly deceptive as the juggler's cup and dice, in which it is the very trickery that pleases me. But show me how the trick is done, and I have lost my interest therein. And I hold the same opinion about these tricky word-plays; for by what other name can one call such sophistries? Not to know them does no harm, and mastering them does no good.

At any rate, if you wish to sift doubtful meanings of this kind, teach us that the happy man is not he whom the crowd deems happy, namely, he into whose coffers mighty sums have flowed, but he whose possessions are all in his soul, who is upright and exalted, who spurns inconstancy, who sees no man with whom he wishes to change places, who rates men only at their value as men, who takes Nature for his teacher, conforming to her laws and living as she commands, whom no violence can deprive of his possessions, who turns evil into good, is unerring in judgment, unshaken, unafraid, who may be moved by force but never moved to distraction, whom Fortune when she hurls at him with all her might the deadliest missile in her armoury, may graze, though rarely, but never wound. For Fortune's other missiles, with which she vanquishes mankind in general, rebound from such a one, like hail which rattles on the roof with no harm to the dweller therein, and then melts away.

Why do you bore me with that which you yourself call the 'liar' fallacy, about which so many books have been written? Come now, suppose that my whole life is a lie; prove that to be wrong and, if you are sharp enough, bring that back to the truth. At present it holds things to be essential of which the greater part is superfluous. And even that which is not superfluous is of no significance in respect to its power of making one fortunate and blest. For if a thing be necessary, it does not follow that it is a good. Else we degrade the meaning of 'good', if we apply that name to bread and barley-porridge and other commodities without which we cannot live.

The good must in every case be necessary; but that which is necessary is not in every case a good, since certain very paltry things are indeed necessary. No one is to such an extent ignorant of the noble meaning of the word 'good', as to debase it to the level of these humdrum utilities.

What, then? Shall you not rather transfer your efforts to making it clear to all men that the search for the superfluous means a great outlay of time, and that many have gone through life merely accumulating the instruments of life? Consider individuals, survey men in general; there is none whose life does not look forward to the morrow.

'What harm is there in this?' you ask. Infinite harm; for such persons do not live, but are preparing to live. They postpone everything. Even if we paid strict attention, life would soon get ahead of us; but as we are now, life finds us lingering and passes us by as if it belonged to another, and though it ends on the final day, it perishes every day.

But I must not exceed the bounds of a letter, which ought not to fill the reader's left hand.[1] So I shall postpone to another day our case against the hair-splitters, those oversubtle fellows who make argumentation supreme instead of subordinate. Farewell.

---

[1] A book was unrolled with the right hand; the reader gathered up the part already perused with the left hand. Nearly all books at this time were papyrus rolls, as were letters of any great length.

CHAPTER FORTY SIX

ON A NEW BOOK BY LUCILIUS

I received the book of yours which you promised me. I opened it hastily with the idea of glancing over it at leisure; for I meant only to taste the volume. But by its own charm the book coaxed me into traversing it more at length. You may understand from this fact how eloquent it was; for it seemed to be written in the smooth style, and yet did not resemble your handiwork or mine, but at first sight might have been ascribed to Titus Livius or to Epicurus. Moreover, I was so impressed and carried along by its charm that I finished it without any postponement. The sunlight called to me, hunger warned, and clouds were lowering, but I absorbed the book from beginning to end.

I was not merely pleased; I rejoiced. So full of wit and spirit it was! I should have added 'force', had the book contained moments of repose, or had it risen to energy only at intervals. But I found that there was no burst of force, but an even flow, a style that was vigorous and chaste. Nevertheless I noticed from time to time your sweetness, and here and there that mildness of yours. Your style is lofty and noble; I want you to keep to this manner and this direction. Your subject also contributed something; for this reason you should choose productive topics, which will lay hold of the mind and arouse it.

I shall discuss the book more fully after a second perusal; meantime, my judgement is somewhat unsettled, just as if I had heard it read aloud, and had not read it myself. You must allow me to examine it also. You need not be afraid; you shall hear the truth. Lucky fellow, to offer a man no opportunity to tell you lies at such long range! Unless perhaps, even now, when excuses for lying are taken away, custom serves as an excuse for our telling each other lies! Farewell.

CHAPTER FORTY SEVEN

ON MASTER AND SLAVE

I am glad to learn, through those who come from you, that you live on friendly terms with your slaves. This befits a sensible and well-educated man like yourself. 'They are slaves,' people declare. Nay, rather they are men. 'Slaves!' No, comrades. 'Slaves!' No, they are unpretentious friends. 'Slaves!' No, they are our fellow-slaves, if one reflects that Fortune has equal rights over slaves and free men alike.

That is why I smile at those who think it degrading for a man to dine with his slave. But why should they think it degrading? It is only because purse-proud etiquette surrounds a householder at his dinner with a mob of standing slaves. The master eats more than he can hold, and with monstrous greed loads his belly until it is stretched and at length ceases to do the work of a belly; so that he is at greater pains to discharge all the food than he was to stuff it down.

All this time the poor slaves may not move their lips, even to speak. The slightest murmur is repressed by the rod; even a chance sound – a cough, a sneeze, or a hiccup – is visited with the lash. There is a grievous penalty for the slightest breach of silence. All night long they must stand about, hungry and dumb.

The result of it all is that these slaves, who may not talk in their master's presence, talk about their master. But the slaves of former days, who were permitted to converse not only in their master's presence, but actually with him, whose mouths were not stitched up tight, were ready to bare their necks for their master, to bring upon their own heads any danger that threatened him; they spoke at the feast, but kept silence during torture.

Finally, the saying, in allusion to this same high-handed treatment, becomes current: 'As many enemies as you have slaves.' They are not enemies when we acquire them; we make them enemies.

I shall pass over other cruel and inhuman conduct towards them; for we maltreat them, not as if they were men, but as if they were beasts of burden. When we recline at a banquet, one slave mops up the disgorged food, another crouches beneath the table and gathers up the leftovers of the tipsy guests.

Another carves the priceless game birds; with unerring strokes and skilled hand he cuts choice morsels along the breast or the rump. Hapless fellow, to live only for the purpose of cutting fat capons correctly – unless, indeed, the other man is still more unhappy than he, who teaches this art for pleasure's sake, rather than he who learns it because he must.

Another, who serves the wine, must dress like a woman and wrestle with his advancing years; he cannot get away from his boyhood; he is dragged back to it; and though he has already acquired a soldier's figure, he is kept beardless by having his hair smoothed away or plucked out by the roots, and he must remain awake throughout the night, dividing his time between his master's drunkenness and his lust; in the chamber he must be a man, at the feast a boy.[1]

Another, whose duty it is to put a valuation on the guests, must stick to his task, poor fellow, and watch to see whose flattery and whose immodesty, whether of appetite or of language, is to get them an invitation for tomorrow. Think also of the poor purveyors of food, who note their masters' tastes with delicate

---

[1] *Glabri, delicati,* or *exoleti* were favourite slaves, kept artificially youthful by Romans of the more dissolute class. Some masters prided themselves on the elegant appearance and graceful gestures of these favourites.

skill, who know what special flavours will sharpen their appetite, what will please their eyes, what new combinations will rouse their cloyed stomachs, what food will excite their loathing through sheer satiety, and what will stir them to hunger on that particular day. With slaves like these the master cannot bear to dine; he would think it beneath his dignity to associate with his slave at the same table! Heaven forfend!

But how many masters is he creating in these very men!

I have seen standing in the line, before the door of Callistus, the former master of Callistus; I have seen the master himself shut out while others were welcomed – the master who once fastened the 'For Sale' ticket on Callistus and put him in the market along with the good-for-nothing slaves. But he has been paid off by that slave who was shuffled into the first lot of those on whom the crier practises his lungs; the slave, too, in his turn has cut *his* name from the list and in his turn has adjudged him unfit to enter his house. The master sold Callistus, but how much has Callistus made his master pay for!

Kindly remember that he whom you call your slave sprang from the same stock, is smiled upon by the same skies, and on equal terms with yourself breathes, lives, and dies. It is just as possible for you to see in him a free-born man as for him to see in you a slave. As a result of the massacres in Marius's day, many a man of distinguished birth, who was taking the first steps towards senatorial rank by service in the army, was humbled by fortune, one becoming a shepherd, another a caretaker of a country cottage. Despise, then, if you dare, those to whose estate you may at any time descend, even when you are despising them.

I do not wish to involve myself in too large a question, and to discuss the treatment of slaves, towards whom we Romans are excessively haughty, cruel, and insulting. But this is the kernel of my advice: treat your inferiors as you would be treated by your betters. And as often as you reflect how much power you have over a slave; remember that your master has just as much power over you.

'But I have no master,' you say. You are still young; perhaps you will have one. Do you not know at what age Hecuba entered captivity, or Croesus, or the mother of Darius, or Plato, or Diogenes?[2]

Associate with your slave on kindly, even on affable, terms; let him talk with you, plan with you, live with

---

[2]Plato was about forty years old when he visited Sicily, whence he was afterwards deported by Dionysius the Elder. He was sold into slavery at Aegina and ransomed by a man from Cyrene. Diogenes, while travelling from Athens to Aegina, is said to have been captured by pirates and sold in Crete, where he was purchased by a certain Corinthian and given his freedom.

you. I know that at this point all the exquisites will cry out against me in a body; they will say: 'There is nothing more debasing, more disgraceful, than this.' But these are the very persons whom I sometimes surprise kissing the hands of other men's slaves.

Do you not see even this – how our ancestors removed from masters everything invidious, and from slaves everything insulting? They called the master 'father of the household', and the slaves 'members of the household', a custom which still holds in the mime. They established a holiday on which masters and slaves should eat together – not as the only day for this custom, but as obligatory on that day in any case. They allowed the slaves to attain honours in the household and to pronounce judgement;[3] they held that a household was a miniature commonwealth.

'Do you mean to say', comes the retort, 'that I must seat all my slaves at my own table?' No, not any more than that you should invite all free men to it. You are mistaken if you think that I would bar from my table certain slaves whose duties are more humble, as, for example, yonder muleteer or yonder herdsman; I propose to value them according to their character, and not according to their duties. Each man acquires his character for himself, but accident assigns his duties.

---

[3] i.e. as the praetor himself was normally accustomed to do.

Invite some to your table because they deserve the honour, and others that they may come to deserve it. For if there is any slavish quality in them as the result of their low associations, it will be shaken off by intercourse with men of gentler breeding.

You need not, my dear Lucilius, hunt for friends only in the forum or in the Senate-house; if you are careful and attentive, you will find them at home also. Good material often stands idle for want of an artist; make the experiment, and you will find it so. As he is a fool who, when purchasing a horse, does not consider the animal's points, but merely his saddle and bridle; so he is doubly a fool who values a man from his clothes or from his rank, which indeed is only a robe that clothes us.

'He is a slave.' His soul, however, may be that of a freeman. 'He is a slave.' But shall that stand in his way? Show me a man who is not a slave; one is a slave to lust, another to greed, another to ambition, and all men are slaves to fear. I will name you an ex-consul who is slave to an old hag, a millionaire who is slave to a serving-maid; I will show you youths of the noblest birth in serfdom to pantomime players! No servitude is more disgraceful than that which is self-imposed.

You should, therefore, not be deterred by these finicky persons from showing yourself to your slaves as an affable person and not proudly superior to them; they ought to respect you rather than fear you.

Some may maintain that I am now offering the liberty-cap to slaves in general and toppling down lords from their high estate, because I bid slaves respect their masters instead of fearing them. They say: 'This is what he plainly means: slaves are to pay respect as if they were clients or early-morning callers!' Anyone who holds this opinion forgets that what is enough for a god cannot be too little for a master. Respect means love, and love and fear cannot be mingled.

So I hold that you are entirely right in not wishing to be feared by your slaves, and in lashing them merely with the tongue; only dumb animals need the thong.

That which annoys us does not necessarily injure us; but we are driven into wild rage by our luxurious lives, so that whatever does not answer our whims arouses our anger.

We don the temper of kings. For they, too, forgetful alike of their own strength and of other men's weakness, grow white-hot with rage, as if they had received an injury, when they are entirely protected from danger of such injury by their exalted station. They are not unaware that this is true, but by finding fault they seize upon opportunities to do harm; they insist that they have received injuries, in order that they may inflict them.

I do not wish to delay you longer; for you need no exhortation. This, among other things, is a mark of good character: it forms its own judgements and abides by them; but badness is fickle and frequently changing, not for the better, but for something different. Farewell.

CHAPTER FORTY EIGHT

ON QUIBBLING AS UNWORTHY OF THE PHILOSOPHER

In answer to the letter which you wrote me while travelling – a letter as long as the journey itself – I shall reply later. I ought to go into retirement, and consider what sort of advice I should give you. For you yourself, who consult me, also reflected for a long time whether to do so; how much more, then, should I myself reflect, since more deliberation is necessary in settling than in propounding a problem! And this is particularly true when one thing is advantageous to you and another to me. Am I speaking again in the guise of an Epicurean?[1]

---

[1]The Epicureans did not regard a friend's advantage as identical to one's own advantage. And yet they laid great stress upon friendship as one of the chief sources of pleasure. For an attempt to reconcile these two positions see Cicero, *De Finibus*, i. 65.

But the fact is, the same thing is advantageous to me which is advantageous to you; for I am not your friend unless whatever is at issue concerning you is my concern also. Friendship produces between us a partnership in all our interests. There is no such thing as good or bad fortune for the individual; we live in common. And no one can live happily who has regard to himself alone and transforms everything into a question of his own utility; you must live for your neighbour, if you would live for yourself.

This fellowship, maintained with scrupulous care, which makes us mingle as men with our fellow-men and holds that the human race have certain rights in common, is also of great help in cherishing the more intimate fellowship which is based on friendship, concerning which I began to speak above. For he that has much in common with a fellow-man will have all things in common with a friend.

And on this point, my excellent Lucilius, I should like to have those subtle dialecticians of yours advise me how I ought to help a friend, or how a fellow-man, rather than tell me in how many ways the word 'friend' is used, and how many meanings the word 'man' possesses. Lo, Wisdom and Folly are

---

Seneca has inadvertently used a phrase that implies a difference between a friend's interest and one's own. This leads him to reassert the Stoic view of friendship.

taking opposite sides. Which shall I join? Which party would you have me follow? On that side, 'man' is the equivalent of 'friend'; on the other side, 'friend' is not the equivalent of 'man'. The one wants a friend for his own advantage; the other wants to make himself an advantage to his friend.[2] What *you* have to offer me is nothing but distortion of words and splitting of syllables.

It is clear that unless I can devise some very tricky premises and by false deductions tack on to them a fallacy which springs from the truth, I shall not be able to distinguish between what is desirable and what is to be avoided! I am ashamed! Old men as we are, dealing with a problem so serious, we make play of it!

'"Mouse" is a syllable.[3] Now a mouse eats cheese; therefore, a syllable eats cheese.' Suppose now that I cannot solve this problem; see what peril hangs over my head as a result of such ignorance! What a scrape I shall be in! Without doubt I must beware, or someday I shall be catching syllables in a mousetrap,

---

[2] To the Stoic the terms 'friend' and 'man' are co-extensive; he is the friend of everybody, and his motive in friendship is to be of service; the Epicurean, however, narrows the definition of 'friend' and regards him merely as an instrument to his own happiness.

[3] In this paragraph Seneca exposes the folly of trying to prove a truth by means of logical tricks, and offers a caricature of those which were current among the philosophers whom he derides.

or, if I grow careless, a book may devour my cheese! Unless, perhaps, the following syllogism is shrewder still: '"Mouse" is a syllable. Now a syllable does not eat cheese. Therefore a mouse does not eat cheese.'

What childish nonsense! Do we knit our brows over this sort of problem? Do we let our beards grow long for this reason? Is this the matter which we teach with sour and pale faces?

Would you really know what philosophy offers to humanity? Philosophy offers counsel. Death calls away one man, and poverty chafes another; a third is worried either by his neighbour's wealth or by his own. So-and-so is afraid of bad luck; another desires to get away from his own good fortune. Some are ill-treated by men, others by the gods.

Why, then, do you frame for me such games as these? It is no occasion for jest; you are retained as counsel for unhappy mankind. You have promised to help those in peril by sea, those in captivity, the sick and the needy, and those whose heads are under the poised axe. Whither are you straying? What are you doing?

This friend, in whose company you are jesting, is in fear. Help him, and take the noose from about his neck. Men are stretching out imploring hands to you on all sides; lives ruined and in danger of ruin are begging for some assistance; men's hopes, men's resources, depend upon you. They ask that you deliver them from all their restlessness; that you reveal to them, scattered and wandering as they are, the clear light of truth.

Tell them what nature has made necessary, and what superfluous; tell them how simple are the laws that she has laid down, how pleasant and unimpeded life is for those who follow these laws, but how bitter and perplexed it is for those who have put their trust in opinion rather than in nature.

I should deem your games of logic to be of some avail in relieving men's burdens, if you could first show me what part of these burdens they will relieve. What among these games of yours banishes lust? Or controls it? Would that I could say that they were merely of no profit! They are positively harmful. I can make it perfectly clear to you whenever you wish, that a noble spirit when involved in such subtleties is impaired and weakened.

I am ashamed to say what weapons they supply to men who are destined to go to war with fortune, and how poorly they equip them! Is this the path to the greatest good? Is philosophy to proceed by such claptrap and by quibbles which would be a disgrace and a reproach even for expounders of the law? For what else is it that you men are doing, when you deliberately ensnare the person to whom you are putting questions, than making it appear that the man has lost his case on a technical error?[4] But just as the judge can reinstate those who have lost a suit in this way, so philosophy has reinstated these victims of quibbling to their former condition.

Why do you men abandon your mighty promises, and, after having assured me in high-sounding language that you will permit the glitter of gold to dazzle my eyesight no more than the gleam of the sword, and that I shall, with mighty steadfastness, spurn both that which all men crave and that which all men fear, why do you descend to the ABCs of scholastic pedants? What is your answer?

Is this the path to heaven?[5]

For that is exactly what philosophy promises to me, that I shall be made equal to God. For this I have been summoned, for this purpose have I come. Philosophy, keep your promise!

---

[4] In certain actions the praetor appointed a judge and established a formula, indicating the plaintiff's claim and the judge's duty. If the statement were false, or the claim excessive, the plaintiff lost his case; under certain conditions the defendant could claim annulment of the formula and have the case tried again. Such cases were not lost on their merits, and for that reason the lawyer who purposely took such an advantage was doing a contemptible thing.

[5] Virgil, *Aeneid*, ix. 641.

CHAPTER FORTY EIGHT

Therefore, my dear Lucilius, withdraw yourself as far as possible from these exceptions and objections of so-called philosophers. Frankness, and simplicity beseem true goodness. Even if there were many years left to you, you would have had to spend them frugally in order to have enough for the necessary things; but as it is, when your time is so scant, what madness it is to learn superfluous things! Farewell.

CHAPTER FORTY NINE

ON THE SHORTNESS OF LIFE

A man is indeed lazy and careless, my dear Lucilius, if he is reminded of a friend only by seeing some landscape which stirs the memory; and yet there are times when the old familiar haunts stir up a sense of loss that has been stored away in the soul, not bringing back dead memories, but rousing them from their dormant state, just as the sight of a lost friend's favourite slave, or his cloak, or his house, renews the mourner's grief, even though it has been softened by time.

Now, lo and behold, Campania, and especially Naples and your beloved Pompeii,[1] struck me, when I viewed them, with a wonderfully fresh sense of longing for you. You stand in full view before my

---

[1]Probably the birthplace of Lucilius.

eyes. I am on the point of parting from you. I see you choking down your tears and resisting without success the emotions that well up at the very moment when you try to check them. I seem to have lost you but a moment ago. For what is not 'but a moment ago' when one begins to use the memory?

It was but a moment ago that I sat, as a lad, in the school of the philosopher Sotion,[2] but a moment ago that I began to plead in the courts, but a moment ago that I lost the desire to plead, but a moment ago that I lost the ability. Infinitely swift is the flight of time, as those see more clearly who are looking backwards. For when we are intent on the present, we do not notice it, so gentle is the passage of time's headlong flight.

Do you ask the reason for this? All past time is in the same place; it all presents the same aspect to us, it lies together. Everything slips into the same abyss. Besides, an event which in its entirety is of brief compass cannot contain long intervals. The time which we spend in living is but a point, nay, even less than a point. But this point of time, infinitesimal as it is, Nature has mocked by making it seem outwardly of longer duration; she has taken one portion thereof and made it infancy, another childhood, another youth, another

---

[2]Pythagorean philosopher and doxographer. Not a great deal is known about him, and none of his works survive. His *Successions*, a summation of previous philosophers and their ideas, is only referred to indirectly by other authors.

the gradual slope, so to speak, from youth to old age, and old age itself is still another. How many steps for how short a climb!

It was but a moment ago that I saw you off on your journey; and yet this 'moment ago' makes up a goodly share of our existence, which is so brief, we should reflect, that it will soon come to an end altogether. In other years, time did not seem to me to go so swiftly; now, it seems fast beyond belief, perhaps, because I feel that the finish-line is moving closer to me, or it may be that I have begun to take heed and reckon up my losses.

For this reason I am all the more angry that some men claim the major portion of this time for super-fluous things – time which, no matter how carefully it is guarded, cannot suffice even for necessary things. Cicero declared that if the number of his days were doubled, he should not have time to read the lyric poets. And you may rate the dialecticians in the same class, but they are foolish in a more melancholy way. The lyric poets are avowedly frivolous, but the dialec-ticians believe that they are themselves engaged upon serious business.

I do not deny that one must cast a glance at di-alectic; but it ought to be a mere glance, a sort of greeting from the threshold, merely that one may not be deceived, or judge these pursuits to contain any hidden matters of great worth.

Why do you torment yourself and lose weight over some problem which it is more clever to have scorned than to solve? When a soldier is undisturbed and travelling at his ease, he can hunt for trifles along his way; but when the enemy is closing in on the rear, and a command is given to quicken the pace, necessity makes him throw away everything which he picked up in moments of peace and leisure.

I have no time to investigate disputed inflections of words, or to try my cunning upon them.

> Behold the gathering clans, the fast-shut gates,
> And weapons whetted ready for the war.[3]
> I need a stout heart to hear without flinching this din of battle which sounds round about.

And all would rightly think me mad if, when grey-beards and women were heaping up rocks for the fortifications, when the armour-clad youths inside the gates were awaiting, or even demanding, the order for a sally, when the spears of the foemen were quivering in our gates and the very ground was rocking with mines and subterranean passages – I say, they would rightly think me mad if I were to sit idle, putting such petty posers as this: 'What you have not lost, you have. But you have not lost any horns. Therefore, you have

---

[3]Virgil, *Aeneid*, viii. 385 f.

horns,'[4] or other tricks constructed after the model of this piece of sheer silliness.

And yet I may well seem in your eyes no less mad, if I spend my energies on that sort of thing; for even now I am in a state of siege. And yet, in the former case it would be merely a peril from the outside that threatened me, and a wall that sundered me from the foe; as it is now, death-dealing perils are in my very presence. I have no time for such nonsense; a mighty undertaking is on my hands. What am I to do? Death is on my trail, and life is fleeting away; teach me something with which to face these troubles. Bring it to pass that I shall cease trying to escape from death, and that life may cease to escape from me. Give me courage to meet hardships; make me calm in the face of the unavoidable. Relax the straitened limits of the time which is allotted me. Show me that the good in life does not depend upon life's length, but upon the use we make of it; also, that it is possible, or rather usual, for a man who has lived long to have lived too little. Say to me when I lie down to sleep: 'You may not wake again!' And when I have waked: 'You may not go to sleep again!' Say to me when I go forth from my

---

[4]Seneca's example of syllogistic nonsense. In syllogisms, you take a general statement (major premise) and a specific statement (minor premise), and from them deduce a conclusion. For instance, if all men are mortal (major premise) and Socrates is a man (minor premise), we can conclude that Socrates is mortal.

house: 'You may not return!' And when I return: 'You may never go forth again!'

You are mistaken if you think that only on an ocean voyage there is a very slight space between life and death. No, the distance between is just as narrow everywhere. It is not everywhere that death shows himself so near at hand; yet everywhere he is as near at hand.

Rid me of these shadowy terrors; then you will more easily deliver to me the instruction for which I have prepared myself. At our birth nature made us teachable, and gave us reason, not perfect, but capable of being perfected.

Discuss for me justice, duty, thrift, and that twofold purity, both the purity which abstains from another's person, and that which takes care of one's own self. If you will only refuse to lead me along by-paths, I shall more easily reach the goal at which I am aiming. For, as the tragic poet[5] says:

The language of truth is simple.

We should not, therefore, make that language intricate; since there is nothing less fitting for a soul of great endeavour than such crafty cleverness. Farewell.

---

[5]Euripides, *Phoenissae*, 469.

ON OUR BLINDNESS AND ITS CURE

I received your letter many months after you had posted it; accordingly, I thought it useless to ask the carrier what you were busied with. He must have a particularly good memory if he can remember that! But I hope by this time you are living in such a way that I can be sure what it is you are busied with, no matter where you may be. For what else are you busied with except improving yourself every day, laying aside some error, and coming to understand that the faults which you attribute to circumstances are in yourself? We are indeed apt to ascribe certain faults to the place or to the time, but those faults will follow us, no matter how we change our place.

You know Harpasté, my wife's female clown; she has remained in my house, a burden incurred from a legacy. I particularly disapprove of these freaks; whenever I wish to enjoy the quips of a clown, I am not compelled to hunt far; I can laugh at myself. Now this clown suddenly became blind. The story sounds incredible, but I assure you that it is true: she does not know that she is blind. She keeps asking her attendant to change her quarters; she says that her apartments are too dark.

You can see clearly that that which makes us smile in the case of Harpasté happens to all the rest of us; nobody understands that he is himself greedy, or that he is covetous. Yet the blind ask for a guide, while we wander without one, saying: 'I am not self-seeking; but one cannot live at Rome in any other way. I am not extravagant, but mere living in the city demands a great outlay. It is not my fault that I have a choleric disposition, or that I have not settled down to any definite scheme of life; it is due to my youth.'

Why do we deceive ourselves? The evil that afflicts us is not external, it is within us, situated in our very vitals; for that reason we attain soundness with all the more difficulty, because we do not know that we are diseased.

Suppose that we have begun the cure; when shall we throw off all these diseases, with all their virulence? At present, we do not even consult the physician, whose work would be easier if he were called in when the complaint was in its early stages. The tender and the inexperienced minds would follow his advice if he pointed out the right way.

No man finds it difficult to return to nature, except the man who has deserted nature. We blush to receive instruction in sound sense, but, by Heaven, if we think it base to seek a teacher of this art, we should also abandon any hope that so great a good could be instilled into us by mere chance.

No, we must work. To tell the truth, even the work is not great, if only, as I said, we begin to mould and reconstruct our souls before they are hardened by sin. But I do not despair even of a hardened sinner.

There is nothing that will not surrender to persistent treatment, to concentrated and careful attention; however much the timber may be bent, you can make it straight again. Heat unbends curved beams, and wood that grew naturally in another shape is fashioned artificially according to our needs. How much more easily does the soul permit itself to be shaped, pliable as it is and more yielding than any liquid! For what else is the soul than air in a certain state? And you see that air is more adaptable than any other matter, in proportion as it is rarer than any other.

There is nothing, Lucilius, to hinder you from entertaining good hopes about us, just because we are even now in the grip of evil, or because we have long been possessed thereby. There is no man to whom a good mind comes before an evil one. It is the evil mind that gets first hold on all of us. Learning virtue means unlearning vice.

We should therefore proceed to the task of freeing ourselves from faults with all the more courage because, when once committed to us, the good is an everlasting possession; virtue is not unlearned. For opposites find difficulty in clinging where they do not belong, therefore they can be driven out and hustled away; but qualities that come to a place which is rightfully theirs abide faithfully. Virtue is according to nature; vice is opposed to it and hostile.

But although virtues, when admitted, cannot depart and are easy to guard, yet the first steps in the approach to them are toilsome, because it is characteristic of a weak and diseased mind to fear that which is unfamiliar. The mind must, therefore, be forced to make a beginning; from then on, the medicine is not bitter; for just as soon as it is curing us it begins to give pleasure. One enjoys other cures only after health is restored, but a draught of philosophy is at the same moment wholesome and pleasant. Farewell.

CHAPTER FIFTY ONE

ON BAIAE AND MORALS

Every man does the best he can, my dear Lucilius! You over there have Etna,[1] that lofty and most celebrated mountain of Sicily (although I cannot make out why Messala – or was it Valgius? for I have been reading in both – has called it 'unique', inasmuch as many regions belch forth fire, not merely the lofty ones where the phenomenon is more frequent – presumably because fire rises to the greatest possible height – but low-lying places also). As for myself, I do the best I can; I have had to be satisfied with Baiae;[2] and

---

[1]Etna was of especial interest to Lucilius. Besides being a Govenor in Sicily, he may have written the poem 'Aetna'.

[2]Baiae was not far from Naples, and across the bay from Puteoli. It was a fashionable and dissolute watering place where the rich built huge villas, had beach parties, and enjoyed the thermal baths.

I left it the day after I reached it; for Baiae is a place to be avoided, because, though it has certain natural advantages, luxury has claimed it for her own exclusive resort.

'What then', you say, 'should any place be singled out as an object of aversion?' Not at all. But just as, to the wise and upright man, one style of clothing is more suitable than another, without his having an aversion for any particular colour, but because he thinks that some colours do not befit one who has adopted the simple life; so there are places also, which the wise man or he who is on the way towards wisdom will avoid as foreign to good morals.

Therefore, if he is contemplating withdrawal from the world, he will not select Canopus[3] (although Canopus does not keep any man from living simply), nor Baiae either; for both places have begun to be resorts of vice. At Canopus luxury pampers itself to the utmost degree; at Baiae it is even more lax, as if the place itself demanded a certain amount of licence.

We ought to select abodes which are wholesome not only for the body but also for the character. Just as I do not care to live in a place of torture, neither do I care to live in a café. To witness persons wandering drunk along the beach, the riotous revelling of sailing

---

[3]Situated at the mouth of the westernmost branch of the Nile, and proverbial in Latin literature for the laxity of its morals.

parties, the lakes a-din with choral[4] song, and all the other ways in which luxury, when it is, so to speak, released from the restraints of law not merely sins, but blazons its sins abroad – why must I witness all this?

We ought to see to it that we flee to the greatest possible distance from provocations to vice. We should toughen our minds, and remove them far from the allurements of pleasure. A single winter relaxed Hannibal's fibre; his pampering in Campania took the vigour out of that hero who had triumphed over Alpine snows. He conquered with his weapons, but was conquered by his vices.

We too have a war to wage, a type of warfare in which there is allowed no rest or furlough. To be conquered, in the first place, are pleasures, which, as you see, have carried off even the sternest characters. If a man has once understood how great is the task which he has entered upon, he will see that there must be no dainty or effeminate conduct. What have I to do with those hot baths or with the sweating-room where they shut in the dry steam which is to drain your strength? Perspiration should flow only after toil.

---

[4]There is considerable doubt whether symphonia was vocal or instrumental music. The passage probably refers either to glee-singers (as in Venice today) or to bands of flute-players playing part-music. Cicero (*In Verrem* iii. 44. 105) mentions them as providing entertainment at banquets.

Suppose we do what Hannibal did – check the course of events, give up the war, and give over our bodies to be coddled. Everyone would rightly blame us for our untimely sloth, a thing fraught with peril even for the victor, to say nothing of one who is only on the way to victory. And we have even less right to do this than those followers of the Carthaginian flag; for our danger is greater than theirs if we slacken, and our toil is greater than theirs even if we press ahead.

Fortune is fighting against me, and I shall not carry out her commands. I refuse to submit to the yoke; nay rather, I shake off the yoke that is upon me – an act which demands even greater courage. The soul is not to be pampered; surrendering to pleasure means also surrendering to pain, surrendering to toil, surrendering to poverty. Both ambition and anger will wish to have the same rights over me as pleasure, and I shall be torn asunder, or rather pulled to pieces, amid all these conflicting passions.

I have set freedom before my eyes; and I am striving for that reward. And what is freedom, you ask? It means not being a slave to any circumstance, to any constraint, to any chance; it means compelling Fortune to enter the lists on equal terms. And on the day when I know that I have the upper hand, her power will be naught. When I have death in my own control, shall I take orders from her?

Therefore, a man occupied with such reflections should choose an austere and pure dwelling-place.

The spirit is weakened by surroundings that are too pleasant, and without a doubt one's place of residence can contribute towards impairing its vigour. Animals whose hoofs are hardened on rough ground can travel any road, but when they are fattened on soft marshy meadows their hoofs are soon worn out. The bravest soldier comes from rock-ribbed regions, but the town-bred and the home-bred are sluggish in action. The hand which turns from the plough to the sword never objects to toil, but your sleek and well-dressed dandy quails at the first cloud of dust.

Being trained in a rugged country strengthens the character and fits it for great undertakings. It was more honourable in Scipio to spend his exile at Liternum[5] than at Baiae; his downfall did not need a setting so effeminate. Those also into whose hands the rising fortunes of Rome first transferred the wealth of the state, Gaius Marius, Gnaeus Pompey, and Caesar, did indeed build villas near Baiae, but they set them on the very tops of the mountains. This seemed more soldier-like, to look down from a lofty height upon lands spread far and wide below. Note the situation, position, and type of building which they chose; you will see that they were not country-places – they were camps.

---

[5]Scipio Africanus (235–183 BCE) was a Roman general and consul who defeated Hannibal at the Battle of Zama, so preceding Seneca by a couple of centuries. At Liternum about 10 miles north of Baiae, Scipio built his famous coastal villa.

Do you suppose that Cato would ever have dwelt in a pleasure-palace, that he might count the lewd women as they sailed past, the many kinds of barges painted in all sorts of colours, the roses which were wafted about the lake, or that he might listen to the nocturnal brawls of serenaders? Would he not have preferred to remain in the shelter of a trench thrown up by his own hands to serve for a single night? Would not anyone who is a man have his slumbers broken by a war-trumpet rather than by a chorus of serenaders?

But I have been haranguing against Baiae long enough; although I never could harangue often enough against vice. Vice, Lucilius, is what I wish you to proceed against, without limit and without end. For it has neither limit nor end. If any vice rend your heart, cast it away from you; and if you cannot be rid of it in any other way, pluck out your heart also. Above all, drive pleasures from your sight. Hate them beyond all other things, for they are like the bandits whom the Egyptians call 'lovers',[6] who embrace us only to garrote us. Farewell.

---

[6]The Egyptians used the word φηλητής in the sense of 'knave' or 'foot-pad'. The word is found in the Hecate of Callimachus. Hesychius defines it as equal to κλώψ 'thief'. It was pronounced in the same way as φιλητής 'lover', and in late Greek was spelt in the same way.

CHAPTER FIFTY TWO

ON CHOOSING OUR TEACHERS

What is this force, Lucilius, that drags us in one direction when we are aiming in another, urging us on to the exact place from which we long to withdraw? What is it that wrestles with our spirit, and does not allow us to desire anything once for all? We veer from plan to plan. None of our wishes is free, none is unqualified, none is lasting.

'But it is the fool', you say, 'who is inconsistent; nothing suits him for long.' But how or when can *we* tear ourselves away from this folly? No man by himself has sufficient strength to rise above it; he needs a helping hand, and someone to extricate him.

Epicurus[1] remarks that certain men have worked their way to the truth without anyone's assistance,

---

[1]Fragment 192, Usener.

carving out their own passage. And he gives special praise to these, for their impulse has come from within, and they have forged to the front by themselves. Again, he says, there are others who need outside help, who will not proceed unless someone leads the way, but who will follow faithfully. Of these, he says, Metrodorus was one; this type of man is also excellent, but belongs to the second grade. We ourselves are not of that first class, either; we shall be well treated if we are admitted into the second. Nor need you despise a man who can gain salvation only with the assistance of another; the will to be saved means a great deal too.

You will find still another class of man – and a class not to be despised – who can be forced and driven into righteousness, who do not need a guide as much as they require someone to encourage and, as it were, to force them along. This is the third variety. If you ask me for a man of this pattern also, Epicurus tells us that Hermarchus was such. And of the two last-named classes, he is more ready to congratulate the one,[2] but he feels more respect for the other; for although both reached the same goal, it is a greater credit to have brought about the same result with the more difficult material upon which to work.

Suppose that two buildings have been erected, unlike as to their foundations, but equal in height

---

[2] i.e. that of Metrodorus, who had the happier nature.

and in grandeur. One is built on faultless ground, and the process of erection goes right ahead. In the other case, the foundations have exhausted the building materials, for they have been sunk into soft and shifting ground and much labour has been wasted in reaching the solid rock. As one looks at both of them, one sees clearly what progress the former has made, but the larger and more difficult part of the latter is hidden.

So with men's dispositions; some are pliable and easy to manage, but others have to be laboriously wrought out by hand, so to speak, and are wholly employed in the making of their own foundations. I should accordingly deem more fortunate the man who has never had any trouble with himself; but the other, I feel, has deserved better of himself, who has won a victory over the meanness of his own nature, and has not gently led himself, but has wrestled his way, to wisdom.

You may be sure that this refractory nature, which demands much toil, has been implanted in us. There are obstacles in our path; so let us fight, and call to our assistance some helpers. 'Whom', you say, 'shall I call upon? Shall it be this man or that?'[3] There is another choice also open to you; you may go to the

---

[3]i.e. a representative of this school or that. Seneca's reply is, in effect, 'No present school; go to the ancients.'

ancients; for they have the time to help you. We can get assistance not only from the living, but from those of the past.

Let us choose, however, from among the living, not men who pour forth their words with the greatest glibness, turning out commonplaces and holding, as it were, their own little private exhibitions[4] – not these, I say, but men who teach us by their lives, men who tell us what we ought to do and then prove it by practice, who show us what we should avoid, and then are never caught doing that which they have ordered us to avoid.

Choose as a guide one whom you will admire more when you see him act than when you hear him speak.

Of course I would not prevent you from listening also to those philosophers who are wont to hold public meetings and discussions, provided they appear before the people for the express purpose of improving themselves and others, and do not practise their profession for the sake of self-seeking. For what is baser than philosophy courting applause? Does the sick man praise the surgeon while he is operating?

---

[4]Circulatores were travelling showmen who performed sword-swallowing and snake-charming feats, or cheap stump speakers who displayed their eloquence at the street-corners in the hope of a few pence. The word is also found in the sense of 'pedlar'.

In silence and with reverent awe submit to the cure. Even though you cry applause, I shall listen to your cries as if you were groaning when your sores were touched. Do you wish to bear witness that you are attentive, that you are stirred by the grandeur of the subject? You may do this at the proper time; I shall of course allow you to pass judgement and cast a vote as to the better course. Pythagoras made his pupils keep silence for five years; do you think that they had the right on that account to break out immediately into applause?

How mad is he who leaves the lecture-room in a happy frame of mind simply because of applause from the ignorant! Why do you take pleasure in being praised by men whom you yourself cannot praise? Fabianus used to give popular talks, but his audience listened with self-control. Occasionally a loud shout of praise would burst forth, but it was prompted by the greatness of his subject, and not by the sound of oratory that slipped forth pleasantly and softly.

There should be a difference between the applause of the theatre and the applause of the school; and there is a certain decency even in bestowing praise. If you mark them carefully, all acts are always significant, and you can gauge character by even the most trifling signs. The lecherous man is revealed by his gait, by a movement of the hand, sometimes by a single answer, by his touching his head with a finger,[5] by the shifting of his eye. The scamp is shown up by his laugh; the madman by his face and general appearance. These qualities become known by certain marks, but you can tell the character of every man when you see how he gives and receives praise.

The philosopher's audience, from this corner and that, stretch forth admiring hands, and sometimes the adoring crowd almost hang over the lecturer's head. But, if you really understand, that is not praise; it is merely applause. These outcries should be left for the arts which aim to please the crowd; let philosophy be worshipped in silence.

Young men, indeed, must sometimes have free play to follow their impulses, but it should only be at times when they act from impulse, and when they cannot force themselves to be silent. Such praise as that gives a certain kind of encouragement to the hearers themselves, and acts as a spur to the youthful mind. But let them be roused to the matter, and not to the style; otherwise, eloquence does them harm, making them enamoured of itself, and not of the subject.

I shall postpone this topic for the present; it demands a long and special investigation, to show how

---

[5]The scratching of the head with one finger was for some reason regarded as a mark of effeminacy or vice.

the public should be addressed, what indulgences should be allowed to a speaker on a public occasion, and what should be allowed to the crowd itself in the presence of the speaker. There can be no doubt that philosophy has suffered a loss, now that she has exposed her charms for sale. But she can still be viewed in her sanctuary, if her exhibitor is a priest and not a pedlar. Farewell.

CHAPTER FIFTY THREE

ON THE FAULTS OF THE SPIRIT

You can persuade me into almost anything now, for I was recently persuaded to travel by water. We cast off when the sea was lazily smooth; the sky, to be sure, was heavy with nasty clouds, such as usually break into rain or squalls. Still, I thought that the few miles between Puteoli and your dear Parthenope[1] might be run off in quick time, despite the uncertain and lowering sky. So, in order to get away more quickly, I made straight out to sea for Nesis,[2] with the purpose of cutting across all the inlets.

---

[1] A poetical or historical name for Naples. Parthenope was a siren who, in desperation at not seducing Ulysses with her voice, threw herself into the sea and drowned. As her body washed up on the shores of Naples, the city is sometimes given her name.

[2] An islet near the mouth of the bay where Baiae was situated. Puteoli was on the opposite side of the bay from Baiae.

But when we were so far out that it made little difference to me whether I returned or kept on, the calm weather, which had enticed me, came to naught. The storm had not yet begun, but the groundswell was on, and the waves kept steadily coming faster. I began to ask the pilot to put me ashore somewhere; he replied that the coast was rough and a bad place to land, and that in a storm he feared a lee shore more than anything else.

But I was suffering too grievously to think of the danger, since a sluggish seasickness which brought no relief was racking me, the sort that upsets the liver without clearing it. Therefore I laid down the law to my pilot, forcing him to make for the shore, willy-nilly. When we drew near, I did not wait for things to be done in accordance with Virgil's orders, until

Prow faced seawards[3]

or

Anchor plunged from bow;[4]

I remembered my profession as a veteran devotee of cold water, and, clad as I was in my cloak, let myself down into the sea, just as a cold-water bather should.

---

[3] Virgil, *Aeneid*, vi. 3. This was the usual method of mooring a ship in ancient times.

[4] *Aeneid*, iii. 277.

What do you think my feelings were, scrambling over the rocks, searching out the path, or making one for myself? I understood that sailors have good reason to fear the land. It is hard to believe what I endured when I could not endure myself; you may be sure that the reason why Ulysses was shipwrecked on every possible occasion was not so much because the sea-god was angry with him from his birth; he was simply subject to seasickness. And in the future I also, if I must go anywhere by sea, shall only reach my destination in the twentieth year.[5]

When I finally calmed my stomach (for you know that one does not escape seasickness by escaping from the sea) and refreshed my body with a rubdown, I began to reflect how completely we forget or ignore our failings, even those that affect the body, which are continually reminding us of their existence – not to mention those which are more serious in proportion as they are more hidden.

A slight ague deceives us, but when it has increased and a genuine fever has begun to burn, it forces even a hardy man, who can endure much suffering, to admit that he is ill. There is pain in the foot, and a tingling sensation in the joints, but we still hide the complaint and announce that we have sprained a joint, or else

---

[5]Ulysses took ten years on his journey, because of seasickness; Seneca will need twice as many.

are tired from overexercise. Then the ailment, uncertain at first, must be given a name; and when it begins to swell the ankles also, and has made both our feet 'right' feet,[6] we are bound to confess that we have the gout.

The opposite holds true of diseases of the soul; the worse one is, the less one perceives it. You need not be surprised, my beloved Lucilius. For he whose sleep is light pursues visions during slumber, and sometimes, though asleep, is conscious that he is asleep; but sound slumber annihilates our very dreams and sinks the spirit down so deep that it has no perception of self.

Why will no man confess his faults? Because he is still in their grasp; only he who is awake can recount his dream, and similarly a confession of sin is a proof of sound mind.

Let us, therefore, rouse ourselves, that we may be able to correct our mistakes. Philosophy, however, is the only power that can stir us, the only power that can shake off our deep slumber. Devote yourself wholly to philosophy. You are worthy of her; she is worthy of you; greet one another with a loving embrace. Say farewell to all other interests with courage and frankness. Do not study philosophy merely during your spare time.

---

[6]That is, they are so swollen that left and right look alike.

If you were ill, you would stop caring for your personal concerns, and forget your business duties; you would not think highly enough of any client to take active charge of his case during a slight abatement of your sufferings. You would try your hardest to be rid of the illness as soon as possible. What, then? Shall you not do the same thing now? Throw aside all hindrances and give up your time to getting a sound mind; for no man can attain it if he is engrossed in other matters. Philosophy wields her own authority; she appoints her own time and does not allow it to be appointed for her. She is not a thing to be followed at odd times, but a subject for daily practice; she is mistress, and she commands our attendance.

Alexander, when a certain state promised him a part of its territory and half its entire property, replied: 'I invaded Asia with the intention, not of accepting what you might give, but of allowing you to keep what I might leave.' Philosophy, likewise, keeps saying to all occupations: 'I do not intend to accept the time which you have left over, but I shall allow you to keep what I myself shall leave.'

Turn to her, therefore, with all your soul, sit at her feet, cherish her; a great distance will then begin to separate you from other men. You will be far ahead of all mortals, and even the gods will not be far ahead of you. Do you ask what will be the difference between

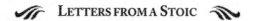

yourself and the gods? They will live longer. But, by my faith, it is the sign of a great artist to have confined a full likeness to the limits of a miniature. The wise man's life spreads out to him over as large a surface as does all eternity to a god. There is one point in which the sage has an advantage over the god; for a god is freed from terrors by the bounty of nature, the wise man by his own bounty.

What a wonderful privilege, to have the weaknesses of a man and the serenity of a god! The power of philosophy to blunt the blows of chance is beyond belief. No missile can settle in her body; she is well-protected and impenetrable. She spoils the force of some missiles and wards them off with the loose folds of her gown, as if they had no power to harm; others she dashes aside, and hurls them back with such force that they recoil upon the sender. Farewell.

CHAPTER FIFTY FOUR

ON ASTHMA AND DEATH

My ill-health had allowed me a long furlough, when suddenly it resumed the attack. 'What kind of ill-health?' you say. And you surely have a right to ask; for it is true that no kind is unknown to me. But I have been consigned, so to speak, to one special ailment. I do not know why I should call it by its Greek name;[1] for it is well enough described as 'shortness of breath'. Its attack is of very brief duration, like that of a squall at sea; it usually ends within an hour. Who indeed could breathe his last for long?

I have passed through all the ills and dangers of the flesh, but nothing seems to me more troublesome than this. And naturally so; for anything else may be

---

[1] i.e. *asthma*. Seneca thinks that the Latin name is good enough.

called illness; but this is a sort of continued 'last gasp'. Hence physicians call it 'practising how to die'. For some day the breath will succeed in doing what it has so often essayed.

Do you think I am writing this letter in a merry spirit, just because I have escaped? It would be absurd to take delight in such supposed restoration to health, as it would be for a defendant to imagine that he had won his case when he had succeeded in postponing his trial. Yet in the midst of my difficult breathing I never ceased to rest secure in cheerful and brave thoughts.

'What?' I say to myself; 'does death so often test me? Let it do so; I myself have for a long time tested death.' 'When?', you ask. Before I was born. Death is non-existence, and I know already what that means. What was before me will happen again after me. If there is any suffering in this state, there must have been such suffering also in the past, before we entered the light of day. As a matter of fact, however, we felt no discomfort then.

And I ask you, would you not say that one was the greatest of fools who believed that a lamp was worse off when it was extinguished than before it was lighted? We mortals also are lighted and extinguished; the period of suffering comes in between, but on either side there is a deep peace. For, unless

I am very much mistaken, my dear Lucilius, we go astray in thinking that death only follows, when in reality it has both preceded us and will in turn follow us. Whatever condition existed before our birth, is death. For what does it matter whether you do not begin at all, or whether you leave off, inasmuch as the result of both these states is non-existence?

I have never ceased to encourage myself with cheering counsels of this kind, silently, of course, since I had not the power to speak; then little by little this shortness of breath, already reduced to a sort of panting, came on at greater intervals, and then slowed down and finally stopped. Even by this time, although the gasping has ceased, the breath does not come and go normally; I still feel a sort of hesitation and delay in breathing. Let it be as it pleases, provided there be no sigh from the soul.[2]

Accept this assurance from me: I shall never be frightened when the last hour comes; I am already prepared and do not plan a whole day ahead. But do you praise[3] and imitate the man whom it does

---

[2]i.e. that the sigh be physical – an asthmatic gasp – and not caused by anguish of the soul.

[3]The argument is: I am ready to die, but do not praise me on that account; reserve your praise for him who is not loath to die, though (unlike me) he finds it a pleasure to live (because he is in good health). There is no more virtue in accepting death

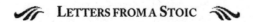

not irk to die, though he takes pleasure in living. For what virtue is there in going away when you are thrust out? And yet there is virtue even in this: I am indeed thrust out, but it is as if I were going away willingly. For that reason the wise man can never be thrust out, because that would mean removal from a place which he was unwilling to leave; and the wise man does nothing unwillingly. He escapes necessity, because he wills to do what necessity is about to force upon him. Farewell.

when one hates life, than there is in leaving a place when one is ejected.

CHAPTER FIFTY FIVE

ON VATIA'S VILLA

I have just returned from a ride in my litter, and I am as weary as if I had walked the distance, instead of being seated. Even to be carried for any length of time is hard work, perhaps all the more so because it is an unnatural exercise; for Nature gave us legs with which to do our own walking, and eyes with which to do our own seeing. Our luxuries have condemned us to weakness; we have ceased to be able to do that which we have long declined to do.

Nevertheless, I found it necessary to give my body a shaking up, in order that the bile which had gathered in my throat, if that was my trouble, might be shaken out, or, if the very breath within me had become, for some reason, too thick, that the jolting, which I have felt was a good thing for me, might make it thinner. So I insisted on being carried longer than usual, along an attractive beach, which bends between Cumae and Servilius Vatia's country house,[1] shut in by the sea on one side and the lake on the other, just like a narrow path. It was packed firm under foot, because of a recent storm; since, as you know, the waves, when they beat upon the beach hard and fast, level it out; but a continuous period of fair weather loosens it, when the sand, which is kept firm by the water, loses its moisture.

As my habit is, I began to look about for something there that might be of service to me, when my eyes fell upon the villa which had once belonged to Vatia. So this was the place where that famous praetorian millionaire passed his old age! He was famed for nothing else than his life of leisure, and he was regarded as lucky only for that reason. For whenever men were ruined by their friendship with Asinius Gallus[2] whenever others were ruined by their hatred of Sejanus, and later[3] by their intimacy with him – for it was no

---

[1] Cumae was on the coast about six miles north of Cape Misenum. Lake Acheron was a saltwater pool between those two points, separated from the sea by a sandbar; it lay near Lake Avernus and probably derived its name from that fact.

[2] Son of Asinius Pollio; his frankness got him into trouble and he died of starvation in a dungeon in 33 CE. Sejanus was an ambitious soldier and confidante of Tiberius. But he was accused of conspiracy and executed in 31 CE.

[3] That is, after his fall.

more dangerous to have offended him than to have loved him – people used to cry out: 'O Vatia, you alone know how to live!'

But what he knew was how to hide, not how to live; and it makes a great deal of difference whether your life be one of leisure or one of idleness. So I never drove past his country place during Vatia's lifetime without saying to myself: 'Here lies Vatia!'

But, my dear Lucilius, philosophy is a thing of holiness, something to be worshipped, so much so that the very counterfeit pleases. For the mass of mankind consider that a person is at leisure who has withdrawn from society, is free from care, self-sufficient, and lives for himself; but these privileges can be the reward only of the wise man. Does he who is a victim of anxiety know how to live for himself? What? Does he even know (and that is of first importance) how to live at all?

For the man who has fled from affairs and from men, who has been banished to seclusion by the unhappiness which his own desires have brought upon him, who cannot see his neighbour more happy than himself, who through fear has taken to concealment, like a frightened and sluggish animal – this person is not living for himself; he is living for his belly, his sleep, and his lust – and that is the most shameful thing in the world. He who lives for no one does not necessarily live for himself. Nevertheless, there is so much in steadfastness and adherence to one's purpose that even sluggishness, if stubbornly maintained, assumes an air of authority with us.

I could not describe the villa accurately; for I am familiar only with the front of the house, and with the parts which are in public view and can be seen by the mere passerby. There are two grottoes, which cost a great deal of labour, as big as the most spacious hall, made by hand. One of these does not admit the rays of the sun, while the other keeps them until the sun sets. There is also a stream running through a grove of plane trees, which draws for its supply both on the sea and on Lake Acheron; it intersects the grove just like a raceway,[4] and is large enough to support fish, although its waters are continually being drawn off. When the sea is calm, however, they do not use the stream, only touching the well-stocked waters when the storms give the fishermen a forced holiday.

But the most convenient thing about the villa is the fact that Baiae is next door, it is free from all the inconveniences of that resort, and yet enjoys its pleasures. I myself understand these attractions, and I believe that it is a villa suited to every season of the year. It fronts the west wind, which it intercepts in such a way

---

[4]Literally, 'like a Euripus', referring to the narrow strait that divides Euboea from Boeotia at Chalcis. Its current is swift.

that Baiae is denied it. So it seems that Vatia was no fool when he selected this place as the best in which to spend his leisure when it was already unfruitful and decrepit.

The place where one lives, however, can contribute little towards tranquillity; it is the mind which must make everything agreeable to itself. I have seen men despondent in a gay and lovely villa, and I have seen them to all appearance full of business in the midst of a solitude. For this reason you should not refuse to believe that your life is well-placed merely because you are not now in Campania. But why are you not there? Just let your thoughts travel, even to this place.

You may hold converse with your friends when they are absent, and indeed as often as you wish and for as long as you wish. For we enjoy this, the greatest of pleasures, all the more when we are absent from one another. For the presence of friends makes us fastidious; and because we can at any time talk or sit together, when once we have parted we give not a thought to those whom we have just beheld.

And we ought to bear the absence of friends cheerfully, just because everyone is bound to be often absent from his friends even when they are present. Include among such cases, in the first place, the nights spent apart, then the different engagements which each of two friends has, then the private studies of

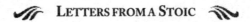

each and their excursions into the country, and you will see that foreign travel does not rob us of much.

A friend should be retained in the spirit; such a friend can never be absent. He can see every day whomsoever he desires to see.

I would, therefore, have you share your studies with me, your meals, and your walks. We should be living within too narrow limits if anything were barred to our thoughts. I see you, my dear Lucilius, and at this very moment I hear you; I am with you to such an extent that I hesitate whether I should not begin to write you notes instead of letters. Farewell.

CHAPTER FIFTY SIX

ON QUIET AND STUDY

Beshrew me if I think anything more requisite than silence for a man who secludes himself in order to study! Imagine what a variety of noises reverberates about my ears! I have lodgings right over a bathing establishment. So picture to yourself the assortment of sounds, which are strong enough to make me hate my very powers of hearing! When your strenuous gentleman, for example, is exercising himself by flourishing leaden weights; when he is working hard, or else pretends to be working hard, I can hear him grunt; and whenever he releases his imprisoned breath, I can hear him panting in wheezy and high-pitched tones. Or perhaps I notice some lazy fellow, content with a cheap rubdown, and hear the crack of the pummelling hand on his shoulder, varying in sound according as the hand is laid on flat or hollow. Then, perhaps, a professional[1] comes along, shouting out the score; that is the finishing touch.

Add to this the arresting of an occasional roysterer or pickpocket, the racket of the man who always likes to hear his own voice in the bathroom, or the enthusiast who plunges into the swimming-tank with unconscionable noise and splashing. Besides all those whose voices, if nothing else, are good, imagine the hair-plucker with his penetrating, shrill voice – for purposes of advertisement – continually giving it vent and never holding his tongue except when he is plucking the armpits and making his victim yell instead. Then the cake-seller with his varied cries, the sausageman, the confectioner, and all the vendors of food hawking their wares, each with his own distinctive intonation.

So you say: 'What iron nerves or deadened ears, you must have, if your mind can hold out amid so many noises, so various and so discordant, when our friend Chrysippus[2] is brought to his death by the continual good-morrows that greet him!' But I assure you that

---

[1] *Pilicrepus* probably means 'ball-counter' – one who keeps a record of the strokes.

[2] It was said that the Stoic philosopher Chrysippus objected to the salutations of his friends.

this racket means no more to me than the sound of waves or falling water; although you will remind me that a certain tribe once moved their city merely because they could not endure the din of a Nile cataract.

Words seem to distract me more than noises; for words demand attention, but noises merely fill the ears and beat upon them. Among the sounds that din round me without distracting, I include passing carriages, a machinist in the same block, a saw-sharpener nearby, or some fellow who is demonstrating with little pipes and flutes at the Trickling Fountain,[3] shouting rather than singing.

Furthermore, an intermittent noise upsets me more than a steady one. But by this time I have toughened my nerves against all that sort of thing, so that I can endure even a boatswain marking the time in high-pitched tones for his crew. For I force my mind to concentrate, and keep it from straying to things outside itself; all outdoors may be bedlam, provided that there is no disturbance within, provided that fear is not wrangling with desire in my breast, provided that meanness and lavishness are not at odds, one harassing the other. For of what benefit

---

[3]A cone-shaped fountain, resembling a turning-post (*meta*) in the circus, from which the water spouted through many jets. Its remains may still be seen now not far from the Colosseum on the Velia.

is a quiet neighbourhood, if our emotions are in an uproar?

'Twas night, and all the world was lulled to rest.[4]

This is not true; for no real rest can be found when reason has not done the lulling. Night brings our troubles to the light, rather than banishes them; it merely changes the form of our worries. For even when we seek slumber, our sleepless moments are as harassing as the daytime. Real tranquillity is the state reached by an unperverted mind when it is relaxed.

Think of the unfortunate man who courts sleep by surrendering his spacious mansion to silence, who, that his ear may be disturbed by no sound, bids the whole retinue of his slaves be quiet and that whoever approaches him shall walk on tiptoe; he tosses from this side to that and seeks a fitful slumber amid his frettings!

He complains that he has heard sounds, when he has not heard them at all. The reason, you ask? His soul is in an uproar; it must be soothed, and its rebellious murmuring checked. You need not suppose that the soul is at peace when the body is still. Sometimes quiet means disquiet.

---

[4]A fragment from the *Argonautica* of Varro Atacinus.

We must therefore rouse ourselves to action and busy ourselves with interests that are good, as often as we are in the grasp of an uncontrollable sluggishness.

Great generals, when they see that their men are mutinous, check them by some sort of labour or keep them busy with small forays. The much occupied man has no time for wantonness, and it is an obvious commonplace that the evils of leisure can be shaken off by hard work. Although people may often have thought that I sought seclusion because I was disgusted with politics and regretted my hapless and thankless position, yet, in the retreat to which apprehension and weariness have driven me, my ambition sometimes develops afresh. For it is not because my ambition was rooted out that it has abated, but because it was wearied or perhaps even put out of temper by the failure of its plans.

And so with luxury, also, which sometimes seems to have departed, and then when we have made a profession of frugality, begins to fret us and, amid our economies, seeks the pleasures which we have merely left but not condemned. Indeed, the more stealthily it comes, the greater is its force. For all unconcealed vices are less serious; a disease also is farther on the road to being cured when it breaks forth from concealment and manifests its power. So with greed, ambition, and the other evils of the mind – you may be sure that they do most harm when they are hidden behind a pretence of soundness.

Men think that we are in retirement, and yet we are not. For if we have sincerely retired, and have sounded the signal for retreat, and have scorned outward attractions, then, as I remarked above, no outward thing will distract us; no music of men or of birds[5] can interrupt good thoughts, when they have once become steadfast and sure.

The mind which starts at words or at chance sounds is unstable and has not yet withdrawn into itself; it contains within itself an element of anxiety and rooted fear, and this makes one a prey to care, as our Virgil says:

> I, whom of yore no dart could cause to flee,
> Nor Greeks, with crowded lines of infantry.
> Now shake at every sound, and fear the air,
> Both for my child and for the load I bear.[6]

This man in his first state is wise; he blenches neither at the brandished spear, nor at the clashing armour of the serried foe, nor at the din of the stricken city. This man in his second state lacks knowledge fearing for his own concerns, he pales at every sound; any

---

[5]An allusion to the Sirens and Ulysses.

[6]Aeneas is escaping from Troy, *Aeneid*, ii. 726 ff.

cry is taken for the battle-shout and overthrows him; the slightest disturbance renders him breathless with fear. It is the load that makes him afraid.[7]

Select anyone you please from among your favourites of Fortune, trailing their many responsibilities, carrying their many burdens, and you will behold a picture of Virgil's hero, 'fearing both for his child and for the load he bears'.

You may therefore be sure that you are at peace with yourself, when no noise reaches you, when no word shakes you out of yourself, whether it be of flattery or of threat, or merely an empty sound buzzing about you with unmeaning din.

'What then?', you say, 'is it not sometimes a simpler matter just to avoid the uproar?' I admit this. Accordingly, I shall change from my present quarters. I merely wished to test myself and to give myself practice. Why need I be tormented any longer, when Ulysses found so simple a cure for his comrades[8] even against the songs of the Sirens? Farewell.

---

[7]Aeneas carries Anchises; the rich man carries his burden of wealth.

[8]Not merely by stopping their ears with wax, but also by bidding them row past the Sirens as quickly as possible. *Odyssey*, xii. 182.

CHAPTER FIFTY SEVEN

ON THE TRIALS OF TRAVEL

When it was time for me to return to Naples from Baiae, I easily persuaded myself that a storm was raging, that I might avoid another trip by sea; and yet the road was so deep in mud, all the way, that I may be thought none the less to have made a voyage. On that day I had to endure the full fate of an athlete; the anointing[1] with which we began was followed by the sand-sprinkle in the Naples tunnel.[2]

No place could be longer than that prison; nothing could be dimmer than those torches, which enabled

---

[1] i.e. an 'anointing' with mud.

[2] After anointing, the wrestler was sprinkled with sand, so that the opponent's hand might not slip. The Naples tunnel provided a shortcut to those who, like Seneca in this letter, did not wish to take the time to travel by the shore route along the promontory of Pausilipum.

us, not to see amid the darkness, but to see the darkness. But, even supposing that there was light in the place, the dust, which is an oppressive and disagreeable thing even in the open air, would destroy the light; how much worse the dust is there, where it rolls back upon itself, and, being shut in without ventilation, blows back in the faces of those who set it going! So we endured two inconveniences at the same time, and they were diametrically different: we struggled both with mud and with dust on the same road and on the same day.

The gloom, however, furnished me with some food for thought; I felt a certain mental thrill, and a transformation unaccompanied by fear, due to the novelty and the unpleasantness of an unusual occurrence. Of course I am not speaking to you of myself at this point, because I am far from being a perfect person, or even a man of middling qualities; I refer to one over whom Fortune has lost her control. Even such a man's mind will be smitten with a thrill and he will change colour.

For there are certain emotions, my dear Lucilius, which no courage can avoid; nature reminds courage how perishable a thing it is. And so he will contract his brow when the prospect is forbidding, will shudder at sudden apparitions, and will become dizzy when he stands at the edge of a high precipice and looks down. This is not fear; it is a natural feeling which reason cannot rout.

That is why certain brave men, most willing to shed their own blood, cannot bear to see the blood of others. Some persons collapse and faint at the sight of a freshly inflicted wound; others are affected similarly on handling or viewing an old wound which is festering. And others meet the sword-stroke more readily than they see it dealt.

Accordingly, as I said, I experienced a certain transformation, though it could not be called confusion. Then at the first glimpse of restored daylight my good spirits returned without forethought or command. And I began to muse and think how foolish we are to fear certain objects to a greater or less degree, since all of them end in the same way. For what difference does it make whether a watchtower or a mountain crashes down upon us? No difference at all, you will find. Nevertheless, there will be some men who fear the latter mishap to a greater degree, though both accidents are equally deadly; so true it is that fear looks not to the effect, but to the cause of the effect.

Do you suppose that I am now referring to the Stoics, who hold that the soul of a man crushed by a great weight cannot abide, and is scattered forthwith, because it has not had a free opportunity to depart? That is not what I am doing; those who think thus are, in my opinion, wrong.

Just as fire cannot be crushed out, since it will escape round the edges of the body which overwhelms it; just as the air cannot be damaged by lashes and blows, or even cut into, but flows back about the object to which it gives place; similarly the soul, which consists of the subtlest particles, cannot be arrested or destroyed inside the body, but, by virtue of its delicate substance, it will rather escape through the very object by which it is being crushed. Just as lightning, no matter how widely it strikes and flashes, makes its return through a narrow opening, so the soul, which is still subtler than fire, has a way of escape through any part of the body.

We therefore come to this question – whether the soul can be immortal. But be sure of this: if the soul survives the body after the body is crushed, the soul can in no wise be crushed out, precisely because it does not perish; for the rule of immortality never admits of exceptions, and nothing can harm that which is everlasting. Farewell.

CHAPTER FIFTY EIGHT

ON BEING

How scant of words our language is, nay, how poverty-stricken, I have not fully understood until today. We happened to be speaking of Plato, and a thousand subjects came up for discussion, which needed names and yet possessed none; and there were certain others which once possessed, but have since lost, their words because we were too nice about their use. But who can endure to be nice in the midst of poverty?

There is an insect, called by the Greeks *oestrus*, which drives cattle wild and scatters them all over their pasturing grounds; it used to be called *asilus* in our language, as you may believe on the authority of Virgil:

Near Silarus groves, and eke Alburnus' shades
Of green-clad oak-trees flits an insect, named

Asilus by the Romans; in the Greek
The word is rendered *oestrus.* With a rough
And strident sound it buzzes and drives wild
The terror-stricken herds throughout the woods.[1]

By which I infer that the word has gone out of use. And, not to keep you waiting too long, there were certain uncompounded words current, like *cernere ferro inter se,* as will be proved again by Virgil:

Great heroes, born in various lands, had come
To settle matters mutually with the sword.[2]

This 'settling matters' we now express by *decernere.* The plain word has become obsolete.

The ancients used to say *iusso,* instead of *iussero,* in conditional clauses. You need not take my word, but you may turn again to Virgil:

The other soldiers shall conduct the fight
With me, where I shall bid.[3]

It is not in my purpose to show, by this array of examples, how much time I have wasted on the study of language; I merely wish you to understand how

---

[1] *Georgics,* iii. 146 ff.

[2] *Aeneid,* xii. 708 f.

[3] *Aeneid,* xi. 467.

many words, that were current in the works of Ennius and Accius, have become mouldy with age; while even in the case of Virgil, whose works are explored daily, some of his words have been filched away from us.

You will say, I suppose: 'What is the purpose and meaning of this preamble?' I shall not keep you in the dark; I desire, if possible, to say the word *essentia* to you and obtain a favourable hearing. If I cannot do this, I shall risk it even though it put you out of humour. I have Cicero[4] as authority for the use of this word, and I regard him as a powerful authority. If you desire testimony of a later date, I shall cite Fabianus,[5] careful of speech, cultivated, and so polished in style that he will suit even our nice tastes. For what can we do, my dear Lucilius? How otherwise can we find a word for that which the Greeks call οὐσία, something that is indispensable, something that is the natural substratum of everything? I beg you accordingly to allow me to use this word *essentia*. I shall nevertheless take pains to exercise the privilege, which you have granted me, with as sparing a hand as possible; perhaps I shall be content with the mere right.

---

[4]Cicero in fact usually says *natura*. The word, according to Quintilian, was first used by a certain Sergius Flavus. It is also found in Apulcius, Macrobius, and Sidonius.

[5]Papirius Fabianus lived in the times of Tiberius and Caligula, and was a pupil of the Sextius. He was praised by the elder Seneca.

Yet what good will your indulgence do me, if, lo and behold, I can in no wise express in Latin the meaning of the word which gave me the opportunity to rail at the poverty of our language? And you will condemn our narrow Roman limits even more, when you find out that there is a word of one syllable which I cannot translate. 'What is this?' you ask. It is the word ὄν. You think me lacking in facility; you believe that the word is ready to hand, that it might be translated by *quod est.* I notice, however, a great difference; you are forcing me to render a noun by a verb.

But if I must do so, I shall render it by *quod est.* There are six ways[6] in which Plato expresses this idea, according to a friend of ours, a man of great learning, who mentioned the fact today. And I shall explain all of them to you, if I may first point out that there is something called *genus* and something called *species.*

For the present, however, we are seeking the primary idea of *genus,* on which the others, the different *species,* depend, which is the source of all classification, the term under which universal ideas are embraced. And the idea of *genus* will be reached if we begin to reckon back from particulars; for in this way we shall be conducted back to the primary notion.

---

[6]Plato's usual division was threefold – αἰσθητά, μαθηματικά, εἴδη (*sensibilia, mathematica, ideae*) – a division that is often quoted by Aristotle.

Now 'man' is a *species*, as Aristotle[7] says; so is 'horse', or 'dog'. We must therefore discover some common bond for all these terms, one which embraces them and holds them subordinate to itself. And what is this? It is 'animal'. And so there begins to be a *genus* 'animal', including all these terms, 'man', 'horse', and 'dog'.

But there are certain things which have life (*anima*) and yet are not 'animals'. For it is agreed that plants and trees possess life, and that is why we speak of them as living and dying. Therefore the term 'living things' will occupy a still higher place, because both animals and plants are included in this category. Certain objects, however, lack life – such as rocks. There will therefore be another term to take precedence over 'living things', and that is 'substance'. I shall classify 'substance' by saying that all substances are either animate or inanimate.

But there is still something superior to 'substance'; for we speak of certain things as possessing substance, and certain things as lacking substance. What, then, will be the term from which these things are derived? It is that to which we lately gave an inappropriate name, 'that which exists'. For by using this term they will be divided into *species*, so that we can say: that which exists either possesses, or lacks, substance.

---

[7]In *Categories* 2 b 11 and often.

This, therefore, is what *genus* is – the primary, original, and (to play upon the word) 'general'. Of course there are the other *genera*, but they are 'special' *genera*: 'man' being, for example, a *genus*. For 'man' comprises species: by nations – Greek, Roman, Parthian; by colours – white, black, yellow. The term comprises individuals also: Cato, Cicero, Lucretius. So 'man' falls into the category *genus*, in so far as it includes many kinds; but in so far as it is subordinate to another term, it falls into the category *species*. But the *genus* 'that which exists' is general, and has no term superior to it. It is the first term in the classification of things, and all things are included under it.

The Stoics would set ahead of this still another *genus*, even more primary; concerning which I shall immediately speak, after proving that the *genus* which has been discussed above, has rightly been placed first, being, as it is, capable of including everything.

I therefore distribute 'that which exists' into these two species – things with, and things without, substance. There is no third class. And how do I distribute 'substance'? By saying that it is either animate or inanimate. And how do I distribute the 'animate'? By saying: 'Certain things have mind, while others have only life.' Or the idea may be expressed as follows: 'Certain things have the power of movement, of progress, of change of position, while others are rooted in the ground; they are fed and they grow only through their roots.' Again, into what species do I divide 'animals'? They are either perishable or imperishable.

Certain of the Stoics regard the primary *genus*[8] as the 'something'. I shall add the reasons they give for their belief; they say: 'in the order of nature some things exist, and other things do not exist. And even the things that do not exist are really part of the order of nature. What these are will readily occur to the mind, for example centaurs, giants, and all other figments of unsound reasoning, which have begun to have a definite shape, although they have no bodily consistency.'

But I now return to the subject which I promised to discuss for you, namely, how it is that Plato divides all existing things in six different ways. The first class of 'that which exists' cannot be grasped by the sight or by the touch, or by any of the senses, but it can be grasped by the thought. Any generic conception, such as the generic idea 'man', does not come within the range of the eyes; but 'man' in particular does; as, for example, Cicero, Cato. The term 'animal' is not seen; it is grasped by thought alone. A particular animal, however, is seen, for example, a horse, a dog.

---

[8] i.e. the genus 'beyond that which exists'.

The second class of 'things which exist', according to Plato, is that which is prominent and stands out above everything else; this, he says, exists in a pre-eminent degree. The word 'poet' is used indiscriminately, for this term is applied to all writers of verse, but among the Greeks it has come to be the distinguishing mark of a single individual. You know that Homer is meant when you hear men say 'the poet'. What, then, is this pre-eminent Being? God, surely, one who is greater and more powerful than anyone else.

The third class is made up of those things which exist in the proper sense of the term; they are countless in number, but are situated beyond our sight. 'What are these?' you ask. They are Plato's own furniture, so to speak; he calls them 'ideas', and from them all visible things are created, and according to their pattern all things are fashioned. They are immortal, unchangeable, inviolable.

And this 'idea', or rather, Plato's conception of it, is as follows: 'The "idea" is the everlasting pattern of those things which are created by nature.' I shall explain this definition, in order to set the subject before you in a clearer light: Suppose that I wish to make a likeness of you; I possess in your own person the pattern of this picture, wherefrom my mind receives a certain outline, which it is to embody in its own handiwork. That outward appearance, then, which gives me instruction and guidance, this pattern for me to imitate, is the 'idea'. Such patterns, therefore, nature possesses in infinite number – of men, fish, trees, according to whose model everything that nature has to create is worked out.

In the fourth place we shall put 'form'. And if you would know what 'form' means, you must pay close attention, calling Plato, and not me, to account for the difficulty of the subject. However, we cannot make fine distinctions without encountering difficulties. A moment ago I made use of the artist as an illustration. When the artist desired to reproduce Virgil in colours he would gaze upon Virgil himself. The 'idea' was Virgil's outward appearance, and this was the pattern of the intended work. That which the artist draws from this 'idea' and has embodied in his own work, is the 'form'.

Do you ask me where the difference lies? The former is the pattern; while the latter is the shape taken from the pattern and embodied in the work. Our artist follows the one, but the other he creates. A statue has a certain external appearance; this external appearance of the statue is the 'form'. And the pattern itself has a certain external appearance, by gazing upon which the sculptor has fashioned his statue; this is the 'idea'. If you desire a further distinction, I will say that the 'form' is in the artist's work, the 'idea' outside his work, and not only outside it, but prior to it.

The fifth class is made up of the things which exist in the usual sense of the term. These things are the first that have to do with us; here we have all such things as men, cattle, and things. In the sixth class goes all that which has a fictitious existence, like void, or time.

Whatever is concrete to the sight or touch, Plato does not include among the things which he believes to be existent in the strict sense of the term. These things are the first that have to do with us: here we have all such things as men, cattle, and things. For they are in a state of flux, constantly diminishing or increasing. None of us is the same man in old age that he was in youth; nor the same on the morrow as on the day preceding. Our bodies are hurried along like flowing waters; every visible object accompanies time in its flight; of the things which we see, nothing is fixed. Even I myself, as I comment on this change, am changed myself.

This is just what Heraclitus says: 'We go down twice into the same river, and yet into a different river.' For the stream still keeps the same name, but the water has already flowed past. Of course this is much more evident in rivers than in human beings. Still, we mortals are also carried past in no less speedy a course; and this prompts me to marvel at our madness in cleaving with great affection to such a fleeting thing as the body, and in fearing lest some day we may die, when every instant means the death of our previous condition. Will you not stop fearing lest that may happen once which really happens every day?

So much for man – a substance that flows away and falls, exposed to every influence; but the universe, too, immortal and enduring as it is, changes and never remains the same. For though it has within itself all that it has had, it has it in a different way from that in which it has had it; it keeps changing its arrangement.

'Very well', say you, 'what good shall I get from all this fine reasoning?' None, if you wish me to answer your question. Nevertheless, just as an engraver rests his eyes when they have long been under a strain and are weary, and calls them from their work, and 'feasts' them, as the saying is; so we at times should slacken our minds and refresh them with some sort of entertainment. But let even your entertainment be work; and even from these various forms of entertainment you will select, if you have been watchful, something that may prove wholesome.

That is my habit, Lucilius: I try to extract and render useful some element from every field of thought, no matter how far removed it may be from philosophy. Now what could be less likely to reform character than the subjects which we have been discussing? And how can I be made a better man by the 'ideas' of Plato? What can I draw from them that will put a check on my appetites? Perhaps the very thought that all these things which minister to our senses, which arouse and excite us, are by Plato denied a place among the things that really exist.

Such things are therefore imaginary, and though they for the moment present a certain external appearance, yet they are in no case permanent or substantial; none the less, we crave them as if they were always to exist, or as if we were always to possess them.

We are weak, watery beings standing in the midst of unrealities; therefore let us turn our minds to the things that are everlasting. Let us look up to the ideal outlines of all things, that flit about on high, and to the God who moves among them and plans how he may defend from death that which he could not make imperishable because its substance forbade, and so by reason may overcome the defects of the body.

For all things abide, not because they are everlasting, but because they are protected by the care of him who governs all things; but that which was imperishable would need no guardian. The Master Builder keeps them safe, overcoming the weakness of their fabric by his own power. Let us despise everything that is so little an object of value that it makes us doubt whether it exists at all.

Let us at the same time reflect, seeing that Providence rescues from its perils the world itself, which is no less mortal than we ourselves, that to some extent our petty bodies can be made to tarry longer upon earth by our own providence, if only we acquire the ability to control and check those pleasures whereby the greater portion of mankind perishes.

Plato himself, by taking pains, advanced to old age. To be sure, he was the fortunate possessor of a strong and sound body (his very name was given him because of his broad chest); but his strength was much impaired by sea voyages and desperate adventures. Nevertheless, by frugal living, by setting a limit upon all that rouses the appetites, and by painstaking attention to himself, he reached that advanced age in spite of many hindrances.

You know, I am sure, that Plato had the good fortune, thanks to his careful living, to die on his birthday, after exactly completing his eighty-first year. For this reason wise men of the East, who happened to be in Athens at that time, sacrificed to him after his death, believing that his length of days was too full for a mortal man, since he had rounded out the perfect number of nine times nine. I do not doubt that he would have been quite willing to forgo a few days from this total, as well as the sacrifice.

Frugal living can bring one to old age; and to my mind old age is not to be refused any more than it is to be craved. There is a pleasure in being in one's own company as long as possible, when a man has made himself worth enjoying. The question, therefore, on which we have to record our judgement is, whether one should shrink from extreme old age and should hasten the end artificially, instead of waiting for it to come. A man who sluggishly awaits his fate is almost a coward, just as he is immoderately given to wine who drains the jar dry and sucks up even the dregs.

But we shall ask this question also: 'Is the extremity of life the dregs, or is it the clearest and purest part of all, provided only that the mind is unimpaired, and the senses, still sound, give their support to the spirit, and the body is not worn out and dead before its time?' For it makes a great deal of difference whether a man is lengthening his life or his death.

But if the body is useless for service, why should one not free the struggling soul? Perhaps one ought to do this a little before the debt is due, lest, when it falls due, he may be unable to perform the act. And since the danger of living in wretchedness is greater than the danger of dying soon, he is a fool who refuses to stake a little time and win a hazard of great gain.

Few have lasted through extreme old age to death without impairment, and many have lain inert, making no use of themselves. How much more cruel, then, do you suppose it really is to have lost a portion of your life, than to have lost your right to end that life?

Do not hear me with reluctance, as if my statement applied directly to you, but weigh what I have to say. It is this: that I shall not abandon old age, if old age preserves me intact for myself, and intact as regards the better part of myself; but if old age begins to shatter my mind, and to pull its various faculties to pieces, if it leaves me, not life, but only the breath of life, I shall rush out of a house that is crumbling and tottering.

I shall not avoid illness by seeking death, as long as the illness is curable and does not impede my soul. I shall not lay violent hands upon myself just because I am in pain; for death under such circumstances is defeat. But if I find out that the pain must always be endured, I shall depart, not because of the pain but because it will be a hindrance to me as regards all my reasons for living. He who dies just because he is in pain is a weakling, a coward; but he who lives merely to brave out this pain is a fool.

But I am running on too long; and, besides, there is matter here to fill a day. And how can a man end his life, if he cannot end a letter? So farewell. This last word[9] you will read with greater pleasure than all my deadly talk about death. Farewell.

---

[9]Since *vale* (farewell) means 'keep well' no less than 'goodbye'.

CHAPTER FIFTY NINE

ON PLEASURE AND JOY

I received great pleasure from your letter; kindly allow me to use these words in their everyday meaning, without insisting upon their Stoic import. For we Stoics hold that pleasure is a vice. Very likely it is a vice, but we are accustomed to use the word when we wish to indicate a happy state of mind.

I am aware that if we test words by our formula, even pleasure is a thing of ill repute, and joy can be attained only by the wise. For 'joy' is an elation of spirit – of a spirit which trusts in the goodness and truth of its own possessions. The common usage, however, is that we derive great 'joy' from a friend's position as consul, or from his marriage, or from the birth of his child, but these events, so far from being matters of joy, are more often the beginnings of sorrow to come. No, it

341

is a characteristic of real joy that it never ceases, and never changes into its opposite.[1]

Accordingly, when our Virgil speaks of

The evil joys of the mind,[2]

his words are eloquent, but not strictly appropriate. For no 'joy' can be evil. He has given the name 'joy' to pleasures, and has thus expressed his meaning. For he has conveyed the idea that men take delight in their own evil.

Nevertheless, I was not wrong in saying that I received great 'pleasure' from your letter; for although an ignorant man may derive 'joy' if the cause be an honourable one, yet, since his emotion is wayward, and is likely soon to take another direction, I call it 'pleasure'; for it is inspired by an opinion concerning a spurious good; it exceeds control and is carried to excess.

But, to return to the subject, let me tell you what delighted me in your letter. You have your words under control. You are not carried away by your language, or borne beyond the limits which you have determined upon.

Many writers are tempted by the charm of some alluring phrase to some topic other than that which

---

[1] i.e. grief.

[2] *Aeneid*, vi. 278.

they had set themselves to discuss. But this has not been so in your case; all your words are compact, and suited to the subject. You say all that you wish, and you mean still more than you say. This is a proof of the importance of your subject matter, showing that your mind, as well as your words, contains nothing superfluous or bombastic.

I do, however, find some metaphors, not, indeed, daring ones, but the kind which have stood the test of use. I find similes also; of course, if anyone forbids us to use them, maintaining that poets alone have that privilege, he has not, apparently, read any of our ancient prose writers, who had not yet learned to affect a style that should win applause. For those writers, whose eloquence was simple and directed only towards proving their case, are full of comparisons; and I think that these are necessary, not for the same reason which makes them necessary for the poets, but in order that they may serve as props to our feebleness, to bring both speaker and listener face to face with the subject under discussion.

For example, I am at this very moment reading Sextius;[3] he is a keen man, and a philosopher who, though he writes in Greek, has the Roman standard of ethics. One of his similes appealed especially to

---

[3] Q. Sextius was a Stoic with Pythagorean leanings, who lived in the days of Julius Caesar.

me, that of an army marching in hollow square,[4] in a place where the enemy might be expected to appear from any quarter, ready for battle. 'This', said he, 'is just what the wise man ought to do; he should have all his fighting qualities deployed on every side, so that wherever the attack threatens, there his supports may be ready to hand and may obey the captain's command without confusion.' This is what we notice in armies which serve under great leaders; we see how all the troops simultaneously understand their general's orders, since they are so arranged that a signal given by one man passes down the ranks of cavalry and infantry at the same moment.

This, he declares, is still more necessary for men like ourselves; for soldiers have often feared an enemy without reason, and the march which they thought most dangerous has in fact been most secure; but folly brings no repose, fear haunts it both in the van and in the rear of the column, and both flanks are in a panic. Folly is pursued, and confronted, by peril. It blenches at everything; it is unprepared; it

---

[4] *Agmen quadratum* was an army in a square formation, with baggage in the middle, ready for battle – as contrasted with *agmen iustum* (close ranks), and *acies triplex* (a stationary formation, almost rectangular). *Agmen quadratum* is first found in the Spanish campaigns of the second century BCE.

is frightened even by auxiliary troops.[5] But the wise man is fortified against all inroads; he is alert; he will not retreat before the attack of poverty, or of sorrow, or of disgrace, or of pain. He will walk undaunted both against them and among them.

We human beings are fettered and weakened by many vices; we have wallowed in them for a long time, and it is hard for us to be cleansed. We are not merely defiled; we are dyed by them. But, to refrain from passing from one figure[6] to another, I will raise this question, which I often consider in my own heart: why is it that folly holds us with such an insistent grasp? It is, primarily, because we do not combat it strongly enough, because we do not struggle towards salvation with all our might; secondly, because we do not put sufficient trust in the discoveries of the wise, and do not drink in their words with open hearts; we approach this great problem in too trifling a spirit.

But how can a man learn, in the struggle against his vices, an amount that is enough, if the time which he gives to learning is only the amount left over from his vices? None of us goes deep below the surface. We

---

[5] i.e. by the troops of the second line, who in training and quality were inferior to the troops of the legion.

[6] i.e. from the metaphor of the 'fetter' to that of the 'dust and dye'. Seneca has earlier praised Lucilius for his judicious employment of metaphors.

skim the top only, and we regard the smattering of time spent in the search for wisdom as enough and to spare for a busy man.

What hinders us most of all is that we are too readily satisfied with ourselves; if we meet with someone who calls us good men, or sensible men, or holy men, we see ourselves in his description. Not content with praise in moderation, we accept everything that shameless flattery heaps upon us, as if it were our due. We agree with those who declare us to be the best and wisest of men, although we know that they are given to much lying. And we are so self-complacent that we desire praise for certain actions when we are especially addicted to the very opposite. Yonder person hears himself called 'most gentle' when he is inflicting tortures, or 'most generous' when he is engaged in looting, or 'most temperate' when he is in the midst of drunkenness and lust. Thus it follows that we are unwilling to be reformed, just because we believe ourselves to be the best of men.

Alexander was roaming as far as India, ravaging tribes that were but little known, even to their neighbours. During the blockade of a certain city, while he was reconnoitring the walls and hunting for the weakest spot in the fortifications, he was wounded by an arrow. Nevertheless, he long continued the siege, intent on finishing what he had begun. The pain of his wound, however, as the surface became dry and as the flow of blood was checked, increased; his leg gradually became numb as he sat his horse; and finally, when he was forced to withdraw, he exclaimed: 'All men swear that I am the son of Jupiter, but this wound cries out that I am mortal.'

Let us also act in the same way. Each man, according to his lot in life, is stultified by flattery. We should say to him who flatters us: 'You call me a man of sense, but I understand how many of the things which I crave are useless, and how many of the things which I desire will do me harm. I have not even the knowledge, which satiety teaches to animals, of what should be the measure of my food or my drink. I do not yet know how much I can hold.'

I shall now show you how you may know that you are not wise. The wise man is joyful, happy and calm, unshaken; he lives on a plane with the gods. Now go, question yourself; if you are never downcast, if your mind is not harassed by any apprehension, through anticipation of what is to come, if day and night your soul keeps on its even and unswerving course, upright and content with itself, then you have attained to the greatest good that mortals can possess. If, however, you seek pleasures of all kinds in all directions, you must know that you are as far short of wisdom as you are short of joy. Joy is the goal which you desire to reach, but you are wandering from the path if you expect to reach your goal while you are in the midst of riches and official titles – in other words, if you seek joy in the midst of cares. These objects for which you strive so eagerly, as if they would give you happiness and pleasure, are merely causes of grief.

All men of this stamp, I maintain, are pressing on in pursuit of joy, but they do not know where they may obtain a joy that is both great and enduring. One person seeks it in feasting and self-indulgence; another, in canvassing for honours and in being surrounded by a throng of clients; another, in his mistress; another, in idle display of culture and in literature that has no power to heal; all these men are led astray by delights which are deceptive and short-lived – like drunkenness for example, which pays for a single hour of hilarious madness by a sickness of many days, or like applause and the popularity of enthusiastic approval which are gained, and atoned for, at the cost of great mental disquietude.

Reflect, therefore, on this, that the effect of wisdom is a joy that is unbroken and continuous.[7] The mind of the wise man is like the ultralunar firmament;[8] eternal calm pervades that region. You have, then, a reason

---

[7]Seneca here returns to his idea that 'True joy never ceases and never changes into its opposite.' It is not subject to ups and downs.

[8]The upper firmament, near the stars, is free from clouds and storms. It is calm, though the lightning plays below.

for wishing to be wise, if the wise man is never deprived of joy. This joy springs only from the knowledge that you possess the virtues. None but the brave, the just, the self-restrained, can rejoice.

And when you query: 'What do you mean? Do not the foolish and the wicked also rejoice?' I reply, no more than lions who have caught their prey. When men have wearied themselves with wine and lust, when night fails them before their debauch is done, when the pleasures which they have heaped upon a body that is too small to hold them begin to fester, at such times they utter in their wretchedness those lines of Virgil:[9]

Thou knowest how, amid false-glittering joys.

We spent that last of nights.

Pleasure-lovers spend every night amid false-glittering joys, and just as if it were their last. But the joy which comes to the gods, and to those who imitate the gods, is not broken off, nor does it cease; but it would surely cease were it borrowed from without. Just because it is not in the power of another to bestow, neither is it subject to another's whims. That which Fortune has not given, she cannot take away. Farewell.

---

[9] *Aeneid*, vi. 513 f. The night is that which preceded the sack of Troy.

CHAPTER SIXTY

ON HARMFUL PRAYERS

I file a complaint, I enter a suit, I am angry. Do you still desire what your nurse, your guardian, or your mother, have prayed for on your behalf? Do you not yet understand what evil they prayed for? Alas, how hostile to us are the wishes of our own folk! And they are all the more hostile in proportion as they are more completely fulfilled. It is no surprise to me, at my age, that nothing but evil attends us from our early youth; for we have grown up amid the curses invoked by our parents. And may the gods give ear to our cry also, uttered in our own behalf – one which asks no favours!

How long shall we go on making demands upon the gods, as if we were still unable to support ourselves? How long shall we continue to fill with grain the marketplaces of our great cities? How long must the people gather it in for us? How long shall many ships convey the requisites for a single meal, bringing them from no single sea? The bull is filled when he feeds over a few acres; and one forest is large enough for a herd of elephants. Man, however, draws sustenance both from the earth and from the sea.

What, then? Did nature give us bellies so insatiable, when she gave us these puny bodies, that we should outdo the hugest and most voracious animals in greed? Not at all. How small is the amount which will satisfy nature? A very little will send her away contented. It is not the natural hunger of our bellies that costs us dear, but our solicitous cravings.

Therefore, those who, as Sallust puts it, 'hearken to their bellies', should be numbered among the animals, and not among men; and certain men, indeed, should be numbered, not even among the animals, but among the dead. He really lives who is made use of by many; he really lives who makes use of himself. Those men, however, who creep into a hole and grow torpid[1] are no better off in their homes than if they were in their tombs. Right there on the marble lintel of the house of such a man you may inscribe his name,[2] for he has died before he is dead. Farewell.

---

[1] i.e. like animals in hibernation.

[2] i.e. you may put an epitaph upon his dwelling as if it were a tomb.

CHAPTER SIXTY ONE

ON MEETING DEATH CHEERFULLY

Let us cease to desire that which we have been desiring. I, at least, am doing this: in my old age I have ceased to desire what I desired when a boy. To this single end my days and my nights are passed; this is my task, this the object of my thoughts – to put an end to my chronic ills. I am endeavouring to live every day as if it were a complete life. I do not indeed snatch it up as if it were my last; I do regard it, however, as if it might even be my last.

The present letter is written to you with this in mind – as if death were about to call me away in the very act of writing. I am ready to depart, and I shall enjoy life just because I am not overanxious as to the future date of my departure.

Before I became old I tried to live well; now that I am old, I shall try to die well; but dying well means dying gladly. See to it that you never do anything unwillingly.

That which is bound to be a necessity if you rebel, is not a necessity if you desire it. This is what I mean: he who takes his orders gladly escapes the bitterest part of slavery – doing what one does not want to do. The man who does something under orders is not unhappy; he is unhappy who does something against his will. Let us, therefore, so set our minds in order that we may desire whatever is demanded of us by circumstances, and above all that we may reflect upon our end without sadness.

We must make ready for death before we make ready for life. Life is well enough furnished, but we are too greedy with regard to its furnishings; something always seems to us lacking, and will always seem lacking. To have lived long enough depends neither upon our years nor upon our days, but upon our minds. I have lived, my dear friend Lucilius, long enough. I have had my fill; I await death. Farewell.

CHAPTER SIXTY TWO

ON GOOD COMPANY

We are deceived by those who would have us believe that a multitude of affairs blocks their pursuit of liberal studies; they make a pretence of their engagements, and multiply them, when their engagements are merely with themselves. As for me, Lucilius, my time is free; it is indeed free, and wherever I am, I am master of myself. For I do not surrender myself to my affairs, but loan myself to them, and I do not hunt out excuses for wasting my time. And wherever I am situated, I carry on my own meditations and ponder in my mind some wholesome thought.

When I give myself to my friends, I do not withdraw from my own company, nor do I linger with those who are associated with me through some special occasion or some case which arises from my official position.

355

But I spend my time in the company of all the best; no matter in what lands they may have lived, or in what age, I let my thoughts fly to them.

Demetrius,[1] for instance, the best of men, I take about with me, and, leaving the wearers of purple and fine linen, I talk with him, half-naked as he is, and hold him in high esteem. Why should I not hold him in high esteem? I have found that he lacks nothing. It is in the power of any man to despise all things, but of no man to possess all things. The shortest cut to riches is to despise riches. Our friend Demetrius, however, lives not merely as if he has learned to despise all things, but as if he has handed them over for others to possess.[2] Farewell.

---

[1]Demetrius of Sunium, the Cynic philosopher, who taught in Rome in the reign of Caligula and was banished by Nero.

[2]i.e. he has achieved the Stoic ideal of independence of all external control; like a king he has all things to bestow upon others, but needs nothing for himself.

CHAPTER SIXTY THREE

ON GRIEF FOR LOST FRIENDS

I am grieved to hear that your friend Flaccus is dead, but I would not have you sorrow more than is fitting. That you should not mourn at all I shall hardly dare to insist; and yet I know that it is the better way. But what man will ever be so blessed with that ideal steadfastness of soul, unless he has already risen far above the reach of Fortune? Even such a man will be stung by an event like this, but it will be only a sting. We, however, may be forgiven for bursting into tears, if only our tears have not flowed to excess, and if we have checked them by our own efforts. Let not the eyes be dry when we have lost a friend, nor let them overflow. We may weep, but we must not wail.

Do you think that the law which I lay down for you is harsh, when the greatest of Greek poets has extended the privilege of weeping to one day only, in the lines where he tells us that even Niobe took thought of food?[1] Do you wish to know the reason for lamentations and excessive weeping? It is because we seek the proofs of our bereavement in our tears, and do not give way to sorrow, but merely parade it. No man goes into mourning for his own sake. Shame on our ill-timed folly! There is an element of self-seeking even in our sorrow.

'What', you say, 'am I to forget my friend?' It is surely a short-lived memory that you vouchsafe to him, if it is to endure only as long as your grief; presently that brow of yours will be smoothed out in laughter by some circumstance, however casual. It is to a time no more distant than this that I put off the soothing of every regret, the quieting of even the bitterest grief. As soon as you cease to observe yourself, the picture of sorrow which you have contemplated will fade away; at present you are keeping watch over your own suffering. But even while you keep watch it slips away from you, and the sharper it is, the more speedily it comes to an end.

Let us see to it that the recollection of those whom we have lost becomes a pleasant memory to us. No man reverts with pleasure to any subject which he will

---

[1] Homer, *Iliad*, xix. 229 and xxiv. 602.

not be able to reflect upon without pain. So too it cannot but be that the names of those whom we have loved and lost come back to us with a sort of sting; but there is a pleasure even in this sting.

For, as my friend Attalus[2] used to say: 'The remembrance of lost friends is pleasant in the same way that certain fruits have an agreeably acid taste, or as in extremely old wines it is their very bitterness that pleases us. Indeed, after a certain lapse of time, every thought that gave pain is quenched, and the pleasure comes to us unalloyed.'

If we take the word of Attalus for it, 'to think of friends who are alive and well is like enjoying a meal of cakes and honey; the recollection of friends who have passed away gives a pleasure that is not without a touch of bitterness. Yet who will deny that even these things, which are bitter and contain an element of sourness, do serve to arouse the stomach?'

For my part, I do not agree with him. To me, the thought of my dead friends is sweet and appealing. For I have had them as if I should one day lose them; I have lost them as if I have them still.

Therefore, Lucilius, act as befits your own serenity of mind, and cease to put a wrong interpretation on the gifts of Fortune. Fortune has taken away, but Fortune has given.

---

[2]Seneca's teacher, often mentioned by him.

Let us greedily enjoy our friends, because we do not know how long this privilege will be ours. Let us think how often we shall leave them when we go upon distant journeys, and how often we shall fail to see them when we tarry together in the same place; we shall thus understand that we have lost too much of their time while they were alive.

But will you tolerate men who are most careless of their friends, and then mourn them most abjectly, and do not love anyone unless they have lost him? The reason why they lament too unrestrainedly at such times is that they are afraid lest men doubt whether they really have loved; all too late they seek for proofs of their emotions.

If we have other friends, we surely deserve ill at their hands and think ill of them, if they are of so little account that they fail to console us for the loss of one. If, on the other hand, we have no other friends, we have injured ourselves more than Fortune has injured us; since Fortune has robbed us of one friend, but we have robbed ourselves of every friend whom we have failed to make.

Again, he who has been unable to love more than one has had none too much love even for that one.[3]

---

[3]Friendship is essentially a social virtue, and is not confined to one object. The pretended friendship for one and only one is a form of self-love, and is not unselfish love.

CHAPTER SIXTY THREE

If a man who has lost his one and only tunic through robbery chooses to bewail his plight rather than look about him for some way to escape the cold, or for something with which to cover his shoulders, would you not think him an utter fool?

You have buried one whom you loved; look about for someone to love. It is better to replace your friend than to weep for him.

What I am about to add is, I know, a very hackneyed remark, but I shall not omit it simply because it is a common phrase: a man ends his grief by the mere passing of time, even if he has not ended it of his own accord. But the most shameful cure for sorrow, in the case of a sensible man, is to grow weary of sorrowing. I should prefer you to abandon grief, rather than have grief abandon you; and you should stop grieving as soon as possible, since, even if you wish to do so, it is impossible to keep it up for a long time.

Our forefathers[4] have enacted that, in the case of women, a year should be the limit for mourning; not that they needed to mourn for so long, but that they should mourn no longer. In the case of men, no rules are laid down, because to mourn at all is not regarded as honourable. For all that, what woman can you show me, of all the pathetic females that

---

[4]According to tradition, from the time of Numa Pompilius.

could scarcely be dragged away from the funeral pile
or torn from the corpse, whose tears have lasted a
whole month? Nothing becomes offensive so quickly
as grief; when fresh, it finds someone to console
it and attracts one or another to itself; but after
becoming chronic, it is ridiculed, and rightly. For it is
either assumed or foolish.

He who writes these words to you is no other
than I, who wept so excessively for my dear friend
Annaeus Serenus[5] that, in spite of my wishes, I must
be included among the examples of men who have
been overcome by grief. Today, however, I condemn
this act of mine, and I understand that the reason
why I lamented so greatly was chiefly that I had never
imagined it possible for his death to precede mine.
The only thought which occurred to my mind was
that he was the younger, and much younger, too – as
if the Fates kept to the order of our ages!

Therefore let us continually think as much about
our own mortality as about that of all those we love. In
former days I ought to have said: 'My friend Serenus is
younger than I; but what does that matter? He would
naturally die after me, but he may precede me.' It was

[5]An intimate friend of Seneca, probably a relative, who died
in the year 63 from eating poisoned mushrooms (Pliny, *Natural History* xxii. 96). Seneca dedicated to Serenus several of his
philosophical essays.

just because I did not do this that I was unprepared when Fortune dealt me the sudden blow. Now is the time for you to reflect, not only that all things are mortal, but also that their mortality is subject to no fixed law. Whatever can happen at any time can happen today.

Let us therefore reflect, my beloved Lucilius, that we shall soon come to the goal which this friend, to our own sorrow, has reached. And perhaps, if only the tale told by wise men is true[6] and there is a bourne to welcome us, then he whom we think we have lost has only been sent on ahead.

---

[6]See for example the closing chapter of the *Agricola* of Tacitus: *si, ut sapientibus placet, non cum corpore exstinguuntur magnae animae,* etc. ('if, as the wise believe, noble souls do not perish with the body').

CHAPTER SIXTY FOUR

ON THE PHILOSOPHER'S TASK

Yesterday you were with us. You might complain if I said 'yesterday' merely. This is why I have added 'with us'. For, so far as I am concerned, you are always with me. Certain friends had happened in, on whose account a somewhat brighter fire was laid – not the kind that generally bursts from the kitchen chimneys of the rich and scares the watch, but the moderate blaze which means that guests have come.

Our talk ran on various themes, as is natural at a dinner; it pursued no chain of thought to the end, but jumped from one topic to another. We then had read to us a book by Quintus Sextius the Elder.[1] He is a

---

[1] Quintus Sextius was a philosopher who combined Stoic, Cynic, and Pythagorean thought. He founded the School of the Sextii in around 50 BCE. Adherents were ascetic, subjected themselves

365

great man, if you have any confidence in my opinion, and a real Stoic, though he himself denies it.

Ye Gods, what strength and spirit one finds in him! This is not the case with all philosophers; there are some men of illustrious name whose writings are sapless. They lay down rules, they argue, and they quibble; they do not infuse spirit simply because they have no spirit. But when you come to read Sextius, you will say: 'He is alive; he is strong; he is free; he is more than a man; he fills me with a mighty confidence before I close his book.'

I shall acknowledge to you the state of mind I am in when I read his works: I want to challenge every hazard; I want to cry: 'Why keep me waiting, Fortune? Enter the lists! Behold, I am ready for you!' I assume the spirit of a man who seeks where he may make trial of himself, where he may show his worth:

And fretting 'mid the unwarlike flocks he prays
Some foam-flecked boar may cross his path, or else
A tawny lion stalking down the hills.[2]

I want something to overcome, something on which I may test my endurance. For this is another

to nightly reflections of conscience, avoided wealth and consumerism, and were vegetarian. Seneca's teacher Sotion was a Sextian.

[2]Virgil, *Aeneid,* iv. 158 f. The boy Ascanius, at Dido's hunt, longs for wilder game than the deer and the goats.

remarkable quality that Sextius possesses: he will show you the grandeur of the happy life and yet will not make you despair of attaining it; you will understand that it is on high, but that it is accessible to him who has the will to seek it.

And Virtue herself will have the same effect upon you, of making you admire her and yet hope to attain her. In my own case, at any rate, the very contemplation of Wisdom takes much of my time; I gaze upon her with bewilderment, just as I sometimes gaze upon the firmament itself, which I often behold as if I saw it for the first time.

Hence I worship the discoveries of wisdom and their discoverers; to enter, as it were, into the inheritance of many predecessors is a delight. It was for me that they laid up this treasure; it was for me that they toiled. But we should play the part of a careful householder; we should increase what we have inherited. This inheritance shall pass from me to my descendants larger than before. Much still remains to do, and much will always remain, and he who shall be born a thousand ages hence will not be barred from his opportunity of adding something further.

But even if the old masters have discovered everything, one thing will be always new – the application and the scientific study and classification of the discoveries made by others. Assume that prescriptions have been handed down to us for the healing of the eyes; there is no need of my searching for others in addition; but for all that, these prescriptions must be adapted to the particular disease and to the particular stage of the disease. Use this prescription to relieve granulation of the eyelids, that to reduce the swelling of the lids, this to prevent sudden pain or a rush of tears, that to sharpen the vision. Then compound these several prescriptions, watch for the right time of their application, and apply the proper treatment in each case. The cures for the spirit also have been discovered by the ancients; but it is our task to learn the method and the time of treatment.

Our predecessors have worked much improvement, but have not worked out the problem. They deserve respect, however, and should be worshipped with a divine ritual. Why should I not keep statues of great men to kindle my enthusiasm, and celebrate their birthdays? Why should I not continually greet them with respect and honour? The reverence which I owe to my own teachers I owe in like measure to those teachers of the human race, the source from which the beginnings of such great blessings have flowed.

If I meet a consul or a praetor, I shall pay him all the honour which his post of honour is wont to receive: I shall dismount, uncover, and yield the road.

CHAPTER SIXTY FOUR

What, then? Shall I admit into my soul with less than the highest marks of respect Marcus Cato, the Elder and the Younger, Laelius the Wise, Socrates and Plato, Zeno and Cleanthes? I worship them in very truth, and always rise to do honour to such noble names. Farewell.

ON THE FIRST CAUSE

I shared my time yesterday with ill health; it claimed for itself all the period before noon; in the afternoon, however, it yielded to me. And so I first tested my spirit by reading; then, when reading was found to be possible, I dared to make more demands upon the spirit, or perhaps I should say, to make more concessions to it. I wrote a little, and indeed with more concentration than usual, for I am struggling with a difficult subject and do not wish to be downed. In the midst of this, some friends visited me, with the purpose of employing force and of restraining me, as if I were a sick man indulging in some excess.

So conversation was substituted for writing; and from this conversation I shall communicate to you the topic which is still the subject of debate; for we have appointed you referee. You have more of a task on your hands than you suppose, for the argument is threefold.

Our Stoic philosophers, as you know, declare that there are two things in the universe which are the source of everything – namely, cause and matter. Matter lies sluggish, a substance ready for any use, but sure to remain unemployed if no one sets it in motion. Cause, however, by which we mean reason, moulds matter and turns it in whatever direction it will, producing thereby various concrete results. Accordingly, there must be, in the case of each thing, that from which it is made, and, next, an agent by which it is made. The former is its material, the latter its cause.

All art is but imitation of nature; therefore, let me apply these statements of general principles to the things which have to be made by man. A statue, for example, has afforded matter which was to undergo treatment at the hands of the artist, and has had an artist who was to give form to the matter. Hence, in the case of the statue, the material was bronze, the cause was the workman. And so it goes with all things – they consist of that which is made, and of the maker.

The Stoics believe in one cause only – the maker; but Aristotle thinks that the word 'cause' can be used in three ways: 'The first cause', he says, 'is the actual matter, without which nothing can be created. The second is the workman. The third is the form, which is impressed upon every work – a statue, for example.' This last is what Aristotle calls the *idos*.[1] 'There is, too', says he, 'a fourth – the purpose of the work as a whole.'

Now I shall show you what this last means. Bronze is the 'first cause' of the statue, for it could never have been made unless there had been something from which it could be cast and moulded. The 'second cause' is the artist; for without the skilled hands of a workman that bronze could not have been shaped to the outlines of the statue. The 'third cause' is the form, inasmuch as our statue could never be called The Lance-Bearer or The Boy Binding his Hair,[2] had not this special shape been stamped upon it. The 'fourth cause' is the purpose of the work. For if this purpose had not existed, the statue would not have been made.

Now what is this purpose? It is that which attracted the artist, which he followed when he made the statue. It may have been money, if he has made it for sale; or

---

[1] The statue metaphor is a frequent one in Roman philosophy; cf. Epicurus ix. 5. The 'form' of Aristotle goes back to the 'idea' of Plato. The four causes are the causes of Aristotle, matter (ὕλη), form (εἶδος), force (τὸ κινοῦν), and the end (τὸ τέλος); when they all concur, we pass from possibility to fact. Aristotle gives eight categories in *Physics* 225 b 5; and ten in *Categories* 1 b 25 – substance, quantity, quality, relation, place, time, situation, possession, action, passion.

[2] Well-known works of Polyclitus, fifth century BCE.

renown, if he has worked for reputation; or religion, if he has wrought it as a gift for a temple. Therefore, this also is a cause contributing towards the making of the statue; or do you think that we should avoid including, among the causes of a thing which has been made, that element without which the thing in question would not have been made?

To these four Plato adds a fifth cause – the pattern which he himself calls the 'idea'; for it is this that the artist gazed upon when he created the work which he had decided to carry out. Now it makes no difference whether he has his pattern outside himself, that he may direct his glance to it, or within himself, conceived and placed there by himself. God has within Himself these patterns of all things, and His mind comprehends the harmonies and the measures of the whole totality of things which are to be carried out; He is filled with these shapes which Plato calls the 'ideas' – imperishable, unchangeable, not subject to decay. And therefore, though men die, humanity itself, or the idea of man, according to which man is moulded, lasts on, and though men toil and perish, it suffers no change.

Accordingly, there are five causes, as Plato says:[3] the material, the agent, the make-up, the model, and the

_____

[3] i.e. the four categories as established by Aristotle, plus the 'idea' of Plato.

end in view. Last comes the result of all these. Just as in the case of the statue – to go back to the figure with which we began – the material is the bronze, the agent is the artist, the make-up is the form which is adapted to the material, the model is the pattern imitated by the agent, the end in view is the purpose in the maker's mind, and, finally, the result of all these is the statue itself.

The universe also, in Plato's opinion, possesses all these elements. The agent is God; the source, matter; the form, the shape, and the arrangement of the visible world. The pattern is doubtless the model according to which God has made this great and most beautiful creation.

The purpose is His object in so doing. Do you ask what God's purpose is? It is goodness. Plato, at any rate, says: 'What was God's reason for creating the world? God is good, and no good person is grudging of anything that is good. Therefore, God made it the best world possible.' Hand down your opinion, then, O judge; state who seems to you to say what is truest, and not who says what is absolutely true. For to do that is as far beyond our ken as truth itself.

This throng of causes, defined by Aristotle and by Plato, embraces either too much or too little.[4] For if

---

[4]The Stoic view, besides making the four categories of 'substance', 'form', 'variety', and 'variety of relation', regarded

they regard as 'causes' of an object that is to be made everything without which the object cannot be made, they have named too few. Time must be included among the causes; for nothing can be made without time. They must also include place; for if there be no place where a thing can be made, it will not be made. And motion too; nothing is either made or destroyed without motion. There is no art without motion, no change of any kind.

Now, however, I am searching for the first, the general cause; this must be simple, inasmuch as matter, too, is simple. Do we ask what cause is? It is surely Creative Reason,[5] – in other words, God. For those elements to which you referred are not a great series of independent causes; they all hinge on one alone, and that will be the creative cause.

Do you maintain that form is a cause? This is only what the artist stamps upon his work; it is part of a cause, but not the cause. Neither is the pattern a cause, but an indispensable tool of the cause. His pattern is as indispensable to the artist as the chisel or the file; without these, art can make no progress.

---

material things as the only things which possessed being. The Stoics thus differ from Aristotle and Plato in holding that nothing is real except matter; besides, they relate everything to one ultimate cause, the acting force or efficient cause.

[5]i.e. the creative force in nature, that is, Providence, or the will of Zeus.

But for all that, these things are neither parts of the art, nor causes of it.

'Then', perhaps you will say, 'the purpose of the artist, that which leads him to undertake to create something, is the cause.' It may be a cause; it is not, however, the efficient cause, but only an accessory cause. But there are countless accessory causes; what we are discussing is the general cause. Now the statement of Plato and Aristotle is not in accord with their usual penetration, when they maintain that the whole universe, the perfectly wrought work, is a cause. For there is a great difference between a work and the cause of a work.

Either give your opinion, or, as is easier in cases of this kind, declare that the matter is not clear and call for another hearing.[6] But you will reply: 'What pleasure do you get from wasting your time on these problems, which relieve you of none of your emotions, rout none of your desires?' So far as I am concerned, I treat and discuss them as matters which contribute greatly towards calming the spirit, and I search myself first, and then the world about me.

And not even now am I, as you think, wasting my time. For all these questions, provided that they be not chopped up and torn apart into such unprofitable refinements, elevate and lighten the

---

[6]i.e. restate the question and hear the evidence again.

soul, which is weighted down by a heavy burden and desires to be freed and to return to the elements of which it was once a part. For this body of ours is a weight upon the soul and its penance; as the load presses down the soul is crushed and is in bondage, unless philosophy has come to its assistance and has bid it take fresh courage by contemplating the universe, and has turned it from things earthly to things divine. There it has its liberty, there it can roam abroad;[7] meantime it escapes the custody in which it is bound, and renews its life in heaven.

Just as skilled workmen, who have been engaged upon some delicate piece of work which wearies their eyes with straining, if the light which they have is niggardly or uncertain, go forth into the open air and in some park devoted to the people's recreation delight their eyes in the generous light of day; so the soul, imprisoned as it has been in this gloomy and darkened house, seeks the open sky whenever it can, and in the contemplation of the universe finds rest.

---

[7]According to the Stoics the soul, which consisted of fire or breath and was a part of the divine essence, rose at death into the ether and became one with the stars. Seneca elsewhere (*Consolatio ad Marciam*) states that the soul went through a sort of purifying process – a view that may have had some influence on Christian thought. The souls of the good, the Stoics maintained, were destined to last until the end of the world; the souls of the bad to be extinguished before that time.

The wise man, the seeker after wisdom, is bound closely, indeed, to his body, but he is an absentee so far as his better self is concerned, and he concentrates his thoughts upon lofty things. Bound, so to speak, to his oath of allegiance, he regards the period of life as his term of service. He is so trained that he neither loves nor hates life; he endures a mortal lot, although he knows that an ampler lot is in store for him.

Do you forbid me to contemplate the universe? Do you compel me to withdraw from the whole and restrict me to a part? May I not ask what are the beginnings of all things, who moulded the universe, who took the confused and conglomerate mass of sluggish matter, and separated it into its parts? May I not inquire who is the Master Builder of this universe, how the mighty bulk was brought under the control of law and order, who gathered together the scattered atoms, who separated the disordered elements and assigned an outward form to elements that lay in one vast shapelessness? Or whence came all the expanse of light? And whether is it fire or something even brighter than fire?

Am I not to ask these questions? Must I be ignorant of the heights whence I have descended? Whether I am to see this world but once, or to be born many times? What is my destination afterwards? What abode awaits my soul on its release from the laws of slavery among men? Do you forbid me to have a share in heaven? In other words, do you bid me live with my head bowed down?

No, I am above such an existence; I was born to a greater destiny than to be a mere chattel of my body, and I regard this body as nothing but a chain[8] which manacles my freedom. Therefore, I offer it as a sort of buffer to fortune, and shall allow no wound to penetrate through to my soul. For my body is the only part of me which can suffer injury. In this dwelling, which is exposed to peril, my soul lives free.

Never shall this flesh drive me to feel fear, or to assume any pretence that is unworthy of a good man. Never shall I lie in order to honour this petty body. When it seems proper, I shall sever my connection with it. And at present, while we are bound together, our alliance shall nevertheless not be one of equality; the soul shall bring all quarrels before its own tribunal. To despise our bodies is sure freedom.

To return to our subject; this freedom will be greatly helped by the contemplation of which we were just speaking. All things are made up of matter and of God; God controls matter, which encompasses Him and follows Him as its guide and leader. And that which creates, in other words, God, is more powerful and precious than matter, which is acted upon by God.

---

[8] The 'prison of the body' is a frequent idea in Stoic philosophy.

God's place in the universe corresponds to the soul's relation to man. World-matter corresponds to our mortal body; therefore let the lower serve the higher. Let us be brave in the face of hazards. Let us not fear wrongs, or wounds, or bonds, or poverty. And what is death? It is either the end, or a process of change. I have no fear of ceasing to exist; it is the same as not having begun. Nor do I shrink from changing into another state, because I shall, under no conditions, be as cramped as I am now. Farewell.